346.73043
S623r
2010

P9-ARG-275

3 5674 05102409 0

Small Business Made Simple

Real Estate
Forms
Simplified

WILDER BRANCH LIBRARY
7140 E. SEVEN MILE RD.
DETROIT, MI 48234

JUN 2010

W1

Small Business Made Simple

Real Estate Forms Simplified

DANIEL SITARZ, ATTORNEY-AT-LAW

Nova Publishing Company
Small Business and Consumer Legal Books
Carbondale Illinois

© 2010 Daniel Sitarz

All rights reserved. This publication may not be reproduced in whole or in part by any means whatsoever without prior written consent.
Adobe®, Adobe® Acrobat®, and Acrobat® logo are trademarks of Adobe®, Inc.
Editorial and research assistance by Janet Harris Sitarz, Caitlin King and Melanie Bray. Cover and interior design by Melanie Bray.
Manufactured in the United States.

ISBN 13: 978-1892949-49-3   Book w/CD   ($29.95)

Cataloging-in-Publication Data

    Real estate forms simplified / by Daniel Sitarz -- 2nd. ed. --
    Carbondale Ill. : Nova Publishing. 2006.
        p.; cm + 1 CD-ROM (4 3/4 in.)
        (Small business made simple)
        ISBN 13: 978-1892949-49-3
        CD-ROM contains forms in both text and PDF formats.
        includes index.
        1. real estate business--United States--Forms. 2. Real
        property--United States--Forms. 3. Real property, Exchange of--
        United States--Forms. 4. Mortgages--United States--Forms.
        5. Vendors and purchasers--United States--Forms. 6. Leases--
        United States--Forms. I. Title. II. Series.
        KF568.1 .S58 2010   346.7304/37--dc22   0210

Nova Publishing Company is dedicated to providing up-to-date and accurate legal information to the public. All Nova publications are periodically revised to contain the latest available legal information.

2nd Edition; 1st Printing   February, 2010
1st Edition; 2nd Printing   May, 2007
1st Edition; 1st Printing   June, 2006

This publication is designed to provide accurate and authoritative information in regard to the subject matter covered. It is sold with the understanding that the publisher and author are not engaged in rendering legal, accounting, or other professional services. If legal advice or other expert assistance is required, the services of a competent professional person should be sought.
—From a Declaration of Principles jointly adopted by a Committee of
the American Bar Association and a Committee of Publishers

DISCLAIMER

Because of possible unanticipated changes in governing statutes and case law relating to the application of any information contained in this book, the author, publisher, and any and all persons or entities involved in any way in the preparation, publication, sale, or distribution of this book disclaim all responsibility for the legal effects or consequences of any document prepared or action taken in reliance upon information contained in this book. No representations, either express or implied, are made or given regarding the legal consequences of the use of any information contained in this book. Purchasers and persons intending to use this book for the preparation of any legal documents are advised to check specifically on the current applicable laws in any jurisdiction in which they intend the documents to be effective.

Nova Publishing Green Business Policies

Nova Publishing Company takes seriously the impact of book publishing on the Earth and its resources. Nova Publishing Company is committed to protecting the environment and to the responsible use of natural resources. As a book publisher, with paper as a core part of our business, we are very concerned about the future of the world's remaining endangered forests and the environmental impacts of paper production. We are committed to implementing policies that will support the preservation of endangered forests globally and to advancing 'best practices' within the book and paper industries. Nova Publishing Company is committed to preserving ancient forests and natural resources. Our company's policy is to print all of our books on 100% recycled paper, with 100% post-consumer waste content, de-inked in a chlorine-free process. In addition, all Nova Publishing Company books are printed using soy-based inks. As a result of these environmental policies, Nova Publishing Company has saved hundreds of thousands of gallons of water, hundreds of thousands of kilowatts of electricity, thousand of pounds of pollution and carbon dioxide, and thousands of trees that would otherwise have been used in the traditional manner of publishing its books. Nova Publishing Company is very proud to be one of the first members of the Green Press Initiative, a nonprofit program dedicated to supporting publishers in their efforts to reduce their use of fiber obtained from endangered forests. (see www.greenpressinitiative.org). Nova Publishing Company is also proud to be an initial signatory on the Book Industry Treatise on Responsible Paper Use. In addition, Nova Publishing Company uses all compact fluorescent lighting; recycles all office paper products, aluminum and plastic beverage containers, and printer cartridges; uses 100% post-consumer fiber, process-chlorine-free, acid-free paper for 95% of in-house paper use; and, when possible, uses electronic equipment that is EPA Energy Star-certified. Nova's freight shipments are coordinated to minimize energy use whenever possible. Finally, all carbon emissions from Nova Publishing Company office energy use are offset by the purchase of wind-energy credits that are used to subsidize the building of wind turbines on the Rosebud Sioux Reservation in South Dakota (see www.nativeenergy.com). We strongly encourage other publishers and all partners in publishing supply chains to adopt similar policies.

Nova Publishing Company
Small Business and Consumer Legal Books and Software
1103 West College St.
Carbondale, IL 62901
Technical support: (800) 748-1175
www.novapublishing.com

Distributed by:
National Book Network
4501 Forbes Blvd., Suite 200
Lanham, MD 20706
Orders: (800) 462-6420

Table of Contents

List of Forms-on-CD

All forms are provided in text and PDF format unless noted otherwise. Additionally, several forms are only provided on the Forms-on-CD and several PDF forms are not fillable using a computer and these are also noted.

The Homebuying Process
      Homebuying Worksheet (PDF only)

Sales of Real Estate
      Agreement to Sell Real Estate
      Contract for Deed (Installment Sales Contract)
      Declaration of Intention to Forfeit and Terminate Contract for Deed
      Option to Buy Real Estate
      Offer to Purchase Real Estate
      Lead Warning Statement
      Federal Lead Warning Brochure (PDF only on Forms-on-CD)
      Appraisal Report
      Appraisal Affidavit
      California Addendum to Contract (only on Forms-on-CD)

Real Estate Disclosure Forms
      Basic Real Estate Disclosure Statement (PDF only)
      State-specific Real Estate Disclosure form (For the states that provide statutory forms. These forms are only provided on Forms-on -CD. They are all PDF forms but are not fillable on your computer and will need to be filled in pen)

Real Estate Closing Documents
      HUD Settlement Statement (PDF only, not fillable on your computer)
      Affidavit of Title
      Quitclaim Deed
      Warranty Deed

Leases of Real Estate
      Rental/Credit Application (PDF version is not fillable on a computer)
      Move In/Move Out Checklist and Acknowledgment (PDF version is not fully fillable on a computer)
      Residential Lease
      Month to Month Rental Agreement
      Commercial Lease
      Lease with Purchase Option

Amendment of Lease
Extension of Lease
Mutual Termination of Lease
Assignment of Lease
Consent to Assignment of Lease
Sublease
Consent to Sublease of Lease
Notice of Rent Default
Notice of Breach of Lease
Notice to Pay Rent or Vacate
Landlord's Notice to Terminate Lease
Final Notice Before Legal Action
Notice of Lease
Receipt for Lease Security Deposit
Rent Receipt
California Addendum to Lease (only on Forms-on-CD)
Chicago Addendum to Lease (only on Forms-on-CD)
Chicago Heating Disclosure Form
     (PDF form only/on Forms-on-CD only/not fillable on a computer)
Chicago Residential Landlord and Tenant Ordinance Summary
     (PDF form only/on Forms-on-CD only/not fillable on a computer)

Sale of Personal Property
Contract for Sale of Personal Property
Bill of Sale, with Warranties
Bill of Sale, without Warranties
Bill of Sale, Subject to Debt

Real Estate Contract Modification Forms
Addendum to Contract
Extension of Contract
Modification of Contract
Termination of Contract
Assignment of Contract
Consent to Assignment of Contract
Notice of Assignment of Contract
Notice of Breach of Contract

Signatures and Notary Acknowledgments (Only provided as text forms)
 Corporate Acknowledgment
 Corporate Signature Line
 Partnership Acknowledgment
 Partnership Signature Line
 Limited Liability Company Acknowledgment
 Limited Liability Company Signature Line
 Sole Proprietorship Acknowledgment
 Sole Proprietorship Signature Line
 Power of Attorney Acknowledgment
 Power of Attorney Signature Line
 Individual Acknowledgment
 Individual Signature Line
 Husband and Wife Acknowledgment
 Husband and Wife Signature Line

Powers of Attorney
 Unlimited Power of Attorney
 Limited Power of Attorney
 Revocation of Power of Attorney

Releases
 General Release
 Mutual Release
 Specific Release

Liens
 Claim of Lien
 Waiver and Release of Lien
 Claim of Lien(Florida) (PDF form only/on Forms-on-CD only)
 Claim of Lien(Georgia) (PDF form only/on Forms-on-CD only)

Miscellaneous Real Estate Documents
 Declaration of Homestead
 Easement and Right of Way Agreement

Chapter 1

Using Real Estate Forms

The business arena in America operates on a daily assortment of legal forms. There are more legal forms in use in American business than are used in the operations and government of many foreign countries. Real estate transactions are not immune to this flood of legal forms. Unfortunately, many people who are confronted with such forms do not understand the legal ramifications of the use of these forms. They simply sign the lease, contract, or bill of sale with the expectation that it is a fairly standard document without any unusual legal provisions. They trust that the details of the particular document will fall within what is generally accepted within the industry or trade. In most cases, this may be true. In many situations, however, it is not. Our court system is clogged with cases in which two people are battling over what was really intended by the incomprehensible legal language in a certain contract.

Much of the confusion over business legal contracts comes from two areas. First, there is a general lack of understanding among many regarding the framework of contract law. Second, many contracts are written in antiquated legal jargon that is difficult for most lawyers to understand and nearly impossible for a layperson to comprehend.

The contracts and various legal documents that are used in this book are, however, written in plain English. Standard legal jargon, as used in most lawyer-prepared documents, is, for most people, totally incomprehensible. Despite the lofty arguments by attorneys regarding the need for such strained and difficult language, the vast majority of legalese is absolutely unnecessary. Clarity, simplicity, and readability should be the goal in legal documents. In most real estate contexts, "buyer" and "seller," "landlord" and "tenant," or some other straightforward term of definition of the parties involved is possible. Unfortunately, certain obscure legal terms are the only words that accurately and precisely describe some things in certain legal contexts. In those few cases, the unfamiliar legal term will be defined when first used. Generally, however, simple terms are used.

All of the legal documents contained in this book have been prepared in essentially the same manner that attorneys create legal forms. Many people believe that lawyers prepare each legal document that they compose entirely from scratch. Nothing could be further from the truth. Invariably, lawyers begin their preparation of a legal document with a standardized legal form book. Every law library has multi-volume sets of these encyclopedic texts that contain blank forms for virtually every conceivable legal situation. Armed with these pre-prepared legal forms, lawyers, in many cases, simply fill in the blanks and have their secretaries retype the form for the client. Of course, the client is generally unaware of this process.

This book provides the reader with a set of legal forms that has been prepared with the problems and issues of normal real estate transactions in mind. These forms are intended to be used in those situations that are clearly described by their terms. Of course, while most real estate transactions will fall within the bounds of standard business practices, some legal circumstances will present non-standard situations. The forms in this book are designed to be readily adaptable to most usual real estate situations. They may be carefully altered to conform to the particular transaction that confronts you. However, if you are faced with a complex or tangled real estate situation, the advice of a competent lawyer is recommended. If you wish, you may also create forms for certain standard real estate transactions and have your lawyer check them for any local legal circumstances.

The proper and cautious use of the forms provided in this book will allow the typical person to save considerable money on legal costs, while complying with legal and governmental regulations. Perhaps more important, these forms will provide a method by which the person can avoid costly misunderstandings about what exactly was intended in a particular situation or transaction. By using the forms provided to clearly set out the terms and conditions of everyday real estate dealings, disputes over what was really meant can be avoided. This protection will allow the reader to avoid many potential lawsuits and operate more efficiently in compliance with the law.

How to Use This Book

In each chapter of this book you will find an introductory section that will give you an overview of the types of situations in which the forms in that chapter will generally be used. Following that overview, there will be a brief explanation of the specific uses for each form. Included in the information provided for each form will be a discussion of the legal terms and conditions provided in the form. Finally, for each form, there is a listing of the information that must be compiled to complete the form.

The preferable manner for using these forms is to use the enclosed Forms-on-CD. Instructions for using the Forms-on-CD are included later in this chapter. However, it is perfectly acceptable to prepare these forms directly from the book by making a copy of the form, filling in the information that is necessary, and then retyping the form in its entirety on clean white letter-sized paper.

For purposes of simplification, most of the forms in this book are set out in a form as would be used by two individuals. However, any of the various forms can be adapted for use between two business entities or an individual and a business entity. Please use the appropriate signature lines from Chapter 9 if you wish to modify the basic form as it is set forth. If businesses are parties to the contract, please identify the name and type of business entity (for example: Jackson Car Stereo, a New York sole proprietorship, etc.) in the first section of the contract. If notary acknowledgments are required for a particular form, please also refer to Chapter 9 for the correct acknowledgment form to use.

Please also note that any forms which begin with "NOTICE" should be sent to the person or company receiving the form by certified U.S. mail. This may be a requirement under various laws, including the Uniform Commercial Code.

Many of the forms in this book have blanks for inserting the state or county. If you are a resident of Louisiana, substitute "parish" for "county." If you are a resident of Pennsylvania, Massachusetts, Virginia, or Kentucky, substitute "Commonwealth" for "state." If you are a resident of Washington D.C., please substitute "District of Columbia" for "state."

In most cases, masculine and feminine terms have been eliminated and the generic "it" or "them" used instead. In the few situations in which this leads to awkward sentence construction, "his or her" or "he or she" may be used instead.

It is recommended that you review the table of contents of this book in order to gain a broad overview of the range and type of legal documents that are available. Then, before you prepare any of the forms for use, you should carefully read the introductory information and instructions in the chapter where the particular form is contained. Try to be as detailed and specific as possible as you fill in these forms. The more precise the description, the less likelihood that later disputes may develop over what was actually intended by the language chosen. The careful preparation and use of the legal forms in this book should provide the typical person with most of the real estate documents necessary for most common transactions relating to real estate. If in doubt as to whether a particular form will work in a specific application, please consult a competent lawyer.

Installation Instructions for the Forms-on-CD

Quick-Start Installation for PCs

1. Insert the enclosed CD in your computer.
2. The installation program will start automatically. Follow the onscreen dialogue and make your appropriate choices.
3 If the CD installation does not start automatically, click on START, then RUN, then BROWSE, and select your CD drive, and then select the file "Install.exe." Finally, click OK to run the installation program.
4. During the installation program, you will be prompted as to whether or not you wish to install the Adobe Acrobat Reader® program. If you do not already have the Adobe Acrobat Reader® program installed on your hard drive, you will need to select the full installation that will install this program to your computer.

Installation Instructions for MACs®

1. Insert the enclosed CD in your computer.
2. Copy the folder "Forms for Macs" to your hard drive. All of the PDF and text-only forms are included in this folder.
3. If you do not already have the Adobe Acrobat Reader® program installed on your hard drive, you will need to download the version of this software that is appropriate for you particular MAC operating system from www.adobe.com. Note: The latest versions of the MAC operating system (OS-X) has PDF capabilities built into it.

Instructions for Using Forms-on-CD

All of the forms which are included in this book have been provided on the Forms-on-CD for your use if you have access to a computer. If you have completed the Forms-on-CD installation program, all of the forms will have been copied to your computer's hard drive. By default, these files are installed in the C:\Real Estate Forms Simplified\Forms folder which is created by the installation program. (Note for MAC users: see instructions above). Opening the Forms folder will provide you with access to folders for each of the topics corresponding to chapters in the book. Within each chapter, the forms are provided in two separate formats:

Text forms which may opened, prepared, and printed from within your own word processing program (such as Microsoft Word®, or WordPerfect®). The text forms all have the file extension: .txt. These forms are located in the TEXT FORMS folders supplied for each chapter's forms. You may wish to use the forms in this format if you will be making changes to text of the forms. To access these forms, please see instructions on page 17.

PDF forms which may be filled in on your computer screen and printed out on any printer. This particular format provides the most widely-used cross-platform format for accessing computer files. Files in this format may be opened as images on your computer and printed out on any printer. The files in Adobe PDF format all have the file extension: .pdf. Although this format provides the easiest method for completing the forms, the forms in this format can not be altered (other than to fill in the information required on the blanks provided). To access the PDF forms, please see below. If you wish to alter the language in any of the forms, you will need to access the forms in their text-only versions. To access these text-only forms, please also see below.

To Access Adobe PDF Forms

1. You must have already installed the Adobe Acrobat Reader® program to your computer's hard drive. This program is installed automatically by the installation program. (MAC users will need to install this program via www.adobe.com).

2. On your computer's desktop, you will find a shortcut icon labeled "Acrobat Reader®" Using your mouse, left double click on this icon. This will open the Acrobat Reader® program. When the Acrobat Reader® program is opened for the first time, you will need to accept the Licensing Agreement from Adobe in order to use this program. Click "Accept" when given the option to accept or decline the Agreement.

3. Once the Acrobat Reader® program is open on your computer, click on FILE (in the upper left-hand corner of the upper taskbar). Then click on OPEN in the drop down menu. Depending on which version of Windows or other operating system you are using, a box will open which will allow you to access files on your computer's hard drive. The files for Real Estate Forms are located on your computer's "C" drive, under the folder "Real Estate Forms Simplified." In this folder, you will find a subfolder "Forms." (Note: if you installed the forms folder on a different drive, access the forms on that particular drive).

4. If you desire to work with one of the forms, you should then left double-click your mouse on the sub-folder: "Forms." This will open two folders: one for text forms and one for PDF forms. Left double click your mouse on the PDF forms folder and a list of the PDF forms for that topic should appear. Left double click your mouse on the form of your choice. This will open the appropriate form within the Adobe Acrobat Reader® program.

To Fill in Forms in the Adobe Acrobat Reader® Program

1. Once you have opened the appropriate form in the Acrobat Reader® program, filling in the form is a simple process. A 'hand tool' icon will be your cursor in the Acrobat Reader® program. Move the 'hand tool' cursor to the first blank space that will need to be completed on the form. A vertical

line or "I-beam" should appear at the beginning of the first space on a form that you will need to fill in. You may then begin to type the necessary information in the space provided. When you have filled in the first blank space, hit the TAB key on your keyboard. This will move the 'hand' cursor to the next space which must be filled in. Please note that some of the spaces in the forms must be completed by hand, specifically the signature blanks.

2. Move through the form, completing each required space, and hitting TAB to move to the next space to be filled in. For information on the information required for each blank on the forms, please read the instructions in this book. When you have completed all of the fill-ins, you may print out the form on your computer's printer. (Please note: hitting TAB after the last fill-in will return you to the first page of the form.)

3. If you wish to save a completed form, you should save it with a new name for the file. This way will allow you to save the original form in its unchanged format for later use if necessary.

To Access and Complete the Text Forms

For your convenience, all of the forms in this book are also provided as text-only forms which may be altered and saved. To open and use any of the text forms:

1. First, open your preferred word processing program. Then click on FILE (in the upper left-hand corner of the upper taskbar). Then click on OPEN in the drop down menu. Depending on which version of Windows or other operating system you are using, a box will open which will allow you to access files on your computer's hard drive. The files for Real Estate Forms are located on your computer's "C" drive, under the folder "Real Estate Forms Simplified." In this folder, you will find a sub-folder: "Forms."

2. If you desire to work with one of the forms, you should then left double-click your mouse on the sub-folder: "Forms." A list of form topics (corresponding to the chapters in the book) will appear and you should then left double-click your mouse on the topic of your choice. This will open two folders: one for text forms and one for PDF forms. Left double click your mouse on the text forms folder and a list of the text forms for that topic should appear. Left double click your mouse on the form of your choice. This will open the appropriate form within your word processing program.

3. You may now fill in the necessary information while the text-only file is open in your word processing program. You may need to adjust margins and/or line endings of the form to fit your particular word processing program. Note that there is an asterisk (*) in every location in these forms where information will need to be included. Replace each asterisk with the necessary information. When the form is complete, you may print out the completed form and you may save the completed form. If you wish to save the completed form, you should rename the form so that your hard drive will retain an unaltered version of the form.

Real Estate Forms Simplified

Technical Support

Nova Publishing will provide technical support for installing the provided software. Please also note that Nova Publishing Company cannot provide legal advice regarding the effect or use of the forms on this software. For questions about installing the Forms-on-CD, you may call Nova Technical Support at 1-800-748-1175.

In addition, Nova cannot provide technical support for the use of the Adobe Acrobat Reader®. For any questions relating to Adobe Acrobat Reader®, please access Adobe Technical Support at www.adobe.com/support/main.html or you may search for assistance in the HELP area of Adobe Acrobat Reader® (located in approximately the center of the top line of the program's desktop).

Chapter 2

The Homebuying Process

Home ownership is becoming a reality for more and more Americans. During 2005, the U.S. home ownership rate reached 69 percent, the highest rate ever. A home is, for most people, the largest single expenditure of their lives. This book will help you understand the entire process of buying and selling a home by looking at the homebuying process and then presenting the various forms used in real estate transactions. The forms in this book may be used for the sale and purchase and even the rental of any type of real estate, not just residential homes. However, to understand the entire process of a real estate transaction, it is useful to look at the most common real estate transaction: buying and selling a single family home.

Participants in the Homebuying Process

- **Lender:** A bank or mortgage company which provides the funds for the purchase of a home
- **Buyer:** A person purchasing a home. The buyer may search for a home with or without the help of a real estate agent (a buyer's agent or seller's agent)
- **Seller:** A person selling a home. The seller usually works closely with a real estate agent to sell his/her home
- **Real Estate Agent:** There are two types of real estate agents. Either real estate agent may be a certified realtor or a lawyer specializing in real estate:
    Selling Agent: A person who earns a commission on the sale of a home from the seller
    Buyer's Agent: A person who earns a commission on the purchase of a home from the buyer
- **Home Inspector:** A real estate professional who inspects a home prior to settlement day. The final result is a report detailing the condition of the house

• **Home Appraiser:** a real estate professional who sets a dollar value for a home's worth, using standard appraisal criteria. The appraisal is one of the important documents required at closing.

Using a Real Estate Professional

Using a real estate agent or broker is often a very good idea. All the details involved in homebuying, particularly the financial ones, can be mind-boggling. A good real estate professional can guide you through the entire process and make the experience much easier. A real estate broker will be well-acquainted with all the important things you'll want to know about a neighborhood you may be considering: the quality of schools, the number of children in the area, the safety of the neighborhood, traffic volume, and more. He or she will help you figure the price range you can afford and will search the classified ads and multiple listing services for homes you'll want to see. With immediate access to homes as soon as they're put on the market, the broker can save you hours of wasted driving-around time. When it's time to make an offer on a home, the broker can point out ways to structure your deal to save you money. He or she will explain the advantages and disadvantages of different types of mortgages, guide you through the paperwork, and be there to hold your hand and answer last-minute questions when you sign the final papers at closing. Generally, the broker or agent's payment comes from the home seller - not from the buyer.

You may also consider using a lawyer for your closing or to help with the complex paperwork and legal contracts. A lawyer can review contracts, make you aware of special considerations, and assist you with the closing process. Your real estate agent may be able to recommend a lawyer. If not, shop around. Find out what services are provided for what fee, and whether the attorney is experienced at representing home buyers.

Are You Ready to Buy?

There are many reasons that make buying your own home a good idea. You can deduct the cost of your mortgage loan interest from your federal income taxes, and usually from your state taxes, too. Interest will compose nearly all of your monthly payments, for over half the number of years you'll be paying your mortgage. This adds up to hefty savings at the end of each year. You're also allowed to deduct the property taxes you pay as a homeowner. If you rent, you write your monthly check and it's gone forever. Another financial plus in owning a home is the possibility that its value will go up through the years.

If you have had bad credit, and don't have much for a down-payment, you may still be able to become a home buyer. You may be a good candidate for one of the federal mortgage programs that are available. A good place for you to start is by contacting one of the HUD-funded housing counseling agencies (HUD is the *U.S. Department of Housing and Urban Development*). Please see **www.hud.gov.** They can help you sort through your options. In addition, contact your local government to see if there are any local home ownership programs that might work for you. Look in the blue pages of your phone directory for your local office of housing and community development. Most people who rent the home that they are living in can afford to buy a home with the right planning. In order to know about your homebuying potential, it will be useful for you to take a look at your income, savings, monthly expenses, and debt. All of these are important factors in how much mortgage you can afford and also in how purchasing a home can affect your monthly budget. Together the following four categories are a guide that will give you a better understanding of your financial situation.

Income: Review your income. Purchasing a home may require that you have a certain amount in savings that can be applied to your down payment and closing costs. If you don't have a lot of cash available, there are loan programs available, especially through FHA (Federal Housing Administration) and VA (Veteran's Administration) mortgage programs that do not require much cash payment at closing. Some questions to consider:

- On average, what is your monthly income?
- Will your income remain stable in the near future?
- Are you expecting any increase or decrease in income in the near future?

Savings: Review your savings. A little savings can help a great deal when planning to purchase a home. There are some costs that you cannot finance through your loan; you have to pay those at closing, the day that you buy your home. Some questions to consider:

- What portion of your income are you saving?
- Can you save more money than you are now?

Monthly expenses: Monthly expenses may increase. The purchase of your home will likely change how much you will need to spend on expenses every month. If you have trouble saving now, your finances may be too tight after the purchase of a home. Some questions to ask yourself:

- How will buying a home affect my monthly budget and my ability to save?
- Can I support the additional expenses that the purchase of a home will bring?
- Do I expect to maintain a stable income for the foreseeable future?

Debt responsibilities: Review your debt responsibilities. Consider how your debt, in relation to your income, will influence a lender's decision on your mortgage loan amount. Carefully consider how additional debt from house payments, on top of your existing debt, will restrict your lifestyle. Some questions to ask yourself:
- How much debt can I afford to manage comfortably?
- Will I be able to manage my debt responsibilities through the life of my loan?

Understanding Mortgage Math

Generally speaking, a mortgage is a loan obtained to purchase real estate. The "mortgage" itself is a *lien* (a legal claim) on the home or property that secures the promise to pay the debt. All mortgages have two features in common: *principal* and *interest*. Principal is the amount of money that you have actually borrowed and interest is the amount of money that the lender will charge you for the privilege of borrowing the principal amount of the loan. There are many types of mortgages, and the more you know about them before you start, the better.

Most people use a *fixed-rate mortgage*. In a fixed-rate mortgage, your interest rate stays the same for the term of the mortgage, which normally is 30 years. The advantage of a fixed-rate mortgage is that you always know exactly how much your mortgage payment will be, and you can plan for it. Another kind of mortgage is an *Adjustable Rate Mortgage* (ARM). With this kind of mortgage, your interest rate and monthly payments usually start lower than those for a fixed rate mortgage. But your rate and payment can change either up or down, as often as once or twice a year. The adjustment is tied to a financial index, such as the U.S. Treasury Securities index. The advantage of an ARM is that you may be able to afford a more expensive home because your initial interest rate will be lower. There are several government mortgage programs that might interest you, too. Most people have heard of FHA mortgages. FHA doesn't actually make loans. Instead, it insures loans so that if buyers default for some reason, the lenders will get their money. This encourages lenders to give mortgages to people who might not otherwise qualify for a loan.

The monthly mortgage payment mainly pays off principal and interest. But most lenders also include local real estate taxes, homeowner's insurance, and mortgage insurance (if applicable). The amount of the down payment, the size of the mortgage loan, the interest rate, the length of the repayment term and payment schedule will all affect the size of your mortgage payment. A lower interest rate allows you to borrow more money than a high rate with the same monthly payment. Interest rates can fluctuate as you shop for a loan, so ask lenders if they offer a rate "lock-in" which guarantees a specific interest rate for a certain period of time. Remember that a lender must disclose the Annual Percentage Rate (APR) of a loan to you. The APR shows the cost of a mortgage loan by expressing it in terms of a yearly interest rate. It is generally higher than the interest rate because it also includes the cost of points, mortgage insurance, and other fees included in the loan. If interest rates drop significantly, you may want to investigate refinancing. Most experts agree that if you plan to be in your house for at least 18 months and you can get a rate two (2) percent less than your current one, refinancing is smart. Refinancing may, however, involve paying many of the same fees that you paid at the original closing, plus origination and application fees. Most loans have four parts:

- **Principal:** The repayment of the amount you actually borrowed
- **Interest:** Payment to the lender for the money you've borrowed
- **Homeowners Insurance:** A monthly amount to insure the property against loss from fire, smoke, theft, and other hazards required by most lenders
- **Property Taxes:** The annual city/county taxes assessed on your property, divided by the number of mortgage payments you make in a year

Most loans are for 30 years, although 15-year loans are available, too. During the life of the loan, you'll pay far more in interest than you will in principal - sometimes two or three times more. Because of the way loans are structured, in the first years you'll be paying mostly interest in your monthly payments. In the final years, you'll be paying mostly principal.

Following are some definitions and calculations that will help you understand some of the terms and figures that lenders use to determine if you can afford to purchase a particular home. Mortgage lenders use many of the following basic mortgage calculations in their mortgage qualification process.

PITI: This figure is the sum of Principal, Interest, Property Taxes, and Insurance payments. For most homeowners, PITI represent the amount of their monthly mortgage payment.

Principal + Interest + Property Tax + Insurance = PITI

PITIO: This figure is the sum of Principal, Interest, Taxes, Insurance, and Other monthly non-housing costs, basically all of the money that you usually spend in a month.

Principal + Interest + Property Tax + Insurance + Total Other Costs = PITIO

Cash Required (or funds required at closing): This is the total of a buyer's closing costs and down payment amount.

Total Closing Costs + Down Payment = Cash Required

Debt Ratio: This is the percentage of monthly income that can be applied toward monthly long-term debt obligations. Loan programs have different guidelines on debt ratio percentages. Government loan programs typically have higher debt ratio percentages, allowing more home buyers to qualify for loans.

Debt Ratio = PITIO ÷ Total Monthly Income

Down Payment: The Down Payment can be shown as the difference between the Home Sales Price and the Loan Amount. This is one of the main parts of the "up-front" cash required at closing. It represents a percentage of the home sales price paid at closing. For example: a 20 percent down payment on a $100,000 sales price is equivalent to a down payment of $20,000 at closing.

Home Sales Price – Loan Amount = Down Payment

Front-End Ratio: This is the percentage of your monthly income that can be applied toward monthly house payments. Each loan program has different guidelines on front-end ratio percentages. Typically, government loan programs have higher front-end ratio percentages, allowing more home buyers to qualify for loans.

Front-End Ratio = PITI ÷ Total Monthly Income

Maximum Loan Amount: This figure is the sum of the total loan amount and other financed fees.

It represents the maximum amount that the lender is willing to offer based on constraints including income, debt, and cash available. This maximum loan amount is set by the lender or by the specific type of loan. For example, a lender offering to finance a $100,000 home with a LTV (Loan to Value ratio) of 97 percent approves a maximum loan amount of $97,000. The buyer must include the remaining 3 percent ($3,000 in this example) in the down payment.

Home Sales Price × Loan to Value (LTV) percent = Maximum Loan Amount

Fixed Rate vs. Adjustable Rate

A Fixed-Rate Mortgage applies the same interest rate toward monthly loan payments for the life of the loan. Fixed-rate mortgages are more straightforward and easier to understand than Adjustable Rate Mortgages (ARMs). They are also more secure for the buyer, and are popular with first-time home buyers. Since the risk to the lender is higher, fixed-rate mortgages generally have higher interest rates than ARMs. For example, a lender can offer a 30-year fixed loan to a home buyer at a 7.0 percent interest rate. The loan is locked in to the 7.0 percent interest rate even if the market interest rate rises to 9.0 percent. Conversely, if the market interest rate decreases to 5.5 percent, you, as the borrower, will continue to pay the 7.0 percent interest rate.

Fixed-Rate benefits include:
- No change in monthly principal and interest payments regardless of fluctuations in interest rates
- More stability may give you "peace-of-mind"

Fixed-Rate disadvantages include:
- Higher initial monthly payments compared to those of adjustable rate mortgages
- Less flexibility

An Adjustable Rate Mortgage (ARM) does not apply the same interest rate toward monthly payments for the life of the loan. Throughout the life of that loan, the home buyer's principal and interest payment will adjust periodically based on fluctuations in the interest rate. For example, a lender could offer a 30-year ARM loan to a home buyer at an initial 6.5 percent interest rate. During an adjustment period for the ARM loan, the market interest rate could rise to 8.0 percent, resulting in a significantly larger interest payment. Similarly, the market interest rate could decrease to 6.0 percent, resulting in lower interest payments.

ARM benefits include:
- Initial payments lower due to lower beginning interest rate, usually about 2 percentage points below the fixed rate
- Ability to qualify for a higher loan amount due to lower initial interest rates
- Lower interest payments if the interest rate drops over time
- Interest rate caps limit the maximum interest payment allowed for the loan

ARM disadvantages include:
- Initial lower interest rate and monthly payments are temporary and apply to the first adjustment period. Typically, the interest rate will rise after the initial adjustment period.
- Higher interest payments if the interest rate rises over time

Buydown vs. Graduated Payment Mortgage (GPM)

While these two mortgage types start the home buyer off at one rate and increase the rate over time, one of these types of mortgages may be right for you:

Buydowns: This is a type of mortgage loan where the loan rate is reduced by paying more up-front at closing and is increased by one percent each year for the period set for the type of loan. For example: For a 2-1 buydown at an 8 percent rate, Year 1 the rate is 6 percent, Year 2 the rate is 7 percent. For Year 3 through the life of the loan, the rate is 8 percent. Qualification rules for the loan programs remain the same. Depending on the lender, though, the buyer can qualify using the reduced rate. (Example: For a 3-2-1 Buydown at a rate of 8 percent, the buyer could qualify using the 5 percent rate.) The difference between the actual payment schedule and the rate schedule is usually paid "up-front" at closing. This can be paid by the seller, the buyer, the home builder, or in some cases, the lender. If the cost is borne by the lender, it is usually offset with increased rates or in points. Generally the funds used to buy down the loan are held in a separate account and are applied with the borrower's payment to equal the true interest rate.

Graduated Payment Mortgage (GPM): This is a type of mortgage loan where the mortgage payments increase gradually for a period established in the loan paperwork, typically five years. This is a negatively amortizing loan, which means that the difference between the interest paid and the interest due is deferred and added to the loan balances. Because of this, your loan amount will increase once you start paying off the loan; it will amortize normally at the end of the loan period. These types of loans are more popular when the interest rates are higher, providing a financial incentive for potential buyers. Since many lenders will qualify a buyer at a lower rate, a buyer can secure a larger mortgage. These loan types are good for those buyers who are fairly certain that their incomes will increase to cover the increase in loan amount.

Interest Rates and Points

The interest rate determines the monthly interest payments over the lifetime of the loan. A "point" or "discount point" is equivalent to 1 percent of the loan amount and usually reduces or "discounts" the loan rate by an eighth of a percentage point. For example: You want to get a loan for $100,000 to buy a home. Each "point" would cost you 1 percent of $100,000 or $1,000 but would reduce your loan's interest rate by .125 percent. The lender might offer you an 8.0 percent loan with zero points, a 7.875 percent loan with one point, or a 7.75 percent loan with 2 points. Points are an up-front payment, in addition to the down payment that is required upon closing. In some cases, lenders will allow borrowers to finance the points over the term of the loan. Lenders sometimes use points to make their interest rates appear lower. Be aware that lower interest rate offered by a lender may translate into higher points requirements.

Mortgage Payment Calculator Chart

The following chart will give you a basic idea of what your monthly principal and interest payments for 30-year, fixed rate mortgage will be. Monthly taxes and mortgage insurance costs are not included. You may combine the payments to find your correct house loan cost (for example to find the payment for a $155,000 home, combine the monthly payments for a $100,000, a $25,000 and a $30,000 mortgage).

Mortgage Payment Calculator Chart

COST	6%	6.5%	7%	7.5%	8%	8.5%	9%	9.5%	10%
$ 25,000	$150	158	166	175	183	192	201	210	219
$ 30,000	$180	190	200	210	220	231	241	252	263
$ 40,000	$240	253	266	280	293	308	322	336	351
$ 50,000	$300	316	333	350	367	384	402	420	439
$ 60,000	$360	379	399	420	440	461	483	505	527
$ 70,000	$420	442	466	489	514	538	563	589	614
$ 80,000	$480	506	532	559	587	615	644	673	702
$ 90,000	$540	569	599	629	660	692	724	757	790
$100,000	$600	632	665	699	734	769	805	841	878
$110,000	$660	695	732	769	807	846	885	925	965
$120,000	$719	758	798	839	880	923	966	1,009	1,053
$130,000	$780	822	865	909	954	1,000	1,046	1,093	1,141
$140,000	$839	885	931	979	1,027	1,076	1,126	1,177	1,229
$150,000	$899	948	998	1,049	1,101	1,153	1,207	1,261	1,316
$160,000	$959	1,011	1,064	1,119	1,174	1,230	1,287	1,345	1,404
$170,000	$1,019	1,075	1,131	1,189	1,247	1,307	1,368	1,429	1,492

Choosing the Best Loan

Your personal situation will determine the best kind of loan for you. By asking yourself a few questions, you can help narrow your search among the many options available and discover which loan suits you best.

• Do you expect your finances to change over the next few years?
• Are you planning to live in this home for a long period of time?
• Are you comfortable with the idea of a changing mortgage payment amount?
• Do you wish to be free of mortgage debt as your children approach college age or as you prepare for retirement?

Loan Application

The first step in securing a loan is to complete a loan application. This section gives you a better understanding of what information is used to determine your ability to qualify for a loan. The information in this section is designed to help you organize all of the information that you will need to gather all of your necessary information and present to a bank or lending institution when you apply for a home loan. By reviewing your own personal information, you should be able to determine your ability to obtain a loan. The actual loan application that you use will come directly from the lender.

When you turn in your application, you'll be required to pay a loan application fee to cover the costs of underwriting the loan. This fee pays for the home appraisal, a copy of your credit report, and any additional charges that may be necessary. The application fee is generally non-refundable. To ensure you won't fall victim to loan fraud, be sure to follow all of these steps as you apply for a loan:

• Be sure to read and understand everything before you sign
• Refuse to sign any blank documents
• Do not buy property for someone else
• Do not overstate your income
• Do not overstate how long you have been employed
• Do not overstate your assets
• Accurately report your debts
• Do not change your income tax returns for any reason
• Tell the whole truth about gifts
• Do not list fake co-borrowers on your loan application
• Be truthful about your credit problems, past and present
• Be honest about your intention to occupy the house
• Do not provide false supporting documents

You will be required to bring various supporting documents with you when you have your loan application meeting with the lender. If you have everything with you when you visit your lender, you'll save a good deal of time. You should have the following with you when you visit with your lender:

- Social Security numbers for both you and your spouse, if both of you are applying for the loan
- Copies of your checking and savings account statements for the past 6 months
- Evidence of any other assets, like bonds or stocks
- A recent paycheck stub detailing your earnings
- List of all credit card accounts and approximate monthly amounts owed on each
- List of account numbers and balances due on outstanding loans, such as a car loan
- Copies of your last 2 years' income tax statements
- Name and address of someone who can verify your employment. Depending on your lender, you may be asked for other information

Lenders will review your income, debt, and savings information to determine how much money they are willing to lend you towards your home purchase. Lenders will provide you with an estimate on how much you can qualify to spend toward the purchase of a home. This estimate is the maximum amount that the lender is willing to lend you. Based on your lifestyle and needs, you should consider how much you are willing to spend on the purchase of a home. In some cases, the home buyer is not willing to invest as much of their income toward a house as he or she can actually afford. Below are further details about the kinds of information used to determine how much you can afford, namely income, debt, and housing-related expenses.

Income: Your income will be critical in computing how much you can afford to pay (using current lending guidelines) for housing-related expenses. Your income information is included in the PITI (Principal, Interest, Taxes, and Insurance) and PITIO debt ratio (PITI and other debt) calculations. Your ability to meet the PITI, or front-end ratio, and the PITIO ratio, or debt ratio, can have an impact on a lender's decision to offer you a loan. Different loan programs have their own rules regarding the percentage of income that can be applied toward monthly house payments. For example, government loan programs such as FHA and VA have ratios that allow you to apply a higher percentage of your income toward the loan. While conventional loan front-end ratios generally run around 28 percent, FHA allows you to apply 29 percent and VA allows you to apply 41 percent. Basically, this means that your monthly loan payment should be no more than 28 percent, 29 percent, or 41 percent of total monthly income, depending on the loan program.

Debt: A lender carefully considers your debt information when it assesses your ability to repay a loan. Your debt information is included in the PITIO, or debt ratio calculation. Loan programs have different rules regarding the percentage of income that can apply towards long-term debt. Your ability to meet the ratio requirements can affect a lender's decision to offer you a loan. Government loan programs such as FHA and VA allow you to apply a higher percentage of your debt requirements towards the loan. While conventional loan debt ratios generally run around 36 percent, FHA and VA allow you to apply 41 percent. Basically, this means that your long-term monthly debt payment plus your monthly loan payment can equal no more than 36 percent or 41 percent of total monthly income, depending on the loan program.

Housing-Related Expenses: Housing-related expenses are another category that lenders consider. These expenses often depend on the location and type of home. This will influence the amount of the loan for which you can qualify and may be one of the most critical factors in your decision to buy a home. You should consider how housing-related expenses could affect your budget. The purchase of a home may increase your monthly expenses and reduce the amount of money you have remaining to support your lifestyle. Typical home expenses include:

Property tax: This expense is dependent on the location of the home. Different counties and states have different property tax requirements. As a home buyer, you would be wise to consider how this additional expense will impact your total monthly expenses.

Maintenance costs: This expense includes anything from washers in the faucets to a new roof or heating system and varies by the geographic location, size, and age of a home.

Utility costs: This expense includes items such as electric, gas, water, and heating and air conditioning, and varies by geographic location, size, season, and age of a home. The type of construction (i.e. gas, electric) may also be a factor in your utility cost estimates.

Mortgage insurance (if applicable): This expense can vary by mortgage insurance company, lender, type of loan, and loan-to-value percentage of the loan.

Other Costs: These expenses vary depending on the type of home and geographic location. These costs can include: homeowner association fees; flood insurance; other required property insurance; condominium assessment fees; and other condominium escrow items.

It usually takes a lender between 1-6 weeks to complete the evaluation of your application. It's not unusual for the lender to ask for more information once the application has been submitted. The sooner you can provide the information, the faster your application will be processed. Once all the information has been verified, the lender will call you to let you know the outcome of your application. If the loan is approved, a closing date is set up and the lender will review the closing with you. After closing, you'll be able to move into your new home.

Checking Your Credit Record

There are three major credit reporting companies: Equifax, Experian, and Trans Union. Obtaining your credit report is as easy as calling and requesting one. Once you receive the report, it's important to verify its accuracy. Double check the "high credit limit," "total loan," and "past due" columns. It's a good idea to get copies from all three companies to assure there are no mistakes, since any of the three could be providing a report to your lender. Fees, ranging from $5-$20, are usually charged to issue credit reports but some states permit citizens to acquire a free one. Contact the reporting companies at the numbers listed for more information:

- Experian: 1-888-243-6951 (www.experian.com)
- Equifax: 1-800-685-1111 (www.equifax.com)
- Trans Union: 1-800-916-8800 (www.tuc.com)

Simple mistakes in your credit record are easily corrected by writing to the reporting company, pointing out the error, and providing proof of the mistake. You can also request to have your own comments added to explain problems. For example, if you made a payment late due to illness, explain that for the record. Lenders are usually understanding about legitimate problems.

A credit bureau score is a number based upon your credit history that represents the possibility that you will be unable to repay a loan. Lenders use it to determine your ability to qualify for a mortgage loan. The better the score, the better your chances are of getting a loan. There are no easy ways to improve your credit score, but you can work to keep it acceptable by maintaining a good credit history. This means paying your bills on time and not overextending yourself by buying more than you can afford.

Homeowner's Tax Benefits

Purchasing a home can provide valuable tax savings to home buyers. Mortgage interest, property tax, and other payments associated with financing a home can apply to your tax deductions. These deductions may decrease the amount of income tax you must pay to the federal government. Another financial advantage to owning a home is that as you begin to pay off your mortgage loan, you build *equity* (the cash value of your home – derived from the market value of your home minus the amount you still owe on the mortgage) in your property. In other words, the value of your home can increase as your total mortgage amount decreases over time. For those who rent, the tax savings of ownership go to the landlord, not to the tenants. Wouldn't you rather build equity for yourself every month instead of paying someone else and giving away "your" tax savings?

Cash Requirements

The amount of money that you will have to come up with to buy a home depends on a number of factors, including the cost of the house and the type of mortgage you get. In general, you need to come up with enough money to cover three costs:

- Earnest Money: the deposit you make on the home when you submit your offer, to prove to the seller that you are serious about wanting to buy the house
- Down Payment: a percentage of the cost of the home that you must pay when you go to to the closing and
- Closing Costs: the costs associated with processing the paperwork to buy a house

When you make an offer on a home, your real estate broker will put your earnest money into an escrow account. If the offer is accepted, your earnest money will be applied to the down payment or closing costs. If your offer is not accepted, your money will be returned to you. The amount of your earnest money varies. If you buy a HUD home, for example, your earnest money deposit generally will range from $500 - $2,000. The more money you can put into your down payment, the lower your mortgage payments will be. Some types of loans require 10-20 percent of the purchase price. That's why many first-time home buyers turn to the FHA for help. FHA loans require only 3.5 percent down - and sometimes less. Closing costs, which you will pay at closing, generally average 3 to 4 percent of the price of your home. These costs cover various fees that your lender charges and other processing expenses. When you apply for your loan, your lender will give you an estimate of the closing costs, so you won't be caught by surprise. If you buy a HUD home, HUD may pay many of your closing costs.

The savings and cash you currently have available can be used to support your up-front payments such as the closing costs and down payment for your home. Consider what savings and cash you will have left after paying your up-front costs to support non-housing-related expenses and emergencies (i.e. unexpected car repairs, credit card payments, car loans). Most lenders prefer that homeowners have three months of living expenses available after closing on the loan. The up-front cash requirements include:

Closing Costs: You need to pay these up-front costs when you close on your home. Closing costs generally depend on the location of the house and the type of loan program. There are opportunities to negotiate closing cost expenses with the seller and lender. Furthermore, there are opportunities to finance some portion of the closing costs as part of the loan amount. Some typical closing costs are:

- Fees paid to the lender
- Fees paid in advance
- Other charges
- Origination fee
- Discount points
- Credit report fee
- Appraisal fee
- Assumption fee if loan is assumed
- Interest from the closing date to the beginning of the 1st payment
- Hazard insurance premium
- Mortgage insurance premium
- Title search and title insurance
- Sales commissions
- Legal and recording fees
- Inspection and survey fees
- Property taxes and other adjustments
- Processing and document preparation fees

Down Payment: This percentage of the sales price must be paid up-front and can vary by lender, location, and loan program. A higher down payment generally translates into lower loan interest rate requirements. While conventional loan down payments may be close to 20 percent of the sales price, government loans typically have lower down payment requirements. This allows potential home buyers who normally can not meet down payment requirements an opportunity to qualify for a mortgage. Keep in mind that down payments less than 20 percent of the sales price typically require mortgage insurance payments.

Example: With an annual income of $45,000 and monthly debt totaling $400, this home buyer may qualify for different loan programs based on a 30-year fixed rate loan with an interest rate of 7.25 percent. Notice that the home buyer can qualify for a more expensive house under the VA program ($141,771) than under either the FHA or conventional loan programs. (The results below are a rough estimate and do not reflect all factors included in the loan qualification calculation.)

	FHA	VA	Conventional
Home Sales Price	$125,507	$141,771	$124,903
Down Payment	$2,858	$0	$12,503
Cash Required	$8,365	$6,132	$17,601
Total Monthly Payment	$1,086	$1,193	$949

These results show that the home buyer can qualify for approximately the same home price for either an FHA or conventional loan. However, there's a big difference in down payment and up-front cash requirements for government loans versus conventional loans. The down payment requirement for the FHA loan is $2,858, approximately 3 percent of the maximum loan amount, out of a total loan for the home of $125,400. To purchase approximately the same house price using a conventional loan, the down payment requirements would total $12,503, an additional $9645. This is about 10 percent of the maximum conventional loan amount. If the home buyer is a veteran, with the same income, the veteran could qualify for a higher home price with no down payment.

Allowable Sources for Down Payment

Most people don't have much money to put toward down payment costs for a home. There are possible solutions to a common cash problem:

- **Co-Borrower:** Income or additional funds from a spouse may provide additional funds to support the down payment costs. You may also want to consider whether a roommate or co-dweller may relieve the financial burden by assisting you with your down payment.

- **Gifts:** Monetary gifts from family members can support your down payment requirements since no funds repayment is required

- **Inheritance/Trust Funds:** Inherited money from family members or a trust fund are also acceptable sources of down payment since no funds repayment is required

- **Borrowing/Loan:** Monetary support from friends or relatives are a solution

- **Retirement Funds:** Some retirement funds like the 401K plans may allow you to borrow a certain percentage from your retirement fund. You should check with your local lenders to see if they allow home buyers to borrow against their retirement funds. *Note*: Borrowing against your 401K plan requires that you repay the amount; therefore, when lenders calculate your loan qualifications, they will add your 401K repayments in calculating your monthly payments

- **Down Payment Assistance Programs:** There are also programs and organizations that can help you with your down payment requirements, such as:

  - **Federal Government Loan Programs:** Federal Housing Administration (FHA) and the Department of Veteran Affairs (VA) may offer assistance in paying your up-front cash requirements. These programs can significantly reduce your down payment requirements. You may also want to contact your local Department of Housing and Urban Development (HUD) Community Builders to find out what local down payment assistance programs are available.

  - **State Housing Authorities:** State agencies may offer down payment assistance programs in your state.

  - **Private Mortgage Insurance:** Private insurance companies that offer you opportunity to finance some of your down payment requirements. This allows lenders to accept lower down payments than they would normally allow.

Mortgage Insurance

Mortgage insurance is a policy that protects lenders against some or most of the losses that result from defaults on home mortgages. It's required primarily for borrowers making a down payment of less than 20 percent. Like home or auto insurance, mortgage insurance requires payment of a premium, is for protection against loss, and is used in the event of an emergency. If a borrower can't repay an insured mortgage loan as agreed, the lender may foreclose on the property and file a claim with the mortgage insurer for some or most of the total losses. You need mortgage insurance only if you plan to make a down payment of less than 20 percent of the purchase price of the home. The FHA offers several loan programs that may meet your needs.

Government Loan Programs

Federal Housing Administration (FHA) Loans

The Federal Housing Administration was established in 1934 to advance opportunities for Americans to own homes. By providing private lenders with mortgage insurance, the FHA gives lenders the security they need to lend to first-time buyers who might not be able to qualify for conventional loans. The FHA has helped more than 26 million Americans buy a home. The FHA works to make home ownership a possibility for more Americans. With the FHA, you don't need perfect credit or a high-paying job to qualify for a loan. The FHA also makes loans more accessible by requiring smaller down payments than conventional loans. In fact, an FHA down payment could be as little as a few months rent. And your monthly payments may not be much more than rent. Lender claims paid by the FHA mortgage insurance program are drawn from the Mutual Mortgage Insurance fund. This fund is made up of premiums paid by FHA-insured loan borrowers. No tax dollars are used to fund the program.

Anyone who meets the credit requirements, can afford the mortgage payments and cash investment, and who plans to use the mortgaged property as a primary residence may apply for an FHA-insured loan. FHA loan limits vary throughout the country, from $115,200 in low-cost areas to $208,800 in high-cost areas. The loan maximums for multi-unit homes are higher than those for single units and also vary by area. Because these maximums are linked to the conforming loan limit and average area home prices, FHA loan limits are periodically subject to change. Ask your lender for details and confirmation of current limits.

With the exception of a few additional forms, the FHA loan application process is similar to that of a conventional loan. There is no minimum income requirement, but you must prove steady income for at least three years, and demonstrate that you've consistently paid your bills on time. Seasonal pay, child support, retirement pension payments, unemployment compensation, VA benefits, military pay, Social Security income, alimony, and rent paid by your family – all qualify as income sources. Part-time pay, overtime, and bonus pay also count as long as they are steady. Special savings plans, such as those set up by a church or community association, also qualify. Income type is not as important as income steadiness with the FHA. Short-term debt doesn't count as long as it can be paid off within 10 months. And some regular expenses, like child care costs, are not considered debt. Talk to your lender or real estate agent about meeting the FHA debt-to-income ratio.

The FHA allows you to use 29 percent of your income towards housing costs and 41 percent towards housing expenses and other long-term debt. With a conventional loan, this qualifying ratio allows only 28 percent toward housing and 36 percent towards housing and other debt. You may qualify to exceed these percentages if you have:

- A large down payment
- A demonstrated ability to pay more toward your housing expenses
- Substantial cash reserves

- Net worth enough to repay the mortgage, regardless of income
- Evidence of acceptable credit history, or limited credit use
- Less-than-maximum mortgage terms funds provided by an organization
- A decrease in monthly housing expenses.

You must have a down payment of at least 3.5 percent of the purchase price of the home. Most affordable loan programs offered by private lenders require between a 3-5 percent down payment, with a minimum of 3 percent coming directly from the borrower's own funds. Besides your own funds, you may use cash gifts or money from a private savings club. If you can do certain repairs and improvements yourself, your labor may be used as part of a down payment (called "sweat equity"). If you are doing a lease purchase, paying extra rent to the seller may also be considered the same as accumulating cash.

The FHA is generally more flexible than conventional lenders in its qualifying guidelines. In fact, the FHA allows you to re-establish credit if:

- Two years have passed since a bankruptcy has been discharged
- All judgments have been paid
- Any outstanding tax liens have been satisfied
- Appropriate arrangements have been made to establish a repayment plan with the IRS or State Department of Revenue
- Three years have passed since a foreclosure
- A deed-in-lieu issue has been resolved.

If you prefer to pay debts in cash or are too young to have established credit, there are other ways to prove your eligibility. Talk to your lender for details. Except for the addition of an FHA mortgage insurance premium, FHA closing costs are similar to those of a conventional loan. The FHA requires a single, up-front mortgage insurance premium equal to 2.25 percent of the mortgage to be paid at closing. This initial premium may be partially refunded if the loan is paid in full during the first seven years of the loan term. After closing, you will then be responsible for an annual premium (paid monthly) if your mortgage is over 15 years or if you have a 15-year loan with an LTV (loan to value ratio) greater than 90 percent. Although you can't roll closing costs into your FHA loan, you may be able to use the amount you pay for them to help satisfy the down payment requirement.

You can *assume* (take over the mortgage payments) an existing FHA-insured loan, or, if you are the one deciding to sell, allow a buyer to assume yours. Assuming a loan can be very beneficial, since the process is streamlined and less expensive compared to that for a new loan. Also, assuming a loan can often result in a lower interest rate. The application process consists basically of a credit check and no property appraisal is required. You must demonstrate that you have enough income to support the mortgage loan. In this way, qualifying to assume a loan is similar to the qualification requirements for a new one.

FHA mortgage programs are available to all buyers. These programs are designed to help creditworthy low-income and moderate-income families who do not meet requirements for conventional loans. FHA loan programs are particularly beneficial to those buyers who don't have much cash available. For more information on the FHA and how you can obtain an FHA loan, visit the HUD web site at:

http://www. hud.gov

or call a HUD-approved counseling agency at 1-800-569-4287. You can also look in the phone book "blue pages" for a listing of the HUD office near you.

FHA loan benefits:

- Only requires a 3.5 percent down payment
- Ability to finance closing costs
- FHA has set limits on the amount lenders can charge for some closing cost fees (e.g. origination no more than 1 percent of mortgage)
- Maximum mortgage amount can vary significantly by area. FHA adjusts this amount periodically. You should check with your local FHA office or approved lender to determine your maximum mortgage amount
- Under certain conditions, automatic cancellation of the FHA mortgage insurance premium

Department of Veteran Affairs (VA) Loans

VA loan programs are available to eligible veterans for the purchase of a home. The VA guaranty loans encourage lenders to offer loans to veterans by protecting lenders against loss if the borrower cannot make the payments. VA loans are particularly beneficial to those veterans who do not have much cash available. VA guidelines allow higher front-end and debt ratios compared to other loan programs. If you are a veteran, contact your local or regional VA office for more details or talk to your lender.

VA loan benefits:

- No down payment requirement
- More favorable interest rates are frequently offered by lenders because of the VA's guarantee backing
- No mortgage insurance premiums
- Maximum loan amount may be 100 percent of appraised value of home, determined by a VA-approved appraiser or up to four times the VA eligibility entitlement (currently $50,750 with a maximum loan amount of $200,300)

Finding the Perfect Home

Your home should fit the way you live, with spaces and features that appeal to the whole family. Before you begin looking at homes, make a list of your priorities, including things like location and size. For example, should the house be:

- Close to certain schools?
- Close to your job?
- Close to public transportation?
- How large should the house be?
- What type of lot do you prefer?
- What kinds of amenities are you looking for?

Establish a set of minimum requirements and a "wish list." Minimum requirements are things that a house must have for you to consider it, while a "wish list" covers things that you'd like to have but that aren't essential. Select a community that will allow you to best live your daily life. Many people choose communities based on schools. When you find places that you like, talk to people who live there. They know the most about the area and will be your future neighbors. More than anything, you want a neighborhood where you feel comfortable. For example:

- Do you want access to shopping and public transportation?
- Is access to local facilities like libraries and museums important to you?
- Do you prefer the peace and quiet of a rural community?

If you ever feel that you are being excluded from certain neighborhoods, sections of a community, or a particular house, immediately contact the *U.S. Department of Housing and Urban Development* (HUD). Also, contact HUD if you believe you are being discriminated against on the basis of race, color, religion, sex, nationality, familial status, or disability. HUD's *Office of Fair Housing* has a hotline for reporting incidents of discrimination: 1-800-669-9777 (or on the HUD website at: www.hud.gov).

You can get information about school systems by contacting the city or county school board or the local schools. Your real estate agent may also be knowledgeable about schools in the area. Contact the local chamber of commerce for promotional literature or talk to your real estate agent about welcome kits, maps, and other information. You may also want to visit the local library. It can be an excellent source for information on local events and resources, and the librarians will probably be able to answer many of the questions you have.

You should look at each home for its individual characteristics. Generally, older homes may be in more established neighborhoods, offer more ambiance, and have lower property tax rates. People who buy older homes, however, shouldn't mind maintaining their home and making some repairs. Newer homes tend to use more modern architecture and systems, are usually easier to maintain, and may be more energy-efficient. People who buy new homes often don't want to worry initially about upkeep and repairs. In addition to comparing the home to your minimum requirement and wish lists, consider the following:

- Is there enough room for both the present and the future?
- Are there enough bedrooms and bathrooms?
- Is the house structurally sound?
- Do the mechanical systems and appliances work?
- Is the yard big enough?
- Do you like the floor plan?
- Will your furniture fit in the space?
- Is there enough storage space? (Bring a tape measure to better answer these questions.)
- Will the seller repair or replace the items?
- Imagine the house in good weather and bad, and in each season.
- Will you be happy with it year-round?
- Does anything need to be replaced?
- What things require ongoing maintenance (e.g., paint, roof, heating, air conditioning, appliances, carpet)?
- Also ask about the house and neighborhood, focusing on quality of life issues.

Be sure the seller's or real estate agent's answers are clear and complete. Ask questions until you understand all of the information they've given. Making a list of questions ahead of time will help you organize your thoughts and arrange all of the information you receive. Take your time and think carefully about each house you see. Ask your real estate agent to point out the pros and cons of each home from a professional standpoint. Many of your questions should focus on potential problems and maintenance issues. If possible, take photographs of each house: the outside, the major rooms, the yard, and extra features that you like or ones you see as potential problems. And don't hesitate to return for a second look. Visit as many homes as it takes to find the one you want. On average, home buyers see fifteen houses before choosing one. Just be sure to communicate often with your real estate agent about everything you're looking for. It will help avoid wasting your time.

Using a Home Inspector

An inspector checks the safety of your potential new home. Home inspectors focus especially on the structure, construction, and mechanical systems of the house and will make you aware of all repairs that are needed. The inspector does not evaluate whether or not you're getting good value for your money. Generally, an inspector checks (and gives prices for repairs on): the electrical system, plumbing and waste disposal, the water heater, insulation and ventilation, the heating and cooling system, water source and quality, the potential presence of pests, the foundation, doors, windows, ceilings, walls, floors, and roof. Be sure to hire a home inspector that is qualified and experienced.

It's a good idea to have an inspection before you sign a written offer since, once the deal is closed, you've bought the house "as is". Or, you may want to include an inspection clause in the offer when negotiating for a home. An inspection clause gives you an "out" on buying the house if serious problems are found, or gives you the ability to renegotiate the purchase price if repairs are needed. An inspection clause can also specify that the seller must fix the problem(s) before you purchase the house. Following the inspection, the home inspector will be able to answer questions about the report and any problem areas. This is also an opportunity to hear an objective opinion on the home you'd like to purchase and it is a good time to ask general maintenance questions. If your home inspector discovers a serious problem, a more specific and detailed inspection may be recommended. It's a good idea to consider having your home inspected for the presence of a variety of health-related risks like radon gas, asbestos, or possible problems with the water or waste disposal system.

You may also consider obtaining a home warranty policy. Home warranties offer you protection for a specific period of time (e.g., one year) against potentially costly problems, like unexpected repairs on appliances or home systems, which are not covered by homeowner's insurance. Warranties are becoming more popular because they offer protection during the time immediately following the purchase of a home, a time when many people find themselves cash-strapped.

Note: Many states now require various disclosure statements that require the sellers of residential real estate to disclose to the buyers any known defects or problems with the home. The use of these type of forms is explained in Chapter 4. The Forms-on-CD included with this book contains real estate disclosure statements that may be used for all states. In addition, the Appendix of this book contains the various state requirements regarding disclosures. Finally, you should also check with your real estate agent or with a local title insurance or abstract company for details on the disclosure requirements for your locale.

Homebuying Worksheet

Included at the end of this chapter is a Homebuying Worksheet. You should fill one out for every home that you are interested in. By completing the information on this worksheet, you will have a clear outline of the advantages and disadvantages of each home that you look at. This will allow you to decide which of the elements of each home and neighborhood are most important to you.

Making an Offer on a Home

You have found the right house. Now, there are several things you should consider:

• Is the asking price in line with prices of similar homes in the area?
• Is the home in good condition or will you have to spend a substantial amount of money making it the way you want it? You probably want to get a professional home inspection before you make your offer.
• How long has the home been on the market? If it's been for sale for awhile, the seller may be more eager to accept a lower offer
• How much mortgage will be required? Make sure you really can afford whatever offer you make
• How much do you really want the home? The closer you are to the asking price, the more likely your offer will be accepted. In some cases, you may even want to offer more than the asking price, if you know you are competing with others for the house

An Offer to Purchase Real Estate Form is included in this book. If you use a real estate agent, they will assist you in making an offer, which will include the following information:

• Complete legal description of the property
• Amount of earnest money
• Down payment and financing details
• Proposed move-in date
• Price you are offering
• Proposed *closing date* (date when you will pay final price and seller will give you the keys to the home)
• Length of time the offer is valid
• Details of the deal

If your offer is rejected, you begin negotiating. You may have to offer more money, but you may ask the seller to cover some or all of your closing costs or to make repairs that wouldn't normally be expected. Often, negotiations on a price go back and forth several times before a deal is made. Just remember, don't get so caught up in negotiations that you lose sight of what you really want and can afford.

Remember that a sale commitment depends on negotiating a satisfactory contract with the seller, not just making an offer. Other ways to lower insurance costs include insuring your home and car(s) with the same company, increasing home security, and seeking group coverage through alumni or business associations. Insurance costs are always lowered by raising your deductibles, but this exposes you to a higher out-of-pocket cost if you have to file a claim.
Unless you have a buyer's agent, remember that the agent works for the seller. Make a point of asking him or her to keep your discussions and information confidential. Listen to your real estate agent's advice, but follow your own instincts on deciding a fair price. Calculating your offer should involve several factors: what homes sell for in the area, the home's condition, how long it's been on the market, financing terms, and the seller's situation. By the time you're ready to make an offer,

you should have a good idea of what the home is worth and what you can afford. Be prepared for give-and-take negotiations, which are very common when buying a home. The buyer and seller may often go back and forth until they can agree on a price.

Earnest money is money put down to demonstrate your seriousness about buying a home. It must be substantial enough to demonstrate good faith and is usually between 1-5 percent of the purchase price (though the amount can vary with local customs and conditions). If your offer is accepted, the earnest money becomes part of your down payment or closing costs. If the offer is rejected, your money is returned to you. If you back out of a deal, you may have to forfeit the entire amount. If your offer is accepted, your next step is to secure financing from a lender. The issues involved in financing have already been covered. With your financing secure, you then proceed to your "closing" on the property.

At Your Closing

Closing is the final step in buying a home. It is the meeting in which the buyer will pay closing costs and sign a mortgage or deed of trust and the seller will turn over the deed to the property and the keys. Before a closing the buyer will have a final walk-through of the home. This will likely be the first opportunity to examine the house without furniture, giving the buyer a clear view of everything. Check the walls and ceilings carefully, as well as any work the seller agreed to do in response to the inspection. Any problems discovered previously that you find uncorrected should be brought up prior to closing. It is the seller's responsibility to fix them.

RESPA stands for Real Estate Settlement Procedures Act. It requires lenders to disclose information to potential customers throughout the mortgage process, By doing so, it protects borrowers from abuses by lending institutions. RESPA mandates that lenders fully inform borrowers about all closing costs, lender servicing, escrow account practices, and business relationships between closing service providers and other parties to the transaction. For more information on RESPA, visit the web page at :

http://www. hud. gov/fha/sfh/res/respa_hm. html

or call 1-800-217-6970 for a local counseling referral.

At your closing, you'll sit at a table with your broker, the broker for the seller, probably the seller, and a closing agent. The closing agent will have a stack of papers for you and the seller to sign. While he or she will give you a basic explanation of each paper, you may want to take the time to read each one and/or consult with your agent to make sure you know exactly what you're signing. After all, this is a large amount of money you're committing to pay for a lot of years. Before you go to closing, your lender is required to give you a booklet explaining the closing costs, a "good faith estimate" of how much cash you'll have to supply at closing, and a list of documents you'll need at closing. If you don't get those items, be sure to call your lender *before* you go to closing.

Don't hesitate to ask questions. You can also look over all of the forms included in this book to get an idea of the basic type of forms that you will be signing at your closing. You'll present your paid homeowner's insurance policy or a binder and receipt showing that the premium has been paid. The closing agent will then list the money you owe the seller (remainder of down payment, prepaid taxes, etc.) and then the money the seller owes you (unpaid taxes and prepaid rent, if applicable). The seller will provide proof of any inspection, warranties, etc. Once you're sure you understand all the documentation, you'll sign the mortgage, agreeing that if you don't make payments the lender is entitled to sell your property and apply the sale price against the amount you owe plus expenses. You'll also sign a mortgage note, promising to repay the loan. The seller will give you the title to the house in the form of a signed deed. You'll pay the lender's agent all closing costs and, in turn, he or she will provide you with a settlement statement of all the items for which you have paid. The deed and mortgage will then be recorded in the state or county Registry of Deeds, and you will be a homeowner. At closing, you should get the following:

• HUD Settlement Statement (itemizes services provided and the fees charged; it is filled out by the closing agent and must be given to you at or before closing. There is a copy included in this book in Chapter 5 and on the Forms-on-CD)
• Truth-in-Lending Statement
• Any required disclosure statements (Many states require various disclosures about the condition of the property, home, or local problems, such as proximity to a landfill. Chapter 4 explains this issue and the Appendix of this book notes state-specific disclosure requirements. Finally, the Forms-on-CD provides both a basic and all necessary state-specific disclosure forms)
• Promissory Note
• Bill of Sale for any personal prooperty included with the sale (see the forms provided in Chapter 7)
• Mortgage or Deed of Trust (explained in Chapter 13)
• Keys to your new home!

Homeowner's Insurance

A paid homeowner's insurance policy (or a paid receipt for one) is required at closing, so arrangements will have to be made prior to that day. Plus, involving the insurance agent early in the homebuying process can save you money. Insurance agents are a great resource for information on home safety and they can give tips on how to keep insurance premiums low. Be sure to shop around among several insurance companies. Also, consider the cost of insurance when you look at homes. Newer homes and homes constructed with materials like brick tend to have lower premiums. Think about avoiding areas prone to natural disasters, like flooding. Choose a home with a fire hydrant or a fire department nearby. If you live in a flood plain, the lender will require that you have flood insurance before lending any money to you. But if you live near a flood plain, you may choose whether or not to get flood insurance coverage for your home. Work with an insurance agent to construct a policy that fits your needs. Always check to see if the house is in a low-lying area, in a high-risk area for natural disasters (like earthquakes, hurricanes, tornadoes, etc.), or in a hazardous materials area. Be sure the house meets building codes. Also consider local zoning laws, which could affect remodeling or making an addition in the future. Your real estate agent should be able to help you with these questions.

Home Buyer's Rights

Here is an overview of some important rights you have as a home buyer:

- **Consumer Credit Protection Act (1960):** Guarantees confidentiality of credit reports and allows customers to correct inaccurate information in their reports

- **Equal Credit Opportunity Act of 1975 (ECOA):** Prohibits the discrimination in any credit action based on race, sex, marital status, color, religion, age, handicap, or national origin

- **Equal Housing Opportunity Act:** Prohibits housing discrimination based on race, sex, marital status, color, religion, age, handicap, family status or national origin

- **Fair Housing Act:** Prohibits the discrimination based on race, sex, marital status, handicap, or national origin in any real estate transaction

- **Federal Consumer Credit Protection Act (commonly known as the Truth in Lending Act) (1969):** Requires that lenders disclose the actual terms and conditions of a loan before an applicant commits to the loan

- **Federal Interstate Land Sales Disclosure Act (1968):** Requires land developers to register subdivisions of 100 or more non-exempt lots with HUD and to provide each purchaser with a disclosure document that contains relevant information about the subdivision.

- **Home Mortgage Disclosure Act (1975):** Provides information to help determine whether public institutions are assisting the housing needs of their communities and neighborhoods

- **Real Estate Settlement Procedures Act of 1974 (RESPA):** Encouraging home ownership through consumer protection, this act regulates certain lending actions related to closing/settlement. Some of its provisions are:

  - RESPA requires lenders to provide buyers a good faith estimate of the cost of the loan, including disclosure of the Annual Percentage Rate (APR)

• RESPA requires lenders to provide buyers with general information about settlement costs. Lenders must provide buyers a copy of the Mortgage Servicing Disclosure Statement, regarding loan servicing and transfer. Within three days after receiving the loan application, lenders must provide the buyer with an estimate of closing costs and monthly payments

• RESPA provides the borrower the opportunity to see the HUD-1 Settlement Statement one day before the actual settlement. Prohibits kickbacks between Real Estate professionals for referrals and prohibits fee-splitting and receiving unearned fees for services not rendered

• **Regulation B of the Consumer Credit Protection Act:** Requires lenders to inform potential borrowers of any adverse actions taken on their loan applications

• **Regulation Z:** Includes regulations related to consumer credit disclosures identified in the *Consumer Credit Protection Act*.

• **Veterans Housing Benefits Act (1978):** Increases the housing benefits for eligible veterans including increased loan amounts.

Homebuying Worksheet

Basic Information
House address _____
General description _____
Asking price _____
Taxes _____
Total sq. footage _____
Lot size _____
Age_____
No. of Bed/Bath_____

Interior
Rooms/Sizes & Features
Living Room_____
Kitchen_____
Dining Room_____
Master Bedroom_____
Bedroom 2_____
Additional Bedrooms_____
Bathroom(s)_____
Closets_____
Basement/Attic_____
Laundry Area_____
Storage_____
Other_____

Appliances/Condition & Comments
Stove/Oven_____
Refrigerator_____
Dishwasher _____
Garbage disposal_____

HVAC
Heat type_____
Forced air, heat pump, baseboard, radiators, etc. _____
System age/condition_____
Heat source_____
Electric, gas, oil_____
Air Conditioning Type _____

Extras Included
Washer/Dryer _____
Ceiling Fans _____
Other _____

Exterior
Condition_____
Surface (Wood, Stucco, Brick, Siding, etc.)_____
Comments_____
Gutters_____

Yard
Comments_____
Natural features_____
Landscaping_____

Additional Features
Porch, Deck, Patio, etc. _____
Garage/Carport_____

Neighborhood
Location/Commute
Close to:_____
Work_____
Schools or Day care_____
Other_____

Utilities
Water source (City or Well)_____
Sewer or Septic_____
Trash pickup_____
Power company _____

Emergency services
Police station_____
Fire station_____
Hospital_____

Comments and Questions

Chapter 3

Sales of Real Estate

In this chapter are various forms for the sale and transfer of real estate. Although most real estate sales today are handled by real estate professionals, it is still perfectly legal to buy and sell property without the use of a real estate broker or lawyer. The forms provided in this chapter allow anyone to prepare the necessary forms for many basic real estate transactions. Please note, however, that there may be various state and local variations on sales contracts, mortgages, or other real estate documents. If in doubt, check with a local real estate professional or an attorney.

The basis of most real estate transactions is an Agreement (or contract) to Sell Real Estate. A *contract* is merely an agreement by which two or more parties each promise to do something. This simple definition of a contract can encompass incredibly complex agreements. The objective of a good contract is to clearly set out the terms of the agreement. Once the parties have reached an oral understanding of what their agreement should be, the terms of the deal should be put in writing. Contrary to what many attorneys may tell you, the written contract should be clearly written and easily understood by both parties. It should be written in precise and unambiguous terms. The most common cause for litigation over contracts is arguments over the meaning of the language used. Remember that both sides to the agreement should be able to understand and agree to the language being used.

A contract has to have certain prerequisites to be enforceable in court. These requirements are relatively simple and most will be present in any standard agreement. However, you should understand what the various legal requirements are before you prepare your own contracts. To be enforceable, a contract must have *consideration*. In the context of contract law, this simply means that both parties to the contract must have promised to do something or forego taking some type of action. If one of the parties has not promised to do anything or forego any action, she or he will not be able to legally force the other party to comply with the terms of the contract. There has to be some form of mutual promise for a contract to be valid. For example: Party A agrees to pay Party B if Party B paints a car. Party A's promise is to pay if the job is completed. Party B's promise is to paint the car. If Party B paints the car and is not paid, Party A's promise to pay can be enforced in court. Similarly, if Party B fails to paint the car, Party A can have the contract enforced in court.

Another requirement is that the parties to the contract be clearly identified and the terms of the contract also be clearly spelled out. The terms and description need not be complicated, but they must be in enough detail to enable the parties to the contract (and any subsequent court) to clearly determine what exactly the parties were referring to when they made the contract. In the above example, the names and addresses of the parties must be included for the contract to be enforceable. In addition, a description of the car must be incorporated in the contract. Finally, a description of the type of paint job and the amount of money to be paid should also be contained in the contract.

Various forms are included in this chapter for transactions relating to the sale of real estate. The two main contract forms are the Agreement to Sell Real Estate and the Contract for Deed. Additional forms are provided for declaring default on a Contract for Deed , an option to buy real estate, an offer to buy real estate, a federal lead brochure, and appraisal of real estate forms. Please read the description of what each form provides and also what information is necessary to complete each form. Also, carefully read through each form itself so that you understand the meaning of each of the terms of the documents.

Instructions

Agreement to Sell Real Estate: This form can be used for setting down an agreement to buy and sell property. It contains the basic clauses to cover situations that will arise in most typical real estate transaction. The various items that are covered in this contract are

- That the sale is conditioned on the buyer being able to obtain financing 30 days prior to the closing
- That if the sale is not completed, the buyer will be given back the earnest money deposit, without interest or penalty
- That the seller will provide a Warranty Deed for the real estate and a Bill of Sale for any personal property included in the sale
- That certain items will be pro-rated and adjusted as of the closing date
- That the buyer and the seller may split the various closing costs
- That the seller represents that it has good title to the property and that the personal property included is in good working order
- That the title to the property will be evidenced by either title insurance or an abstract of title
- That the buyer has the right to a termite inspection
- That the buyer has a right to a complete home inspection at least 30 days prior to closing

- That the seller provide a radon statement and lead paint disclosure
- That the seller will provide the buyer with the U.S. EPA pamphlet: "Protect Your Family from Lead in Your Home." *Note*: This document is necessary *only* if the residential dwelling was built prior to 1978
- That the seller will provide a Real Estate Disclosure Statement to the buyer within 5 days and that the buyer has the right to rescind the agreement within 5 days after the receipt of the disclosure statement

In order to prepare this agreement, please fill in the following information:

1. Date of Agreement
2. Name of seller
3. Address of seller
4. Name of buyer
5. Address of buyer
6. Address of property
7. City of property
8. State of property
9. A legal description of the property involved
10. A description of any personal property to be included in the sale
11. The purchase price of the property
12. The amount of any mortgage which will be arranged 30 days prior to closing
13. Number of monthly payments of this mortgage
14. Annual interest rate of this mortgage
15. Write out percent
16. Amount of earnest money deposit
17. Description and amount of any other deposits
18. Amount of balance due at closing
19. Total purchase price of the property
20. Amount of earnest money paid upon signing the contract
21. Date for closing sale
22. Time for closing
23. am or pm
24. Address of closing
25. City of closing
26. State of closing
27. Any other documents to be provided to buyer at closing
28. Any other items that will be adjusted and pro-rated at closing
29. Closing costs which will be paid for by seller
30. Closing costs which will be paid for by buyer
31. Whether there are any outstanding claims, liabilities, indebtedness and/or restrictions pertaining to the property

㉜ Seller's initials on 'presence of lead paint' disclosure
㉝ Seller's initials on records or reports of lead paint
㉞ Buyer's initials on lead paint acknowledgment
㉟ Whether there are any additional terms
㊱ Which state's laws will be used to interpret contract
㊲ Signature of seller
㊳ Printed Name of seller
㊴ Signature of witness for seller
㊵ Printed name of witness for seller
㊶ Signature of witness for seller
㊷ Printed name of witness for seller
㊸ Signature of buyer
㊹ Printed name of buyer
㊺ Signature of witness for buyer
㊻ Printed name of witness for buyer
㊼ Signature of witness for buyer
㊽ Printed name of witness for buyer

Title insurance or an abstract of title will need to be obtained from a local title company or attorney. A Bill of Sale for any personal property (Chapter 7) and a Warranty Deed (later in this chapter) will need to be prepared for use at the closing of the sale. Finally, a federal lead brochure will need to be provided to the buyer if the dwelling was built before 1978 (also later in this chapter). Both the seller's and buyer's signatures should be witnessed by two witnesses. Note: California residents will need to include the California Addendum to Contract that is included on the Forms-on-CD as well as the appropriate disclosure forms.

Contract for Deed: This form is also known in some localities as an Installment Real Estate Sales Contract, a Land Contract, or a Conditional Sales Contract. This form is used in real estate situations where it is desired that the Buyer receives possession of the property, but does not receive actual title to the property until the entire sales price has been paid to the Seller. Under this type of contract, the Buyer agrees to make periodic installment payments until the sales price of the property has been paid in full. The reason that some real estate transactions are handled in this manner is that it is much easier for the property to be returned to the Seller in the case of a *default* (failure to make an installment payment when due) by the Buyer. Most Contracts for Deed (as does the one provided in this book) provide for the complete forfeiture of all money paid if the Buyer misses even one payment. This harsh remedy also precludes the need for any foreclosure proceedings against a defaulting Buyer in order to regain possession of the property, as the Buyer does not have legal title to the property until all payments have been made. This type of real estate transaction is generally only used for the sale of undeveloped vacant land. Although a Contract for Deed can be used for the sale of improved property as well, the lack of the legal protections that a mortgage provides make this type of real estate contract a bad choice for a Buyer of residential or commercial property that has a home or business already erected on the property.

This contract provides that a Buyer pay a down payment of some amount and that the remaining balance due for the sale of the real estate be paid in equal monthly installment payments, which include principal and interest at a certain percentage rate. The Buyer also has the right to pay off part of or the entire balance due at any time, without penalty. The Buyer and Seller will need to determine a sales price, what the annual interest rate will be, the amount of a down payment, and also how many monthly payments will be required. For example, the Buyer and Seller agree that the property will be sold for $50,000.00 and that this total amount includes an annual interest rate of 6%. They also agree that there will be 60 monthly payments (five years) and that the Buyer will make a $2,000.00 down payment, leaving $48,000.00 remaining to be paid. Thus, the Buyer will be required to make 60 monthly installment payments of $800.00 per payment for a total of $48,000.00.

The contract also provides that the Buyer agrees to forfeit all of the payments made if any payment has been missed for a period of 30 days and another 30-day period has elapsed after the Buyer has received from the Seller, via Certified U.S. Mail, a Declaration of Intent to Forfeit and Terminate Contact for Deed (explained below). The forfeited payments will be then retained by the Seller as accumulated rent for the property. The Buyer also agrees to immediately vacate the property if the Contract for Deed is terminated. The Buyer agrees to pay all real estate property taxes and assessments on the property when due. The contract allows for the Buyer to build new construction on the property as long as the building complies with all applicable zoning laws and health and building codes. Finally, the Buyer has the right, under this contract, to examine an abstract of title to the property to determine that the Seller actually has title to the property. If and when the Buyer has made all payments and is up-to-date on payment of all taxes and assessments on the property, the Seller agrees to transfer full title to the Buyer by the use of a Warranty Deed. A Bill of Sale for any personal property (Chapter 7) and a Warranty Deed (Chapter 5) will need to be prepared for use at the closing of the sale. Finally, a federal lead brochure will need to be provided to the buyer if the dwelling was built before 1978 (explained later in this chapter). Both the seller's and buyer's signatures should be witnessed by two witnesses. Note: California residents will need to include the California Addendum to Contract that is included on the Forms-on-CD as well as the appropriate disclosure forms.

To complete this form, you will need the following information:

① Date of Contract for Deed
② Name of seller
③ Address of seller
④ Name of buyer
⑤ Address of buyer
⑥ Address of property
⑦ City of property
⑧ State of property
⑨ A legal description of the property involved
⑩ A description of any personal property to be included in the sale

⑪ The purchase price of the property
⑫ The total purchase price of the property
⑬ Amount of the down payment
⑭ Balance due from the buyer
⑮ Number of monthly payments
⑯ Amount of each monthly payments
⑰ Day of the month on which payment will be due
⑱ Due date of first monthly payment
⑲ Percent of interest rate
⑳ Amount of down payment paid upon signing the contract
㉑ Any other documents to be provided to buyer at closing
㉒ Tax year for which buyer will begin paying taxes
㉓ Whether there are any outstanding claims, liabilities, indebtedness and/or restrictions pertaining to the property
㉔ Seller's initials on presence of lead paint disclosure
㉕ Seller's initials on records or reports of lead paint
㉖ Buyer's initials on lead paint acknowledgment
㉗ Whether there are any additional terms
㉘ Which state's laws will be used to interpret contract
㉙ Signature of seller
㉚ Printed Name of seller
㉛ Signature of witness for seller
㉜ Printed name of witness for seller
㉝ Signature of witness for seller
㉞ Printed name of witness for seller
㉟ Signature of buyer
㊱ Printed name of buyer
㊲ Signature of witness for buyer
㊳ Printed name of witness for buyer
㊴ Signature of witness for buyer
㊵ Printed name of witness for buyer

Declaration of Intent to Forfeit and Terminate Contract for Deed: This form is to be used by a Seller under a Contract for Deed to notify the Buyer that they are in default of a term of the contract and that the Seller is declaring that the Buyer's payments under the contract thus far are forfeited and that the Contract will be terminated by the Seller for non-compliance by the Buyer. Under the terms of the above Contract for Deed, the Seller must provide this Declaration to the Buyer by Certified U.S. Mail. The Buyer then has 30 days to become current with their payments under the contract. If the Buyer does not make the past-due payments within 30 of receipt of this Declaration, the Buyer's prior payments will be forfeited to the Seller, the Contract for Deed will be terminated, and the Buyer will be required to vacate the property immediately. To complete this document, you will need the following information:

① Date of original Contract for Deed
② Name of seller
③ Address of seller
④ Name of buyer
⑤ Address of buyer
⑥ Address of property involved
⑦ City of property involved
⑧ State of property involved
⑨ A legal description of the property involved
⑩ Date of Declaration
⑪ Reason buyer is in default on Contract for Deed (if buyer has missed a payment or payments, you will need to specify the due date of the payment(s) and the exact amount of any past due amounts)
⑫ Date of mailing of this Declaration
⑬ Date of this Declaration
⑭ Signature of seller
⑮ Printed name of seller

Option to Buy Real Estate: This form is designed to be used to offer an interested buyer a time period in which to have an exclusive option to purchase a parcel of real estate. It should be used in conjunction with a filled-in but unsigned copy of the above Agreement to Sell Real Estate. Through the use of this option agreement, the seller can offer the buyer a time during which he or she can consider the purchase without concern of a sale to another party.

This agreement provides that in exchange for a payment (which will be applied to the purchase price if the option is exercised), the buyer is given a period of time to accept the terms of a completed real estate contract. If the buyer accepts the terms and exercises the option in writing, the seller agrees to complete the sale. If the option is not exercised, the seller is then free to sell the property on the market and to retain the money that the potential buyer paid for the option. To complete this form, please fill in the following information:

① Date of Option
② Name of seller
③ Address of seller
④ Name of buyer
⑤ Address of buyer
⑥ Address of property
⑦ City of property
⑧ State of property
⑨ Legal description of property
⑩ Price buyer will pay for option

⑪ Date that option period will end
⑫ Price buyer will pay seller for property if option is exercised
⑬ State whose laws will govern the agreement
⑭ Date of option agreement
⑮ Signature of seller
⑯ Printed name of seller
⑰ Signature of buyer
⑱ Printed name of buyer

In addition, an Agreement to Sell Real Estate covering the property subject to the option to buy should be completed and attached to the option agreement. This contract will provide all of the essential terms of the actual agreement to sell the property.

Offer to Purchase Real Estate: This document is used by a potential buyer of real estate to make an offer to purchase the property. It is *not* a contract or agreement for the purchase of the real estate. It is an offer to pay a certain price for a parcel of real estate, based on the meeting of certain conditions.

The conditions that must be met are as follows: The buyer must be able to arrange for suitable financing prior to closing. The buyer must receive a satisfactory termite inspection report. The property to be purchased will be transferred to the buyer free of any debts or liabilities. The parties agree to sign a standard Agreement to Sell Real Estate. The date of the closing is set forth in the Offer. Any other terms that the buyer would like should be included. The Offer is only open for acceptance by the Owner until the time and date set in the Offer. To complete this form, please fill in the following information:

① Date of Offer
② Name of buyer
③ Address of buyer
④ Name of owner
⑤ Address of owner
⑥ Address of property
⑦ City of property
⑧ State of property
⑨ Legal description of property
⑩ Purchase price offered for property
⑪ Escrow deposit included with Offer
⑫ Any additional deposit anticipated
⑬ Balance of price due to owner at closing
⑭ Total purchase price
⑮ Amount of mortgage commitment required within 90 days
⑯ Number of monthly payments of mortgage commitment

54

⑰ Annual interest rate percentage of mortgage commitment
⑱ Date for closing
⑲ Time for closing (time and am or pm)
⑳ Address for closing
㉑ City for closing
㉒ State for closing
㉓ Any other terms
㉔ Expiration time (time and am or pm) of Offer
㉕ Expiration date of Offer
㉖ Signature of buyer
㉗ Date of buyer's signature
㉘ Printed name of buyer
㉙ Signature of owner
㉚ Date of owner's signature
㉛ Printed name of owner

Lead Warning Statement: Under the Federal Real Estate Disclosure and Notification Rule, if you are a seller of a residential property that has a home built before 1978, you are required to notify the buyer of the risk of lead exposure and provide them with a copy of the enclosed brochure: "Protect Your Family from Lead in Your Home." In addition, you must disclose your knowledge of any risk of lead hazards in the home. Clauses in the Agreement to Purchase Real Estate, the Contract for Deed, and the Residential Lease forms that are included in this book satisfy the federal requirement. The Lead Warning Statement form included in this chapter is for use in any real estate transaction for residential property built prior to 1978, for which the main sale or lease document does not already contain the required Lead Warning Statement. To complete this form, the following must be done:

① Seller should initial the appropriate choices regarding knowledge of lead paint and/or hazards in the building
② If available, seller should also provide buyer with any records or reports pertaining to lead paint and/or hazards
③ Buyer should initial the appropriate choices regarding receipt of copies of any seller-provided information, receipt of the Federal Lead Brochure (Protect Your Family From Lead in Your Home).
④ Buyer either accepts or waives the right to conduct an inspection of the building within the following 10 days (or any other agreed upon period).
⑤ Date of signing of statement
⑥ Signature of seller (change to Landlord if using this Statement with a lease)
⑦ Printed name of seller (change to Landlord if using this Statement with a lease)
⑧ Signature of buyer (change to Tenant if using this Statement with a lease)
⑨ Printed name of buyer (change to Tenant if using this Statement with a lease)

Federal Lead Brochure: A PDF-format copy of the U.S. EPA's pamphlet, "Protect Your Family from Lead in Your Home," is provided *only* on the included Forms-on-CD. A copy of this brochure must be provided to every potential buyer (or renter) of any residential dwelling that was built prior to 1978.

Appraisal Report: An appraisal of real estate is an impartial evaluation of real estate by a knowledgeable and qualified person after they have performed a careful inspection and study of the property and have used certain techniques to compare the property to other properties. There are three generally-accepted approaches to estimating real estate values. The 'Cost' approach arrives at a value by estimating the replacement value of the property. The 'Market' approach compares the property with similar properties and uses the comparison to determine what the property would sell for on the open market. The 'Income' approach looks at what the net return for a piece of property would be. This approach is generally used for commercial property. Appraisers will use various combinations of these approaches to come to a reasonable estimate of a property's value. Real estate brokers are qualified to perform appraisals and there are professional appraisers who are also qualified. An appraisal report can range from a short 1 or 2 page opinion to a detailed bound document with a survey, photos, plot plans, etc.

The form provided is a simple version of an Appraisal Report and provides that the appraiser certifies that he or she has investigated a certain piece of property and has determined the market value of the property to be a certain amount. The report then provides a list of conditions which the appraiser has used to limit the market determination. To complete this form, an appraiser will need to insert the following:

1. Date of appraisal
2. Name of appraiser
3. Address of appraiser
4. Name of person requesting appraisal
5. Address of property appraised
6. Legal description of property appraised
7. Market value of land only
8. Market value of improvements to land
9. Total market value
10. Qualifications of appraiser
11. Signature of appraiser
12. Printed name of appraiser

Appraisal Affidavit: An appraisal affidavit provides the basic details of an appraisal that is signed and sworn to before a notary public. This type of document is often required by financing institutions at the closing of a real estate transaction. This documents supplies essentially the same information as the basic Appraisal Report, but in a more formal affidavit. To complete this form, the following needs to be completed:

① Date of appraisal
② Name of appraiser
③ Address of appraiser
④ Name of person requesting appraisal
⑤ Address of property appraised
⑥ Legal description of property appraised
⑦ Market value of land only
⑧ Market value of improvements to land
⑨ Total market value
⑩ Qualifications of appraiser
⑪ Signature of appraiser
⑫ Printed name of appraiser
⑬ The following must be completed by a Notary Public*

*Note: California residents must use the California Notary box available on the Forms-on-CD

Agreement to Sell Real Estate

This agreement is made on ① _____ , 20 ___ , between ② _____ , seller, address: ③

and ④ _____ , buyer, address: ⑤

The seller now owns the following described real estate, located at
⑥ _____ , City of ⑦ _____ , State of ⑧ _____ , and legally described as follows: ⑨

For valuable consideration, the seller agrees to sell and the buyer agrees to buy this property for the following price and on the following terms:

1. The seller will sell this property to the buyer, free from all claims, liabilities, and indebtedness, unless noted in this agreement.

2. The following personal property is also included in this sale: ⑩

3. The buyer agrees to pay the seller the sum of $ ⑪ _____ , which the seller agrees to accept as full payment. This agreement, however, is conditional upon the buyer being able to arrange suitable financing on the following terms at least thirty (30) days prior to the closing date for this agreement: A mortgage in the amount of
    $ ⑫ _____ , payable in ⑬ _____ monthly payments, with an annual interest rate of ⑭ _____ % (⑮ _____ percent) .

4. The purchase price will be paid as follows:
    Earnest deposit .... $ ⑯ _____
    Other deposit: .... $ ⑰ _____
    Cash or certified check on closing .... $ ⑱ _____
    (subject to any adjustments or prorations on closing)
    Total Purchase Price .... $ ⑲ _____

5. The seller acknowledges receiving the earnest money deposit of $ ⑳ _____ from the buyer. If buyer fails to perform this agreement, the seller shall retain this money. If seller fails to perform this agreement, this money shall be returned to the buyer or the buyer may have the right of specific performance. If buyer is unable to obtain suitable financing at

least thirty (30) days prior to closing, then this money will be returned to the buyer without penalty or interest.

6. This agreement will close on ㉑_____ , 20 _____ , at ㉒_____ o'clock
    ㉓____ . m., at ㉔_____ ,
    City of ㉕_____ , State of ㉖_____ . At that time, and upon
    payment by the buyer of the portion of the purchase price then due, the seller will deliver to
    buyer the following documents:

    (a) A Bill of Sale for all personal property
    (b) A Warranty Deed for the real estate
    (c) A Seller's Affidavit of Title
    (d) A closing statement
    (e) Other documents: ㉗

7. At closing, pro-rated adjustments to the purchase price will be made for the following items:

    (a) Utilities
    (b) Property taxes
    (c) The following other items: ㉘

8. The following closing costs will be paid by the seller: ㉙

9. The following closing costs will be paid by the buyer: ㉚

10. Seller represents that it has good and marketable title to the property and will supply the buyer
    with either an abstract of title or a standard policy of title insurance. Seller further represents
    that the property is free and clear of any restrictions on transfer, claims, indebtedness, or li-
    abilities except the following:

    (a) Zoning, restrictions, prohibitions, or requirements imposed by any governmental
         authority
    (b) Any restrictions appearing on the plat of record of the property
    (c) Public utility easements of record
    (d) Other: ㉛

    Seller warrants that there shall be no violations of zoning or building codes as of the date of
    closing. Seller also warrants that all personal property included in this sale will be delivered
    in working order on the date of closing.

11. At least thirty (30) days prior to closing, buyer shall have the right to obtain a written report from a licensed termite inspector stating that there is no termite infestation or termite damage to the property. If there is such evidence, seller shall remedy such infestation and/or repair such damage, up to a maximum cost of two (2) percent of the purchase price of the property. If the costs exceed two (2) percent of the purchase price and seller elects not to pay for the costs over two (2) percent, buyer may cancel this agreement and the escrow shall be returned to buyer without penalty or interest.

12. At least thirty (30) days prior to closing, buyer or their agent shall have the right to inspect all heating, air conditioning, electrical, and mechanical systems of the property, the roof and all structural components of the property, and any personal property included in this agreement. If any such systems or equipment are not in working order, seller shall pay for the cost of placing them in working order prior to closing. Buyer or their agent may again inspect the property within forty-eight (48) hours of closing to determine if all systems and equipment are in working order.

13. Between the date of this agreement and the date for closing, the property shall be maintained in the condition as existed on the date of this agreement. If there is any damage by fire, casualty, or otherwise, prior to closing, seller shall restore the property to the condition as existed on the date of this agreement. If seller fails to do so, buyer may:
    (a) accept the property, as is, along with any insurance proceeds due seller, *or*
    (b) cancel this agreement and have the escrow deposit returned, without penalty or interest.

14. As required by law, the seller makes the following statement: "Radon gas is a naturally occurring radioactive gas that, when accumulated in sufficient quantities in a building, may present health risks to persons exposed to it. Levels of radon gas that exceed federal and state guidelines have been found in buildings in this state. Additional information regarding radon gas and radon gas testing may be obtained from your county health department."

15. As required by law, the seller makes the following Lead Warning Statement: "Every purchaser of any interest in residential real property on which a residential dwelling was built prior to 1978 is notified that such property may present exposure to lead from lead-based paint that may place young children at risk of developing lead poisoning. Lead poisoning in young children may produce permanent neurological damage, including learning disabilities, reduced intelligence quotient, behavioral problems, and impaired memory. Lead poisoning also poses a particular threat to pregnant women. The seller of any interest in residential real estate is required to provide the buyer with any information on lead-based paint hazards from risk assessments or inspection in the seller's possession and notify the buyer of any known lead-based paint hazards. A risk assessment or inspection for possible lead-based paint hazards is recommended prior to purchase."

Seller's Disclosure

㉜Presence of lead-based paint and/or lead-based paint hazards: (Seller to initial one).

_____ Known lead-based paint and/or lead-based paint hazards are present in building (explain):

_____ Seller has no knowledge of lead-based paint and/or lead-based paint hazards in building.

㉝Records and reports available to seller: (Seller to initial one).

_____ Seller has provided buyer with all available records and reports pertaining to lead-based paint and/or lead-based paint hazards are present in building (list documents):

_____ Seller has no records and reports pertaining to lead-based paint and/or lead-based paint hazards in building.

Buyer's Acknowledgment

㉞(Buyer to initial all applicable).

_____ Buyer has received copies of all information listed above.
_____ Buyer has received the pamphlet "Protect Your Family From Lead in Your Home."
_____ Buyer has received a ten (10)-day opportunity (or mutually agreed-on period) to conduct a risk assessment or inspection for the presence of lead-based paint and/or lead-based paint hazards in building.
_____ Buyer has waived the opportunity to conduct a risk assessment or inspection for the presence of lead-based paint and/or lead-based paint hazards in building.

The seller and buyer have reviewed the information above and certify, by their signatures at the end of this agreement, that to the best of their knowledge, the information they have provided is true and accurate.

16. Seller agrees to provide Buyer with a Real Estate Disclosure Statement (or its equivalent that is acceptable in the State in which the property is located) within five (5) days of the signing of this Agreement. Upon receipt of the Real Estate Disclosure Statement from Seller, Buyer shall have five (5) business days within which to rescind this Agreement by providing Seller with a written and signed statement rescinding this Agreement. The disclosures in the Real Estate Disclosure Statement are made by the seller concerning the condition of the property and are provided on the basis of the seller's actual knowledge of the property on the date of this disclo-

sure. These disclosures are not the representations of any real estate agent or other party. The disclosures themselves are not intended to be a part of any written agreement between the buyer and seller. In addition, the disclosure shall not, in any way, be construed to be a warranty of any kind by the seller.

17. The parties also agree to the following additional terms: ㉟

18. No modification of this agreement will be effective unless it is in writing and is signed by both the buyer and seller. This agreement binds and benefits both the buyer and seller and any successors. Time is of the essence of this agreement. This document, including any attachments, is the entire agreement between the buyer and seller. This agreement is governed by the laws of the State of ㊱_____ .

㊲_____
Signature of Seller

㊳_____
Printed Name of Seller

㊴_____
Signature of Witness for Seller

㊵_____
Printed Name of Witness for Seller

㊶_____
Signature of Witness for Seller

㊷_____
Printed Name of Witness for Seller

㊸_____
Signature of Buyer

㊹_____
Printed Name of Buyer

㊺_____
Signature of Witness for Buyer

㊻_____
Printed Name of Witness for Buyer

㊼_____
Signature of Witness for Buyer

㊽_____
Printed Name of Witness for Buyer

Contract For Deed

This contract is made on ①_____ , 20 ____ , between ②_____ ,
seller,
address: ③

and ④_____ , buyer,
address: ⑤

The seller now owns the following described real estate, located at ⑥_____
,
City of ⑦_____ , State of ⑧_____: and legally described as follows: ⑨

For valuable consideration, the seller agrees to sell and the buyer agrees to buy this property for
the following price and on the following terms:

1. The seller agrees to sell this property to the buyer, free from all claims, liabilities, and indebted-
    ness, unless noted in this contract.

2. The following personal property is also included in this sale: ⑩

3. The buyer agrees to pay the seller the sum of $ ⑪_____ , which the seller agrees to ac-
    cept as full payment, such total purchase price includes interest as noted below in Paragraph
    #4.

4. The purchase price will be paid as follows:
    Total Purchase Price .... $ ⑫_____
    Less Down Payment .... $ ⑬_____
    Balance Due .... $ ⑭_____
    (subject to any adjustments or prorations on closing)

    Balance Due will be paid in ⑮_____ equal monthly payments of $⑯_____ each, until
    the Balance is paid in full. The monthly payments will be due and payable on the ⑰_____
    day of each month, beginning on ⑱_____20____. The total purchase price includes
    principal and interest of ⑲_____ % (percent) per year on the unpaid balance. The balance
    due under this contract is prepayable at any time, in whole or in part, without penalty

5. The seller acknowledges receiving the down payment of $⑳ _____ from the buyer.

6. If buyer fails to perform any duties under this contract, including the failure to make any of the required payments within 30 days of when such payment is due, this contact shall be forfeited and terminated 30 days after the receipt by the buyer of a Declaration of Intent to Forfeit and Terminate Contract for Deed, which shall be sent to the buyer via Certified U.S. Mail. During the 30-day period after the receipt of this Declaration, Buyer shall have the right to cure the default. If the default is not satisfied within the 30-day period, then on the 31st day after receipt of the Declaration, Buyer shall forfeit all monies paid to the Seller under the Contract for Deed and Buyer shall immediately vacate the property. Seller shall, on that date, have the right to reenter and take full possession of the property, without being liable for any action or any costs incurred by the Buyer. Upon termination of this contract by the seller, the seller shall retain all money paid by the buyer to the seller as accumulated rent for the property.

7. If seller fails to perform this contract, all money paid to the seller by the buyer shall be returned to the buyer or, at buyer's option, the buyer may have the right of specific performance, including the performance by the seller of delivering a warranty deed to the buyer for full title to the property.

8. All closing costs will be paid by the buyer: Upon payment by the buyer of the entire purchase price when due and the fulfillment of all other contracts under this contract by the buyer, the seller will deliver to buyer the following documents:

    (a) A Bill of Sale for all personal property included in this sale
    (b) A Warranty Deed for the real estate
    (c) A Seller's Affidavit of Title
    (d) A closing statement
    (e) Other documents: ㉑

9. The buyer agrees to pay all property taxes and assessments against the property beginning with the tax year of ㉒_____.

10. Seller represents that it has good and marketable title to the property and, on request, will supply the buyer with an abstract of title. Seller further represents that the property is free and clear of any restrictions on transfer, claims, indebtedness, or liabilities except the following:

    (a) Zoning, restrictions, prohibitions, or requirements imposed by any governmental authority
    (b) Any restrictions appearing on the plat of record of the property

(c) Public utility easements of record

(d) Other: ㉓

Seller warrants that there shall be no violations of zoning or building codes as of the date of this contract. Seller also warrants that all personal property included in this sale has been delivered to the buyer in working order.

11. Between the date of this contract and the date for closing, the property shall be maintained by the buyer in the condition as existed on the date of this contract. In addition, if there is a structure on this property as of the date of this contract, the buyer agrees to maintain both general liability insurance and property insurance in the amount of the balance due under this contract, as specified in Paragraph #4 of this contract, naming the seller as owner of the property and recipient of all insurance settlements, If there is any damage by fire, casualty, or otherwise, prior to closing, buyer shall restore the property to the condition as existed on the date of this contract, and buyer shall be have the right to use any casualty or fire insurance proceeds for such restoration. If buyer fails to do so within a reasonable time, seller may declare this contract forfeit and terminated.

12. As required by law, the seller makes the following statement: "Radon gas is a naturally occurring radioactive gas that, when accumulated in sufficient quantities in a building, may present health risks to persons exposed to it. Levels of radon gas that exceed federal and state guidelines have been found in buildings in this state. Additional information regarding radon gas and radon gas testing may be obtained from your county health department."

13. As required by law, the seller makes the following Lead Warning Statement: "Every purchaser of any interest in residential real property on which a residential dwelling was built prior to 1978 is notified that such property may present exposure to lead from lead-based paint that may place young children at risk of developing lead poisoning. Lead poisoning in young children may produce permanent neurological damage, including learning disabilities, reduced intelligence quotient, behavioral problems, and impaired memory. Lead poisoning also poses a particular threat to pregnant women. The seller of any interest in residential real estate is required to provide the buyer with any information on lead-based paint hazards from risk assessments or inspection in the seller's possession and notify the buyer of any known lead-based paint hazards. A risk assessment or inspection for possible lead-based paint hazards is recommended prior to purchase."

Seller's Disclosure

㉔Presence of lead-based paint and/or lead-based paint hazards: (Seller to initial one).

_____ Known lead-based paint and/or lead-based paint hazards are present in building (explain):

_____ Seller has no knowledge of lead-based paint and/or lead-based paint hazards in building.

㉕Records and reports available to seller: (Seller to initial one).

_____ Seller has provided buyer with all available records and reports pertaining to lead-based paint and/or lead-based paint hazards are present in building (list documents):

_____ Seller has no records and reports pertaining to lead-based paint and/or lead-based paint hazards in building.

Buyer's Acknowledgment
㉖(Buyer to initial all applicable).

_____ Buyer has received copies of all information listed above.
_____ Buyer has received the pamphlet "Protect Your Family From Lead in Your Home."
_____ Buyer has received a ten (10)-day opportunity (or mutually agreed-on period) to conduct a risk assessment or inspection for the presence of lead-based paint and/or lead-based paint hazards in building.
_____ Buyer has waived the opportunity to conduct a risk assessment or inspection for the presence of lead-based paint and/or lead-based paint hazards in building.

The seller and buyer have reviewed the information above and certify, by their signatures at the end of this contract, that to the best of their knowledge, the information they have provided is true and accurate.

14. Seller agrees to provide Buyer with a Real Estate Disclosure Statement (or its equivalent that is acceptable in the State in which the property is located) within five (5) days of the signing of this Agreement. Upon receipt of the Real Estate Disclosure Statement from Seller, Buyer shall have five (5) business days within which to rescind this Agreement by providing Seller with a written and signed statement rescinding this Agreement. The disclosures in the Real Estate Disclosure Statement are made by the seller concerning the condition of the property and are provided on the basis of the seller's actual knowledge of the property on the date of this disclosure. These disclosures are not the representations of any real estate agent or other party. The disclosures themselves are not intended to be a part of any written agreement between the buyer and seller. In addition, the disclosure shall not, in any way, be construed to be a warranty of any kind by the seller

15. The parties also agree to the following additional terms: ㉗

16. The buyer and seller agree that this contract or any assignment of this contract may not be re-

corded without the express written permission of the seller. If this contract is recorded contrary to the above provision, then any existing balance shall become immediately due and payable.

17. Buyer agrees that any construction on this property be limited to residences built of new materials and that all construction comply with all applicable building, health and zoning codes and laws.

18. No modification of this contract will be effective unless it is in writing and is signed by both the buyer and seller. No assignment of this contract by buyer will be effective without the written permission of the seller. This contract binds and benefits both the buyer and seller and any successors. Time is of the essence of this contract. This document, including any attachments, is the entire contract between the buyer and seller. This contract is governed by the laws of the State of ㉘_____ .

㉙_____
Signature of Seller

㉚_____
Printed Name of Seller

㉛_____
Signature of Witness for Seller

㉜_____
Printed Name of Witness for Seller

㉝_____
Signature of Witness for Seller

㉞_____
Printed Name of Witness for Seller

㉟_____
Signature of Buyer

㊱_____
Printed Name of Buyer

㊲_____
Signature of Witness for Buyer

㊳_____
Printed Name of Witness for Buyer

㊴_____
Signature of Witness for Buyer

㊵_____
Printed Name of Witness for Buyer

Declaration of Intent to Forfeit and Terminate Contract for Deed

Under the terms of the Contract for Deed, dated① _____ , 20___ which exists between
② _____ , seller
address:③

and ④ _____ , buyer,
address:⑤

The seller now owns the following described real estate, located at ⑥ _____ , City
of ⑦ _____ , State of ⑧ _____ : and legally described as follows:⑨

The seller declares that as of the date of ⑩ _____ , 20 _____ ,
Buyer is in default of this Contract for Deed for the following reasons:⑪

Due to this default, Seller declares the existing Contract for Deed between Seller and Buyer to be forfeit and terminated 30 days after the receipt of this Declaration by the Buyer. Seller shall send a copy of this Declaration to Buyer at the above address, via Certified U.S. Mail, on the date of ⑫ _____ , 20 ____ .

During the 30-day period after the receipt of this Declaration, Buyer shall have the right to cure the default noted above. If the default is not satisfied within the 30-day period, then on the 31st day after receipt of this Declaration, Buyer shall forfeit all monies paid to the Seller under the Contract for Deed and shall immediately vacate the property. Seller shall, on that date, have the right to reenter and take full possession of the property, without being liable for any action or any costs incurred by the Buyer.

Dated: ⑬ _____

⑭ _____
Signature of Seller
⑮ _____
Printed Name of Seller

Option to Buy Real Estate

This option agreement is made on ①_____ , 20 _____ , between ②_____ , seller,
address: ③
and ④_____ , buyer,
address: ⑤

The seller now owns the following described real estate, located at ⑥_____ ,
City of ⑦_____ , State of ⑧_____ , and legally described as follows: ⑨

For valuable consideration, the seller agrees to give the buyer an exclusive option to buy this property for the following price and on the following terms:

1. The buyer will pay the seller $ ⑩_____ for this option. This amount will be credited against the purchase price of the property if this option is exercised by the buyer. If the option is not exercised, the seller will retain this payment.
2. The option period will be from the date of this agreement until ⑪_____ , 20 ___ , at which time it will expire unless exercised.
3. During this period, the buyer has the option and exclusive right to buy the seller's property mentioned above for the purchase price of $ ⑫_____ . The buyer must notify the seller, in writing, of the decision to exercise this option.
4. Attached to this Option Agreement is a completed Agreement to Sell Real Estate. If the buyer notifies the seller, in writing, of the decision to exercise the option within the option period, the seller and buyer agree to sign the Agreement to Sell Real Estate and complete the sale on the terms contained in the Agreement.
5. No modification of this Option Agreement will be effective unless it is in writing and is signed by both the buyer and seller. This Option Agreement binds and benefits both the buyer and seller and any successors. Time is of the essence of this Option Agreement. This document, including any attachments, is the entire agreement between the buyer and seller. This Option Agreement is governed by the laws of the State of ⑬_____ .

Dated ⑭_____

⑮_____
Signature of Seller

⑯_____
Signature of Buyer

⑰_____
Printed Name of Seller

⑱_____
Printed Name of Buyer

Offer to Purchase Real Estate

This offer is made on ①_____ 20 _____ , by ②_____ , buyer,
address:③

to ④_____ , owner,
address:⑤

The owner now owns the following described real estate, located at ⑥ _____ ,
City of ⑦_____ , State of ⑧_____ , and legally described as
follows: ⑨

The buyer offers to purchase the above property under the following terms:

The following price is offered for the property: $ ⑩_____
Escrow deposit paid to the Owner with this Offer: $ ⑪_____
Further deposit to Owner upon signing of Sales Agreement: $ ⑫_____
Balance due at closing: $ ⑬_____
Total purchase price: $ ⑭_____

This Offer is conditioned on the following terms:

1. This Offer is conditional upon the Buyer being able to arrange a firm commitment for suitable
financing on the following terms within ninety (90) days of acceptance of this Offer by the Owner:

Mortgage amount: $⑮_____
Term of Mortgage: ⑯_____ monthly payments
Interest rate of Mortgage: ⑰_____% (percent) per annum

2. This offer is conditional upon the Buyer obtaining a satisfactory termite report and upon a
satisfactory inspection of the property by Buyer within ninety (90) days of acceptance of this Offer
by the Owner.

3. Property will be sold free and clear of all encumbrances and with good and marketable title.

4. The parties agree to execute a standard Agreement to Sell Real Estate within ninety (90) days of acceptance of this Offer by the Owner.

5. The closing for this sale shall occur on or before ⑱_____ , at ⑲_____m. , at
⑳_____ , City of ㉑_____ , State of ㉒_____.

6. Other terms: ㉓

7. This Offer shall remain open until ㉔_____m. , on ㉕_____
_____. If not accepted by the Owner by this time, this Offer is rescinded and the deposit money shall be returned.

㉖_____
Signature of Buyer

㉗_____
Date signed

㉘_____
Printed Name of Buyer

㉙_____
Signature of Owner

㉚_____
Date Signed

㉛_____
Printed Name of Owner

Lead Warning Statement

Every purchaser of any interest in residential real property on which a residential dwelling was built prior to 1978 is notified that such property may present exposure to lead from lead-based paint that may place young children at risk of developing lead poisoning. Lead poisoning in young children may produce permanent neurological damage, including learning disabilities, reduced intelligence quotient, behavioral problems, and impaired memory. Lead poisoning also poses a particular threat to pregnant women. The seller of any interest in residential real estate is required to provide the buyer with any information on lead-based paint hazards from risk assessments or inspection in the seller's possession and notify the buyer of any known lead-based paint hazards. A risk assessment or inspection for possible lead-based paint hazards is recommended prior to purchase. Initial your correct choices.

SELLER'S DISCLOSURE
①Presence of lead-based paint and/or lead-based paint hazards: (Seller to initial one).
_____ Known lead-based paint and/or lead-based paint hazards are present in building (explain).②
_____ Seller has no knowledge of lead-based paint and/or lead-based paint hazards in building.

RECORDS AND REPORTS AVAILABLE TO SELLER: (Seller to initial one).
_____ Seller has provided Buyer with all available records and reports pertaining to lead-based paint and/or lead-based paint hazards that are present in building (list documents).②
_____ Seller has no records and reports pertaining to lead-based paint and/or lead-based paint hazards in building.

③BUYER'S ACKNOWLEDGMENT (Buyer to initial all applicable).
_____ Buyer has received copies of all information listed above.
_____ Buyer has received the pamphlet "Protect Your Family From Lead in Your Home."
④_____ Buyer has received a 10-day opportunity (or mutually-agreed on period) to conduct a risk assessment or inspection for the presence of lead-based paint and/or lead-based paint hazards in building.
④_____ Buyer has waived the opportunity to conduct a risk assessment or inspection for the presence of lead-based paint and/or lead-based paint hazards in building.

Dated: ⑤_____

⑥_____
Signature of Seller
⑦_____
Printed Name of Seller

⑧_____
Signature of Buyer
⑨_____
Printed Name of Buyer

Appraisal Report

This Appraisal Report is made on ① _____ , 20 _____ , by② _____
_____ , Appraiser,
address:③ _____.

Appraiser states that at the request of ④ _____ , who employed him/her to appraise the property commonly known as⑤ _____
_____ , and whose legal description is: ⑥

and after a careful and thorough inspection of the property and to the best of his or her knowledge,
it is the professional opinion of the Appraiser that the market value of the property is as follows:

Land	$⑦ _____
Improvements	$⑧ _____
Total Market Value	$⑨ _____

The physical conditions of the improvements are based on a visual inspection only and no liability
is assumed for the soundness of the structure as no engineering test were done or requested. Appraiser also states that he or she has no financial interest whatsoever in the property, and that his
or her findings are in no way contingent upon the payment that he or she is to receive for making
the appraisal, and that he or she is qualified to make the appraisal for the following reasons:
⑩

⑪ _____
Signature of Appraiser

⑫ _____
Printed Name of Appraiser

73

Appraisal Affidavit

This Appraisal Affidavit is made on ①_____ , 20 _____ , by②_____ , Appraiser, address:③_____.

Appraiser states that, at the request of ④_____ , who employed him/her to appraise the property commonly known as⑤_____ , and whose legal description is:⑥

and that after a careful and thorough inspection of the property and to the best of his or her knowledge, it is the professional opinion of the Appraiser that the market value of the property is as follows:

Land $⑦_____

Improvements $⑧_____

Total Market Value $⑨_____

Appraiser also states that he or she has no financial interest whatsoever in the property, and that his or her findings are in no way contingent upon the payment that he or she is to receive for making the appraisal, and that he or she is qualified to make the appraisal for the following reasons: ⑩

⑪_____   ⑫_____

Signature of Appraiser   Printed Name of Appraiser

⑬State of _____

County of _____

On _____ , 20 _____ , _____ personally came before me and, being duly sworn, did state that he or she is the person described in the above document and that he or she signed the above document in my presence.

_____

Signature of Notary Public

Notary Public, In and for the County of _____

State of _____

My commission expires: _____   Notary Seal

Chapter 4

Real Estate Disclosure Forms

In addition to the federal requirement to disclose information regarding lead in a home, many states have adopted laws requiring some form of disclosure regarding sales of residential real estate. In general, sales of commercial, industrial, or multi-family residences do not require disclosure statements. In addition, condominiums, vacation properties or time-share properties may require additional disclosures. At press time, about 33 states have varying requirements for disclosure regarding residential real estate and 31 states have specific forms. The official state disclosure forms are contained on the Forms-on-CD that accompanied this book. A basic real estate disclosure form is included in this chapter (and on the Forms-on-CD) for the following states that either do not have a specific statutory disclosure requirement or have not provided official forms: Alabama, Arkansas, District of Columbia (Washington D.C.), Florida, Georgia, Hawaii, Kansas, Massachusetts, Minnesota, Missouri, Montana, New Hampshire, New Jersey, New Mexico, North Dakota, Rhode Island, Utah, Vermont, West Virginia, and Wyoming. The states that have official state forms (on the Forms-on-CD) and the names of the forms are listed below (Note: California requires several different disclosure statements):

Alaska: Residential Real Property Transfer Disclosure Statement
Arizona: Affidavit of Disclosure
California: Smoke Detector Statement of Compliance, Military Ordnance Disclosure, Industrial Use Disclosure, Earthquake Hazards,Disclosure,Real Estate Transfer Disclosure Statement, Natural Hazard Disclosure Statement
Colorado: Seller's Property Disclosure
Connecticut: Residential Property Condition Disclosure Report
Delaware: Seller's Disclosure of Real Property Condition Report
Florida: Use the Basic Real Estate Disclosure Form and the Florida Property Tax Disclosure Summary
Idaho: Seller Property Disclosure Form

Illinois: Residential Real Property Disclosure Report
Indiana: Seller's Residential Real Estate Sales Disclosure
Iowa: Residential Property Seller Disclosure Statement
Kentucky: Seller's Disclosure of Property Conditions
Louisiana: Property Disclosure Document for Residential Real Estate
Maine: Property Disclosure Statement
Maryland: Residential Property Disclosure and Disclaimer Statement
Michigan: Seller's Disclosure Statement
Mississippi: Seller's Disclosure Statement
Nebraska: Seller Property Condition Disclosure Statement
Nevada: Seller's Real Property Disclosure Form
New York: Property Condition Disclosure Statement
North Carolina: Residential Property Disclosure Statement
Ohio: Residential Property Disclosure Form
Oklahoma: Residential Property Condition Disclosure Statement
Oregon: Seller's Property Disclosure Statement or Statement of Exclusion
Pennsylvania: Seller's Property Disclosure Statement
South Carolina: Residential Property Condition Disclosure Statement
South Dakota: Seller's Property Condition Disclosure Statement
Tennessee: Residential Property Condition Disclosure
Texas: Seller's Disclosure of Property Condition
Virginia: Residential Property Disclosure Statement
Washington: Seller's Residential Property Disclosure Statement
Wisconsin: Real Estate Condition Report

Under the strictest laws, the seller is required to disclose all facts that materially affect the value or desirability of the property which are known or are accessible only to him or her. Please note that there may also be local or municipal disclosure requirements. You are cautioned to consult a local real estate professional, lawyer, or your state's own statutes to determine if the following form fulfills your state's requirements. The following basic disclosure statement provides a detailed statement regarding most provisions required by most states. The provided statement covers questions relating to ownership of the property, water/sewer issues, possible site problems, possible defects in the home itself, and any prior inspections which may have been performed. The Agreement to Sell Real Estate and the Contract for Deed that are used in this book both contain a paragraph that provides tha the seller will provide buyer with a Real Estate Disclosure Statement within five (5) days of the signing of the documents and that the disclosures will be made by the seller concerning the condition of the property and are provided on the basis of the seller's actual knowledge of the property on the date of this disclosure. The agreements also provide that the disclosures are not, in any way, be construed to be a warranty of any kind by the seller."

Basic Real Estate Disclosure Statement: Any seller that uses the included Agreement to Sell Real Estate or Contract for Deed must provide the buyer with a real estate disclosure statement, even if not required by statute in the seller's particular state. For those states that do not have an official disclosure statement, sellers may use the following form. To complete the following form, you will need the following information:

① Provide a legal description of the property
② Do you have the legal right to sell this property?
③ Are there any leases or rental agreements?
④ Is there a survey for this property available?
⑤ Are there any encroachments or boundary disputes?
⑥ Any written easement or rights of way?
⑦ Any assessments against the property?
⑧ Any zoning or code violations or non-conforming uses?
⑨ Any covenants, conditions, or restrictions?
⑩ Any legal disputes?
⑪ Any liens?
⑫ Any planned zoning or use changes?
⑬ Any planned changes in adjacent property?
⑭ Any landslides or erosion present?
⑮ Any landfill or dumps present?
⑯ Any hazards or hazardous waste present?
⑰ Any soil or drainage problems?
⑱ Any fill material present?
⑲ Any damage from fire, wind, floods, earthquakes, or landslides?
⑳ Any environmental hazards present?
㉑ Any storage tanks present?
㉒ Any greenbelt or utility easement present?
㉓ Is there a homeowner's association? Provide details.
㉔ Has the property been flooded?
㉕ Is it in a flood plain?
㉖ What is the source of household water? Any problems?
㉗ If serviced by well, provide details.
㉘ Are there any irrigation rights?
㉙ Is there an outdoor sprinkler system? Provide details.
㉚ What is the sewage disposal system for property? Provide details.
㉛ What is the age of roof? Provide details.
㉜ Any additions, conversions, or remodeling? Provide details.
㉝ What is the age of the home? Provide details.
㉞ Are you aware of any defects in the structure or of any other improvements?
㉟ Has there been a termite or pest inspection? Provide details.
㊱ Has there been a dry rot or structural inspection? Provide details.
㊲ Are you aware of any other conditions or defects to the property?
㊳ Date of seller's signing of disclosure statement

㊴ Signature of seller
㊵ Printed name of seller
㊶ Signature of seller (second seller if needed)
㊷ Printed name of seller (second seller if needed)
㊸ Date of buyer's receipt of disclosure statement
㊹ Signature of buyer
㊺ Printed name of buyer
㊻ Signature of buyer (second buyer if needed)
㊼ Printed name of buyer (second buyer if needed)

Real Estate Disclosure Statement

Notice to the Buyer:

The following disclosures are made by the seller concerning the condition of the property and are provided on the basis of the seller's actual knowledge of the property on the date of this disclosure. These disclosures are not the representations of any real estate agent or other party. These disclosures are not intended to be a part of any written agreement between the buyer and seller. Unless you have waived the right of cancellation in your real estate sales agreement, you have five (5) business days from the date you receive this disclosure form to cancel your agreement by delivering to the seller a separate signed statement canceling your agreement. For a more comprehensive examination of this property, you are advised to obtain the services of a qualified specialists to inspect the property on your behalf. Examples of specialists are: architects, engineers, surveyors, plumbers, electricians, roofers, or real estate inspection services. The buyer and seller may wish to provide appropriate provisions in the sales agreement regarding any defects, repairs, or warranties. This disclosure shall not be construed to be a warranty of any kind by the seller.

This disclosure concerns the following property: ①

This disclosure is intended to satisfy the real estate disclosure requirements of the state in which this property is located. If additional information is required, I have attached an explanation or information to this statement and intend that such attachments be considered as part of this disclosure statement.

YES or NO

1. Do you have legal authority to sell this property? ②
2. Is the title to this property subject to any leases or rental agreements?
    a. If yes, explain: ③
3. Is there a boundary survey available for this property?
    b. If yes, explain ④
4. Are you aware of any of the following:
    If yes to any, please explain on an attachment.
    a. Encroachments or boundary disputes? ⑤
    b. Any written agreements for easements or rights of way? ⑥
    c. Pending or existing assessments against the property? ⑦

d. Zoning or building code violations, or non-conforming uses? ⑧
e. Covenants, conditions, or restrictions that affect the property? ⑨
f. Any pending or anticipated legal disputes concerning the property? ⑩
g. Any liens against the property? ⑪
h. Any major changes planned in neighborhood zoning or uses? ⑫
i. Any planned or anticipated changes in adjacent properties? ⑬
j. Any landslides or erosion on this or adjacent property? ⑭
k. Any landfills or dumps within one mile of the property? ⑮
l. Any hazards or hazardous materials on or near the property? ⑯
m. Any soil settling, standing water, or drainage problems on the property? ⑰
n. Any fill material in or under the property? ⑱
o. Any damage to property from fire, wind, floods, earthquakes, or landslides? ⑲
p. Any environmental hazards on or near the property? ⑳
q. Any underground or aboveground storage tanks on the property? ㉑
r. Any greenbelt or utility easements affecting the property? ㉒

5. Is there a Home Owners' Association? ㉓
   a. If yes, the name of it is:
   b. Are there any regular assessments?
          Amount: $
   c. Are there any pending special assessments?
   d. Are there any association or other joint maintenance agreements?
          If yes, explain or attach:

6. Has the property ever been flooded? ㉔

7. Is the property within a designated flood plain or flood way? ㉕

8. The source of household water is: ㉖
   a. Are there any water pressure problems?

9. If the property is serviced by a water well: ㉗
   a. Is the well solely owned or shared?
   b. Are there any written agreements regarding well usage?
          If yes, explain or attach:
   c. Are there any known problems or repairs needed?
   d. Does the well provide adequate year-round water supply?
   e. Has water been tested recently?
   f. Is water treated before use?

10. Are there any irrigation water rights for the property? ㉘

11. Is there an outdoor sprinkler system for the property? ㉙
   a. Are there any defects in the system?

12. The sewage disposal system for this property is: ㉚
   a. Are there any known problems with this system?
   b. Do all plumbing fixtures, including floor or laundry drains, go to this system?
   c. If a septic tank system, when was it last pumped?
   d. If a septic tank system, when was it last inspected?
   e. If a septic tank system, is the drainfield located entirely on this property?
   f. If a septic tank system, was it approved and is the permit available?

13. What is the approximate age of the roof? ㉛
   a. Is there a roof warranty?
         If yes, explain or attach:
   b. If yes, is the warranty transferable?
   c. Does the roof leak?
   d. Has the roof ever been repaired?

14. Have there been any additions, conversions, or remodeling of the property? ㉜
   a. If yes, were all building permits and inspections obtained?

15. What is the age of the house? ㉝
   a. Has there been any settling or sliding of the house or any other structures?

16. Are you aware of any defects in any of the following: ㉞
      If yes to any, explain:
   a. Foundations?
   b. Decks or patios?
   c. Exterior walls?
   d. Chimneys and fireplaces?
   e. Interior walls?
   f. Fire alarms and smoke detectors?
   g. Windows or doors?
   h. Pools, hot tubs, or saunas?
   i. Sidewalks?
   j. Garage?
   k. Floors or walkways?
   l. Wood stoves?
   m. Electrical system?
   n. Plumbing system?
   o. Hot water tanks?

p. Garbage disposal?
q. Appliances?
r. Sump pump?
s. Heating and cooling system?
t. Security system?
u. Other (explain)?

17. Has a termite and/or pest inspection been performed recently? ㉟
    a. If yes, when:

18. Has a dry rot or structural inspection been performed recently? ㊱
    a. If yes, when:

19. Are you aware of any other conditions or defects which affect this property? ㊲

The foregoing answers and attached explanations (if any) are complete and correct to the best of my knowledge on the date signed. I authorize all of my real estate licensees or agents to deliver a copy of this disclosure statement to other real estate licensees or agents and to all prospective buyers of the property.

㊳_____
Date of Seller's signing

㊴_____
Signature of seller

㊵_____
Printed Name of seller

㊶_____
Signature of seller

㊷_____
Printed Name of seller

Buyer's Acknowledgment

1. As buyer, I acknowledge my duty to pay diligent attention to any material defects which are known to me or can be known to me by using diligent attention and observation.

2. I understand that the disclosures set forth in this statement and any amendments and attachments are made only by the seller.

3. I hereby acknowledge receipt of a copy of this disclosure statement and any attachments bearing seller's signature.

Unless you have waived the right of cancellation in your real estate sales agreement, you have five (5) business days from the date you receive this disclosure form to cancel your agreement by delivering to the seller a separate signed statement canceling your agreement.

㊸_____
Date of receipt by Buyer

㊹_____
Signature of buyer

㊺_____
Printed Name of buyer

㊻_____
Signature of buyer

㊼_____
Printed Name of buyer

Chapter 5

Real Estate Closing Documents

Closing a real estate transaction is simply the meeting at which the buyer pays the down payment and signs the various paperwork agreeing to pay the balance of the purchase price and the seller delivers the deed and keys to the property. The HUD settlement form that is included in this book is required to be used (in some form) at most real estate closings. It details the various monetary pluses and minuses that take place for most real estate closing settlements regarding the costs payable by both seller and buyer at the time of settlement. These costs can be up to ten percent of the mortgage amount and usually include but are not limited to the following:

- Fees paid to the lender, including those paid in advance
- Loan origination fee
- Discount points
- Credit report fee
- Appraisal fee
- Assumption fee if loan is assumed
- Interest from the closing date to the beginning of the 1st payment
- Hazard insurance premium
- Mortgage insurance premium
- Title search and title insurance
- Sales commissions paid to realtors
- Legal and recording fees
- Inspection and survey fees
- Property taxes and other adjustments
- Processing and document preparation fees

The buyer may also get credit off the purchase price for taxes that the seller has not yet paid, or for repairs that the seller has agreed to pay for. It can often be difficult for an inexperienced buyer or seller to follow exactly what the various credits and debits refer to that are listed on a settlement statement. The best way to understand the settlement form is to study it carefully.

If you will be attempting to handle your own closing as a seller, your local title insurance or abstract company is often an excellent source of assistance. Many such offices will handles all of the paper-work requirements for a very minimal fee (sometimes as little as $100). They will often also assist you in making certain that all of the required forms will be present at your closing and are signed correctly. They will also normally have a notary public present if notarization will be required for any forms. If your buyer will be obtaining a loan from a bank or other lending institution, in many cases the bank or lender will handle the closing of the transaction in their own offices and using their own trained staff. Make sure that you have arranged all of the details and documents of your closing well in advance of the date that you have agreed will be your closing date. Don't forget that certain of the documents that will be signed at the closing may need to be recorded in your local court house recording office. If in doubt, ask your local title insurance or abstract company. Finally, if you are unsure of how to handle your closing, you may request the assistance of an attorney skilled in real estate law. Their costs for handling the paperwork requirements of a real estate sale are often far less than the cost of a real estate broker's commission.

There are certain real estate documents that come into play at the time of the closing of the sale of a piece of real property. A real estate closing is when many of the other documents relating to a real estate transaction are signed. Many other chapters in this book contain documents that may be used in a typical real estate closing, for example: documents relating to real estate disclosure forms (Chapter 4), bills of sale (Chapter 7), and documents pertaining to liens (Chapter 12). The four forms included in this chapter are specific and relate directly to the closing meeting. The first is an Affidavit of Title through which a seller acknowledges full ownership of a piece of real estate. The second is the required federal form that must be used at all residential real estate closings: the HUD Settlement Statement. Finally, two real estate deed forms are included: a Quitclaim Deed and a Warranty Deed.

Affidavit of Title: This specialized type of affidavit is used in real estate transactions to verify certain information regarding a piece of property. This documents is generally used at the closing of the sale of a piece of property. An Affidavit of Title is often required by a mortgage lender prior to approving a mortgage. With an Affidavit of Title, a landowner or seller states, under oath, that he or she has full possession and ownership of the property being sold. The seller also states the existence of any liens or claims against the property and that he or she has full authority to sell the property. This form should be notarized as it may be required to be recorded. If the person making the affirmed statement is acting in other than an individual capacity (such as the director of a corporation, for example), substitute the appropriate signature and acknowledgment forms from Chapter 9.

To complete this form, fill in the following information:
① Date of Affidavit of Title
② Name of Seller

③ Address of Seller
④ Name of Buyer
⑤ Address of Buyer
⑥ Legal description of the property
⑦ List any liens, contracts, debts, or existing lawsuits against property
⑧ Date Affidavit of Title signed
⑨ Signature of Seller
⑩ Printed Name of Seller
⑪ The following must be completed by a Notary Public*
Note: California residents must use the California Notary box available on the Forms-on-CD

HUD Settlement Statement: The official Settlement Statement from the U.S. Department of Housing and Urban Development is used in most real estate closings. It provides a clear and standardized method for detailing the various financial transactions that comprise a typical closing. It provides spaces for detailing the amounts due from the buyer/borrower for the contracted sales price of the real estate, plus any additional costs for personal property or additional closing costs that the buyer has agreed to pay. Similar spaces are provided for the seller's costs and deductions. Adjustment spaces for prepaid taxes, hazard or mortgage insurance, or other assessments are also provided. Look this form over very carefully to gain an understanding of how a typical closing transaction is handled.

Quitclaim Deed: This form is used to transfer property from the seller (called the *'grantor'* on the deed) to the buyer (called the *'grantee'* on the deed) without any warranties that he or she actually owns the property involved. Any transfers of real estate must be in writing. This type of Quitclaim Deed is intended to be used when the seller is merely selling whatever interest she or he may have in the property. By using a Quitclaim Deed, a seller is not, in any way, guaranteeing that she or he actually owns any interest in the property. This type of Deed may be used to settle any claims that a person may have to a piece of real estate, to settle disputes over property, or to transfer property between co-owners. For this deed form to be recorded, it must be properly notarized.

To prepare this deed, simply fill in the following information:
① Name of person requesting recording of deed (generally, you)
② Name and address of person who prepared the deed
③ Name and address of person to whom the recorded deed should be mailed by the recorder's office (not necessary if you bring the deed to the recorder's office personally)
④ Property Tax Parcel number or Tax account number (generally found on latest tax bill)
⑤ Date of signing deed
⑥ Name of grantor (the one transferring the property)
⑦ Address of grantor
⑧ Name of grantee (the one receiving the property)
⑨ Address of grantee
⑩ Street address of property itself

⑪ Legal description of property (should be taken from current deed)
⑫ Current year for property taxes (taxes will be prorated between grantor and grantee for the portion of the tax year that each party owned the property)
⑬ Date of signing of deed by grantor
⑭ Signature of grantor (signed in the front of notary public)
⑮ Printed Name of grantor
⑯ Signatures and printed names of two witnesses (signed in front of notary public)
⑰ Notary Acknowledgement to be completed by notary public*
Note: California residents must use the California Notary box available on the Forms-on-CD

Warranty Deed: This form is used to transfer property from the seller (called the *'grantor'* in the deed) to a buyer (called the *'grantee'* in the deed) with various standard warranties that he or she actually owns the property involved. Any transfers of real estate must be in writing. This type of Warranty Deed is intended to be used when the seller is selling his or her entire legal interest in the property. By using a Warranty Deed, a seller is guaranteeing that she or he actually owns any interest in the property. This type of deed is used in most real estate situations. It provides that the seller is conveying to the buyer a full and complete title to the land without any restrictions or debts. If the property will be subject to any restrictions or debts, these should be noted in the legal description area provided. For the transfer to actually take place, the grantor must give the actual deed to the grantee. In addition, in order for this document to be recorded, this form should be properly notarized. To prepare this Deed, simply fill in the following information:

① Name of person requesting recording of deed (generally, you)
② Name and address of person who prepared the deed
③ Name and address of person to whom the recorded deed should be mailed by the recorder's office (not necessary if you bring the deed to the recorder's office personally)
④ Property Tax Parcel number or Tax account number (generally found on latest tax bill)
⑤ Date of signing deed
⑥ Name of grantor (the one transferring the property)
⑦ Address of grantor
⑧ Name of grantee (the one receiving the property)
⑨ Address of grantee
⑩ Street address of property itself
⑪ Legal description of property (should be taken from current deed)
⑫ Current year for property taxes (taxes will be prorated between grantor and grantee for the portion of the tax year that each party owned the property)
⑬ Date of signing of deed by grantor
⑭ Signature of grantor (signed in the front of notary public)
⑮ Printed Name of grantor
⑯ Signatures and printed names of two witnesses (signed in front of notary public)
⑰ Notary Acknowledgement to be completed by notary public*
Note: California residents must use the California Notary box available on the Forms-on-CD

Affidavit of Title

This affidavit of title is made on ①_____ , 20 _____ , between ②_____ ,
seller,
address: ③

for ④_____ , buyer,
address: ⑤

1. Seller certifies that it is now in possession of and is the absolute owner of the following prop-
    erty: ⑥
2. Seller also states that its possession has been undisputed and that seller knows of no fact or
    reason that may prevent transfer of this property to the buyer.
3. Seller also states that no liens, contracts, debts, or lawsuits exist regarding this property,
    except the following:⑦
4. Seller finally states that it has full power to transfer full title to this property to the buyer.

Dated: ⑧_____ , 20 _____

⑨_____   ⑩_____
Signature of Seller   Printed Name of Seller

⑪State of _____
County of _____

On _____ , 20 _____ , _____ personally came
before me and, being duly sworn, did state that he or she is the person described in the above
document and that he or she signed the above document in my presence.

_____
Signature of Notary Public

Notary Public, In and for the County of _____
State of _____

My commission expires: _____   Notary Seal

OMB Approval No. 2502-0265

A. **Settlement Statement (HUD-1)**

B. Type of Loan

1. ☐ FHA	2. ☐ RHS	3. ☐ Conv. Unins.	6. File Number:	7. Loan Number:	8. Mortgage Insurance Case Number:
4. ☐ VA	5. ☐ Conv. Ins.				

C. Note: This form is furnished to give you a statement of actual settlement costs. Amounts paid to and by the settlement agent are shown. Items marked "(p.o.c.)" were paid outside the closing; they are shown here for informational purposes and are not included in the totals.

D. Name & Address of Borrower:	E. Name & Address of Seller:	F. Name & Address of Lender:

G. Property Location:	H. Settlement Agent:	I. Settlement Date:
	Place of Settlement:	

J. Summary of Borrower's Transaction

100. Gross Amount Due from Borrower

101. Contract sales price	
102. Personal property	
103. Settlement charges to borrower (line 1400)	
104.	
105.	

Adjustment for items paid by seller in advance

106. City/town taxes to	
107. County taxes to	
108. Assessments to	
109.	
110.	
111.	
112.	

120. Gross Amount Due from Borrower

200. Amount Paid by or in Behalf of Borrower

201. Deposit or earnest money	
202. Principal amount of new loan(s)	
203. Existing loan(s) taken subject to	
204.	
205.	
206.	
207.	
208.	
209.	

Adjustments for items unpaid by seller

210. City/town taxes to	
211. County taxes to	
212. Assessments to	
213.	
214.	
215.	
216.	
217.	
218.	
219.	

220. Total Paid by/for Borrower

300. Cash at Settlement from/to Borrower

301. Gross amount due from borrower (line 120)	
302. Less amounts paid by/for borrower (line 220)	( )

303. Cash ☐ From ☐ To Borrower

K. Summary of Seller's Transaction

400. Gross Amount Due to Seller

401. Contract sales price	
402. Personal property	
403.	
404.	
405.	

Adjustment for items paid by seller in advance

406. City/town taxes to	
407. County taxes to	
408. Assessments to	
409.	
410.	
411.	
412.	

420. Gross Amount Due to Seller

500. Reductions In Amount Due to seller

501. Excess deposit (see instructions)	
502. Settlement charges to seller (line 1400)	
503. Existing loan(s) taken subject to	
504. Payoff of first mortgage loan	
505. Payoff of second mortgage loan	
506.	
507.	
508.	
509.	

Adjustments for items unpaid by seller

510. City/town taxes to	
511. County taxes to	
512. Assessments to	
513.	
514.	
515.	
516.	
517.	
518.	
519.	

520. Total Reduction Amount Due Seller

600. Cash at Settlement to/from Seller

601. Gross amount due to seller (line 420)	
602. Less reductions in amounts due seller (line 520)	( )

603. Cash ☐ To ☐ From Seller

The Public Reporting Burden for this collection of information is estimated at 35 minutes per response for collecting, reviewing, and reporting the data. This agency may not collect this information, and you are not required to complete this form, unless it displays a currently valid OMB control number. No confidentiality is assured; this disclosure is mandatory. This is designed to provide the parties to a RESPA covered transaction with information during the settlement process.

Previous edition are obsolete   Page 1 of 3   HUD-1

L. Settlement Charges

700. Total Real Estate Broker Fees		Paid From Borrower's Funds at Settlement	Paid From Seller's Funds at Settlement
Division of commission (line 700) as follows :			
701. $ to			
702. $ to			
703. Commission paid at settlement			
704.			

800. Items Payable in Connection with Loan			
801. Our origination charge	$	(from GFE #1)	
802. Your credit or charge (points) for the specific interest rate chosen	$	(from GFE #2)	
803. Your adjusted origination charges		(from GFE #A)	
804. Appraisal fee to		(from GFE #3)	
805. Credit report to		(from GFE #3)	
806. Tax service to		(from GFE #3)	
807. Flood certification to		(from GFE #3)	
808.			
809.			
810.			
811.			

900. Items Required by Lender to be Paid in Advance			
901. Daily interest charges from to @ $ /day		(from GFE #10)	
902. Mortgage insurance premium for months to		(from GFE #3)	
903. Homeowner's insurance for years to		(from GFE #11)	
904.			

1000. Reserves Deposited with Lender			
1001. Initial deposit for your escrow account		(from GFE #9)	
1002. Homeowner's insurance months @ $ per month $			
1003. Mortgage insurance months @ $ per month $			
1004. Property Taxes months @ $ per month $			
1005. months @ $ per month $			
1006. months @ $ per month $			
1007. Aggregate Adjustment -$			

1100. Title Charges			
1101. Title services and lender's title insurance		(from GFE #4)	
1102. Settlement or closing fee	$		
1103. Owner's title insurance		(from GFE #5)	
1104. Lender's title insurance	$		
1105. Lender's title policy limit $			
1106. Owner's title policy limit $			
1107. Agent's portion of the total title insurance premium to	$		
1108. Underwriter's portion of the total title insurance premium to	$		
1109.			
1110.			
1111.			

1200. Government Recording and Transfer Charges			
1201. Government recording charges		(from GFE #7)	
1202. Deed $ Mortgage $ Release $			
1203. Transfer taxes		(from GFE #8)	
1204. City/County tax/stamps Deed $ Mortgage $			
1205. State tax/stamps Deed $ Mortgage $			
1206.			

1300. Additional Settlement Charges			
1301. Required services that you can shop for		(from GFE #6)	
1302. $			
1303. $			
1304.			
1305.			

1400. Total Settlement Charges (enter on lines 103, Section J and 502, Section K)			

Comparison of Good Faith Estimate (GFE) and HUD-1 Charrges

Charges That Cannot Increase	HUD-1 Line Number	Good Faith Estimate	HUD-1
Our origination charge	# 801		
Your credit or charge (points) for the specific interest rate chosen	# 802		
Your adjusted origination charges	# 803		
Transfer taxes	# 1203		

Charges That In Total Cannot Increase More Than 10%		Good Faith Estimate	HUD-1
Government recording charges	# 1201		
	#		
	#		
	#		
	#		
	#		
	#		
	#		
	Total		
Increase between GFE and HUD-1 Charges		$	or	%

Charges That Can Change		Good Faith Estimate	HUD-1
Initial deposit for your escrow account	# 1001		
Daily interest charges $ /day	# 901		
Homeowner's insurance	# 903		
	#		
	#		
	#		

Loan Terms

Your initial loan amount is	$
Your loan term is	years
Your initial interest rate is	%
Your initial monthly amount owed for principal, interest, and any mortgage insurance is	$ includes ☐ Principal ☐ Interest ☐ Mortgage Insurance
Can your interest rate rise?	☐ No ☐ Yes, it can rise to a maximum of %. The first change will be on and can change again every after . Every change date, your interest rate can increase or decrease by %. Over the life of the loan, your interest rate is guaranteed to never be **lower** than % or **higher** than %.
Even if you make payments on time, can your loan balance rise?	☐ No ☐ Yes, it can rise to a maximum of $
Even if you make payments on time, can your monthly amount owed for principal, interest, and mortgage insurance rise?	☐ No ☐ Yes, the first increase can be on and the monthly amount owed can rise to $. The maximum it can ever rise to is $
Does your loan have a prepayment penalty?	☐ No ☐ Yes, your maximum prepayment penalty is $
Does your loan have a balloon payment?	☐ No ☐ Yes, you have a balloon payment of $ due in years on .
Total monthly amount owed including escrow account payments	☐ You do not have a monthly escrow payment for items, such as property taxes and homeowner's insurance. You must pay these items directly yourself. ☐ You have an additional monthly escrow payment of $ that results in a total initial monthly amount owed of $. This includes principal, interest, any mortgage insurance and any items checked below: ☐ Property taxes ☐ Homeowner's insurance ☐ Flood insurance ☐ ☐

Note: If you have any questions about the Settlement Charges and Loan Terms listed on this form, please contact your lender.

Recording requested by: ①
When recorded, mail to:

Name: ② _____

Address: _____

City: _____

State/Zip: _____

Space above reserved for use by Recorder's Office

Document prepared by:

Name ③ _____

Address _____

City/State/Zip _____

Property Tax Parcel/Account Number: ④

QUITCLAIM DEED

This Quitclaim Deed is made on ⑤ _____ , between

⑥ _____ , Grantor, of ⑦ _____ ,

City of _____ , State of _____ , and

⑧ _____ , Grantee, of ⑨ _____ ,

City of _____ , State of _____ .

For valuable consideration, the Grantor hereby quitclaims and transfers all right, title, and interest held by the Grantor in the following described real estate and improvements to the Grantee, and his or her heirs and assigns, to have and hold forever, located at ⑩ _____ ,

City of _____ , State of _____ : ⑪

Subject to all easements, rights of way, protective covenants, and mineral reservations of record, if any. Taxes for the tax year of ⑫ _____ shall be prorated between the Grantor and Grantee as of the date of recording of this deed.

Dated: ⑬ _____

⑭ _____
Signature of Grantor

⑮ _____
Name of Grantor

⑯ _____   ⑯ _____
Signature of Witness #1   Printed Name of Witness #1

⑯ _____   ⑯ _____
Signature of Witness #2   Printed Name of Witness #2

⑰ State of _____ County of _____
On _____ , the Grantor, _____ ,
personally came before me and, being duly sworn, did state and prove that he/she is the person described in the above
document and that he/she signed the above document in my presence.

_____
Notary Signature

Notary Public,
In and for the County of _____ State of _____

My commission expires: _____   Seal

Send all tax statements to Grantee.

Recording requested by: ① _____
When recorded, mail to:

Name: ② _____

Address: _____

City: _____

State/Zip: _____

Space above reserved for use by Recorder's Office

Document prepared by:

Name ③ _____

Address _____

City/State/Zip _____

Property Tax Parcel/Account Number: ④

WARRANTY DEED

This Warranty Deed is made on ⑤ _____ , between

⑥ _____ , Grantor, of ⑦ _____ ,

City of _____ , State of _____ ,

and ⑧ _____ , Grantee, of ⑨ _____ ,

City of _____ , State of _____ .

For valuable consideration, the Grantor hereby sells, grants, and conveys the following described real estate, in fee simple, to the Grantee to have and hold forever, along with all easements, rights, and buildings belonging to the described property, located at ⑩ _____ , City of

_____ , State of _____ : ⑪

The Grantor warrants that it is lawful owner and has full right to convey the property, and that the property is free from all claims, liabilities, or indebtedness, and that the Grantor and its successors will warrant and defend title to the Grantee against the lawful claims of all persons. Taxes for the tax year of ⑫ _____ shall be prorated between the Grantor and Grantee as of the date of recording of this deed.

Dated: ⑬ _____

⑭ _____
Signature of Grantor

⑮ _____
Name of Grantor

⑯ _____   ⑯ _____
Signature of Witness #1   Printed Name of Witness #1

⑯ _____   ⑯ _____
Signature of Witness #2   Printed Name of Witness #2

⑰ State of _____ County of _____
On _____ , the Grantor, _____ ,
personally came before me and, being duly sworn, did state and prove that he/she is the person described in the above
document and that he/she signed the above document in my presence.

_____
Notary Signature

Notary Public,
In and for the County of _____ State of _____

My commission expires: _____   Seal

Send all tax statements to Grantee.

Chapter 6

Leases of Real Estate

A lease of real estate is simply a written contract for one party to rent a specific property from another for a certain amount and certain time period. As such, all of the general legal ramifications that relate to contracts also relate to leases. However, all states have additional requirements which pertain only to leases. If the rental period is to be for one year or more, most states require that leases be in writing. Leases can be prepared for *periodic tenancies* (that is, for example, month-to-month or week-to-week) or they can be for a fixed period. There are leases contained in this chapter that provide for both fixed-period tenancies and for month-to-month tenancies.

There are also general guidelines for security deposits in most states. These most often follow a reasonable pattern and should be adhered to. Most states provide for the following with regard to lease security deposits:

- Should be no greater than one month's rent and should be fully refundable
- Should be used for the repair of damages only, and not applied for the nonpayment of rent (an additional month's rent may be requested to cover potential nonpayment of rent situations)
- Should be kept in a separate, interest-bearing account and returned, with interest, to the tenant within 10 days of termination of a lease (minus, of course, any deductions for damages)

In addition to state laws regarding security deposits, many states have requirements relating to the time periods required prior to terminating a lease. These rules have evolved over time to prevent both the landlord or the tenant from being harmed by early termination of a lease. In general, if the lease is for a fixed time period, the termination of the lease is governed by the lease itself. Early termination of a fixed-period lease may, however, be governed by individual state law. For periodic leases (month-to-month, etc.), there are normally state rules as to how much advance notice must be given prior to termination of a lease. If early lease termination is anticipated you should check your state law in the Real Estate Appendix, located on the CD, regarding this issue. This Appendix provides a state-by-state listing of the main provisions of landlord-tenant law for all 50 states and Washington D.C., including details of state laws regarding security deposits, entry into leased premises, and other rental issues. Please see the Real Estate Appendix on the CD for information on the requirements in your state. In addition, be advised that there may also be specific local laws that pertain to landlord and tenant relationships that may be applicable. You are advised to check any local ordinances or state laws for any possible additional requirements. You will also need to supply your tenant with a copy of the enclosed federal form: "Protect Your Family from Lead in Your Home," if the rental unit was built before 1978.

Instructions

Credit/Rental Application: This form is the basis of a check into the credit history of a potential tenant (or customer). With this form, an applicant furnishes various information which may be checked further to ascertain the reliability and background of the credit or tenant applicant. The applicant is requested to furnish personal information, two credit references, two bank references, two personal references, and answer a few basic questions. The form also provides for information to be entered regarding the verification of the references.

The Applicant will furnish the following information:

1. Name, address, phone number, fax number, and e-mail address of applicant
2. Creditor #1- Name, account number, phone, and address of creditor #1
3. Creditor #2- Name, account number, phone, and address of creditor #2
4. Bank #1- Name, account number, phone, and address of bank #1
5. Bank #2- Name, account number, phone, and address of bank #2
6. Personal Reference #1- Name, relationship, phone, and address of personal reference #1
7. Personal Reference #2- Name, relationship, phone, and address of personal reference #2
8. Other informations (bankruptcy, felony, eviction, etc.)
9. Applicant's driver's license number and state issuing driver's license
10. Date of Application
11. Signature of Applicant
12. Printed Name of Applicant

Landlord (or Creditor) to fill in the following information:

13. Person at Credit reference #1 contacted
14. Remarks
15. Person at Credit reference #2 contacted
16. Remarks

17 Person at Bank reference #1 contacted
18 Remarks
19 Person at Bank reference #2 contacted
20 Remarks
21 Person at Personal reference #1 contacted
22 Remarks
23 Person at Personal reference #2 contacted
24 Remarks
25 Person contacting references
26 Date references contacted
27 Applicant approval
28 Person making approval
29 Date of approval

Move-in/Move-out Checklist and Acknowledgment: This form is to be used to catalog and note the condition of all of the furniture, furnishings, appliances, and personal property that are present at the leased property. The tenant is responsible for returning all of the following property in as good a condition as is noted on the Move-in section of this form, except for normal wear and tear. Landlord should complete this form prior to move-in and Tenant should check this form upon move-in, noting any disagreements with landlord's assessment. Both Tenant and Landlord should sign the form at move-in. When the Tenant moves out, the Landlord should again check the presence and condition of the items listed on this form and note the condition of such items on the form. The Tenant should then check the items and note any disagreements with the Landlord's assessment of the condition or presence of any of the items listed. Both the Tenant and Landlord should sign this form again at the moving out of the Tenant. This form may be used to determine any deductions from the security deposit of the Tenant. Both the Landlord and the Tenant should get a copy of this form. To complete this form, enter the following information:

1 Name of landlord
2 Name of tenant
3 Address of leased property
4 Term of the lease
5 Date tenant moves into property
6 Date tenant moves out of property
7 Listing of all items and their condition (Complete at time of move-in and again at move-out)
8 Date of landlord signature for move-in condition
9 Signature of landlord for move-in condition
10 Date of tenant signature for move-in condition
11 Signature of tenant for move-in condition
12 Date of landlord signature for move-out condition
13 Signature of landlord for move-out condition
14 Date of tenant signature for move-out condition
15 Signature of tenant for move-out condition

Residential Lease: This form should be used when renting a residential property for a fixed period. Although the landlord and tenant can agree to any terms they desire, this particular lease provides for the following basic terms to be included:

- A fixed-period term for the lease
- A security deposit for damages, which will be returned within 10 days after the termination of the lease, but without interest unless required by state law
- An additional month's rent as security for payment of the rent, which will be returned within 10 days after the termination of the lease, but without interest unless required by state law
- That the tenant agrees to keep the property in good repair and not make any alterations without consent
- Tenant agrees not to conduct any business without permission of the landlord
- Tenant agrees not to have any pets without permission of the landlord
- That landlord and tenant agree on who will pay utilities
- That the tenant agrees not to assign the lease or sublet the property without the landlord's consent
- That the landlord has the right to inspect the property on a reasonable basis, and that the tenant has already inspected it and found it satisfactory
- That the landlord has the right to re-enter and take possession upon breach of the lease (as long as it is in accordance with state law)
- Once the lease term has expired, any continued occupancy will be as a month-to month tenancy
- That the landlord will provide tenant with the U.S. EPA lead pamphlet: "Protect Your Family from Lead in Your Home." *Note*: This document is provided on the Forms-on-CD and is necessary *only* if the rental dwelling was built prior to 1978
- Any other additional terms that the parties agree upon

You will also need to supply your tenant with a copy of the enclosed federal form: "Protect Your Family from Lead in Your Home" if the property was built prior to 1978. (Note: Residents of California will need to include the California Addendum to Lease form that is included on the Forms-on-CD. Residents of Chicago will need to include the Chicago Addendum to Lease and other required Chicago forms that are included on the Forms-on-CD).

To prepare this form, fill in the following information:

1. Date of lease
2. Name of landlord
3. Address of landlord
4. Name of tenant
5. Address of tenant
6. Complete address of leased property
7. Beginning date of lease

⑧ End date of lease
⑨ Amount of the rental payment
⑩ Day of the period when rent will be due and length of period (usually, month)
⑪ Due date of first rental payment
⑫ Amount of security deposit for damages
⑬ Which state's laws will be used
⑭ Amount of additional rent held as rental default deposit
⑮ Which state's laws will be used
⑯ Maximum number of tenants
⑰ Which state's laws will be used
⑱ Utilities that landlord will supply
⑲ Utilities that tenant will provide
⑳ Which state's laws will be used
㉑ Landlord's initials on presence of lead paint disclosure
㉒ Landlord's initials on records and/or reports of lead paint
㉓ Tenant's initials on lead paint acknowledgment
㉔ Any other additional terms
㉕ Which state's laws will be used to interpret lease
㉖ Signature of landlord
㉗ Printed name of landlord
㉘ Signature of tenant
㉙ Printed name of tenant

Month-to-Month Rental Agreement: This rental agreement provides for a month-to-month tenancy: one that continues each month indefinitely or until terminated by either party. For a fixed tenancy lease, please see the Residential Lease, explained above. Although the landlord and tenant can agree to any terms they desire, this particular lease provides for the following basic terms to be included:

- A month-to-month tenancy for the agreement
- A security deposit for damages, to be returned within 10 days after the termination of the agreement, but without interest unless required by state law
- An additional month's rent as security for payment of the rent, which will be returned within 10 days after the termination of the agreement, but without interest unless required by state law
- That the tenant agrees to keep the property in good repair and not make any alterations without consent
- Tenant agrees not to conduct any business without permission of the landlord
- Tenant agrees not to have any pets without permission of the landlord
- That landlord and tenant agree on who will pay utilities
- That the tenant agrees not to assign or sublet the property without the landlord's consent
- That the landlord has the right to inspect the property on a reasonable basis, and that the tenant has already inspected it and found it satisfactory

- That the landlord has the right to re-enter and take possession upon breach of the agreement (as long as it is in accordance with state law)
- That the landlord will provide tenant with the U.S. EPA lead pamphlet: "Protect Your Family from Lead in Your Home." *Note*: This document is provided on the Forms-on-CD and is necessary *only* if the rental dwelling was built prior to 1978
- Any other additional terms that the parties agree upon

You will also need to supply your tenant with a copy of the enclosed federal form: "Protect Your Family from Lead in Your Home" if the property was built prior to 1978. (Note: Residents of California will need to include the California Addendum to Lease form that is included on the Forms-on-CD. Residents of Chicago will need to include the Chicago Addendum to Lease and other required Chicago forms that are included on the Forms-on-CD).

To prepare this form, fill in the following information:

1. Date of rental agreement
2. Name of landlord
3. Address of landlord
4. Name of tenant
5. Address of tenant
6. Complete address of rental property
7. Beginning date of rental agreement
8. Number of days required for termination of rental agreement
9. Amount of rental payment
10. Day of the month when rent will be due and period of tenancy
11. Due date of first rent payment
12. Amount of security deposit for damages
13. Which state's laws will be used
14. Amount of additional rent held as rental default deposit
15. Which state's laws will be used
16. Maximum number of tenants
17. Which state's laws will be used
18. Utilities that landlord will supply
19. Utilities that tenant will provide
20. Which state's laws will be used
21. Landlord's initials on presence of lead paint disclosure
22. Tenant's initials on lead paint acknowledgment
23. Any other additional terms
24. Which state's laws will be used to interpret agreement
25. Signature of landlord
26. Printed name of landlord
27. Signature of tenant
28. Printed name of tenant

Commercial Lease: This form should be used when renting a commercial property. Although the landlord and tenant can agree to any terms they desire, this particular lease provides for the following basic terms to be included:

- An initial fixed-period term for the lease, with the lease continuing on after this term as a month-to-month lease
- A five percent late charge for rent payments over five days late
- A limitation on what business the tenant may conduct on the property
- A security deposit for damages, which will be returned within 10 days after the termination of the lease
- An additional month's rent as security for payment of the rent, which will be returned within 10 days after the termination of the lease
- That the tenant agrees to keep the property in good repair and not make any alterations without consent
- That the tenant agrees not to assign the lease or sublet the property without the landlord's consent
- That the landlord has the right to inspect the property on a reasonable basis, and that the tenant has already inspected it and found it satisfactory
- That the landlord has the right to re-enter and take possession upon breach of the lease (as long as it is in accordance with state law)
- That the landlord is responsible for the upkeep of the exterior and the tenant for the upkeep of the interior of the property
- That the landlord will carry fire and casualty insurance on the property, and that the tenant will carry casualty insurance on their own equipment and fixtures and also carry general business liability insurance
- That the lease is subject to any mortgage or deed of trust and that the tenant agrees to sign any future subordination documents
- Any other additional terms that the parties agree upon

To prepare this form, fill in the following information:

1. Date of lease
2. Name of landlord
3. Address of landlord
4. City of landlord
5. State of landlord
6. Name of tenant
7. Address of tenant
8. City of tenant
9. State of tenant
10. Complete address and description of leased property
11. Amount of rental payment

⑫ Day of the month when rent will be due
⑬ Due date of first rent payment
⑭ Beginning date of lease
⑮ End date of lease
⑯ Additional lease term upon renewal of lease
⑰ Amount of rent upon renewal
⑱ Amount of rent if tenancy is extended as month-to-month
⑲ Amount of security deposit for damages
⑳ Amount of additional rent held as rental default deposit
㉑ Description of tenant's business
㉒ Description of equipment or fixtures tenant will install
㉓ Number of days tenant allowed to correct violation or rent default
㉔ Number of days required for termination of lease if violation or default
㉕ Minimum amount of business liability insurance tenant will carry
㉖ Number of days required for termination of lease for other than violation or default
㉗ Any other additional terms
㉘ Any attachments to lease
㉙ Which state's laws will be used to interpret lease
㉚ Signature of landlord
㉛ Printed name of landlord
㉜ Signature of tenant
㉝ Printed name of tenant

Lease with Purchase Option: This lease provides for a fixed-period tenancy and contains a "purchase option" which offers the tenant a time period in which to have an exclusive option to purchase a parcel of real estate. Through the use of this agreement, the landlord can offer the tenant a time period with which to consider the purchase without concern of a sale to another party. This option provides that in exchange for a percentage of the rent (which will be applied to the purchase price if the option is exercised), the tenant is given a period of time to exercise the option and accept the terms of a completed real estate contract. If the tenant accepts the terms and exercises the option in writing, the landlord agrees to complete the sale. If the option is not exercised, the landlord is then free to sell the property on the market and retain the money paid for the option as rent. You will also need to supply your tenant with a copy of the enclosed federal form: "Protect Your Family from Lead in Your Home," if the rental unit was built before 1978. (Note: Residents of California will need to include the California Addendum to Lease form that is included on the Forms-on-CD. Residents of Chicago will need to include the Chicago Addendum to Lease and other required Chicago forms that are included on the Forms-on-CD).

To prepare this form, fill in the following information:

① Date of lease
② Name of landlord

Real Estate Forms Simplified

3. Address of landlord
4. City of landlord
5. State of landlord
6. Name of tenant
7. Address of tenant
8. City of tenant
9. State of tenant
10. Complete address of leased property
11. Beginning date of lease
12. End date of lease
13. Amount of rental payment
14. Period of time between payments
15. Day of the month when rent will be due
16. Due date of first rental payment
17. Percentage of each rental payment which will be applied to purchase price if option exercised
18. Date option period expires
19. Anticipated purchase price of property
20. Anticipated rental payment deposit held in trust for option (use full term of lease amount)
21. Type of any other deposit
22. Amount of any other deposit
23. Balance of purchase price due at closing
24. Total purchase price
25. Amount of mortgage commitment required
26. Number of monthly payments of mortgage commitment
27. Annual interest rate of mortgage commitment
28. Amount of security deposit for damages
29. Amount of additional rent held as rental default deposit
30. Maximum number of tenants
31. Utilities that landlord will supply
32. Utilities that tenant will provide
33. Landlord's initials on presence of lead paint disclosure
34. Landlord's initials on records and/or reports of lead paint
35. Tenant's initials on lead paint acknowledgment
36. Any other additional terms
37. State where property is located
38. Signature of landlord
39. Printed name of landlord
40. Signature of tenant
41. Printed name of tenant

Amendment of Lease: Use this form to modify any terms of a lease. A copy of the original lease should be attached to this form. The amendment can be used to change any portion of the lease.

104

Simply note what changes are being made in the appropriate place on this form. If a portion of the lease is being deleted, make note of the deletion. If certain language is being substituted, state the substitution clearly. If additional language is being added, make this clear. For example, you may wish to use language as follows:

"Paragraph _____ is deleted from this lease."

"Paragraph _____ is deleted from this lease and the following paragraph is substituted in its place:

"The following new paragraph is added to this lease:"

In order to prepare this Amendment, please fill in the following information:

① Date of amendment
② Name of landlord and address
③ Name of tenant and address
④ Description of original lease (including date of lease and description of property involved)
⑤ Terms of amendment
⑥ Signature of landlord
⑦ Printed name of landlord
⑧ Signature of tenant
⑨ Printed name of tenant

Extension of Lease: This document should be used to extend the effective time period during which a lease is in force. The use of this form allows the time limit to be extended without having to entirely re-draft the lease. Under this document, all of the other terms of the lease will remain the same, with only the expiration date changing. A copy of the original lease should be attached to this form.

To complete this form, fill in the following information:

① Date of extension
② Name of landlord and address
③ Name of tenant and address
④ Description of original lease (including date of lease and description of property involved)
⑤ Date on which original lease will end
⑥ Date on which extension of lease will end
⑦ Signature of landlord
⑧ Printed name of landlord
⑨ Signature of tenant
⑩ Printed name of tenant

Mutual Termination of Lease: This form should be used when both the landlord and tenant desire to terminate a lease. This document releases both parties from any claims that the other may have against them for any actions under the lease. It also states that the landlord agrees that the rent has been paid in full and that the property has been delivered in good condition.

To complete this form, fill in the following information:

① Date of termination
② Name of landlord and address
③ Name of tenant and address
④ Description of original lease (including date of lease and description of property involved)
⑤ Signature of landlord
⑥ Printed name of landlord
⑦ Signature of tenant
⑧ Printed name of tenant

Assignment of Lease: This form is for use if one party to a lease is assigning its full interest in the lease to another party. This effectively substitutes one party for another under a lease. This particular assignment form has both of the parties agreeing to indemnify and hold each other harmless for any failures to perform under the lease while they were the party liable under it. This Assignment of Lease may be used by a seller of real estate to assign their interest in any lease that covers the property for sale to the new buyer. This *indemnify and hold harmless* clause simply means that if a claim arises for failure to perform, each party agrees to be responsible for the period of their own performance obligations. A description of the lease which is assigned should include the parties to the lease, a description of the property, and the date of the lease. Other information that is necessary to complete the assignment is the name and address of the *assignor* (the party who is assigning the lease), the name and address of the *assignee* (the party to whom the lease is being assigned), and the date of the assignment. A copy of the original lease should be attached to this form.

In order to prepare this Assignment, please fill in the following information:

① Date of assignment
② Name of assignor
③ Address of assignor
④ Name of assignee
⑤ Address of assignee
⑥ Description of original lease (including date of lease and description of property involved)
⑦ Signature of assignor
⑧ Printed name of assignor
⑨ Signature of assignee
⑩ Printed name of assignee

Consent to Assignment of Lease: This form is used if the original lease states that the consent of the landlord is necessary for the assignment of the lease to be valid. A landlord may wish to supply a copy of this form to a tenant if a tenant requests the landlord's consent for an assignment of the lease to another party. A copy of the original lease should be attached to this form.

To complete this form, the following information is needed:

①　Date of consent to assignment
②　Name of tenant requesting consent
③　Address of tenant requesting consent
④　Name of tenant requesting consent
⑤　Description of lease, including date of lease and location of leased premises
⑥　Signature of landlord
⑦　Printed name of landlord

Sublease: This form is used if the tenant subleases the property covered by an original lease. This particular sublease form has both of the parties agreeing to indemnify and hold each other harmless for any failures to perform under the lease while they were the party liable under it. This *indemnify and hold harmless* clause simply means that if a claim arises for failure to perform, each party agrees to be responsible for the period of their own performance obligations. A description of the lease which is subleased should include the parties to the lease, a description of the property, and the date of the lease. Note that the *subtenant* is the party to whom the property is being subleased. A copy of the original lease should be attached to this form. A copy of a Consent to Sublease of Lease should also be attached, if necessary.

To complete this form, enter the following information:

①　Date of sublease
②　Name of tenant
③　Address of tenant
④　Name of subtenant
⑤　Address of subtenant
⑥　Description of property covered by lease
⑦　Description of original lease (including date of lease and name and address of landlord)
⑧　Beginning date of sublease
⑨　Ending date of sublease
⑩　Amount of subrental payments
⑪　Period for each subrental payment (generally, per month)
⑫　Day of month each subrental payment is due
⑬　Beginning date for first subrental payment
⑭　Any additional terms of sublease
⑮　State law which will govern the sublease

⑯ Signature of tenant
⑰ Printed name of tenant
⑱ Signature of subtenant
⑲ Printed name of subtenant

Consent to Sublease: This form is used if the original lease states that the consent of the landlord is necessary for a sublease to be valid. A landlord may wish to supply a copy of this form to a tenant if a tenant requests the landlord's consent for a sublease of the lease to another party. A copy of the original lease should be attached to this form and a copy should be attached to any sublease of a property.

To complete this form, the following information is needed:

① Date of consent to sublease
② Name of tenant requesting consent
③ Address of tenant requesting consent
④ Name of tenant requesting consent
⑤ Description of lease, including date of lease and location of leased premises
⑥ Signature of landlord
⑦ Printed name of landlord

Notice of Rent Default: This form allows for notice to a tenant of default in the payment of rent. It provides for the amount of the defaulted payments to be specified and for a time limit to be placed on payment before further action is taken. Most states have laws relating to the time limits that must be allowed to a tenant to pay the late rent after the landlord's notice of a rent default. You should check your state's listing in the Real Estate Appendix on the CD for the time limit that you should use in this form. If the breach is not taken care of within the time period allowed, you may send the tenant a Notice to Pay Rent or Vacate (shown later in this book). In addition, a lawyer should be consulted for further action, which may involve a lawsuit to enforce the lease terms. A copy of the original lease should be attached to this form.

To complete this form, fill in the following information:

① Date of notice
② Name of tenant
③ Address of tenant
④ Name of tenat
⑤ Description of lease (address of property, dates covered, etc.)
⑥ Date of this notice
⑦ Exact amount of rent past due
⑧ Number of days allowed to pay rent (Check the Appendix for your state's requirements)
⑨ Signature of landlord
⑩ Printed Name of landlord

Notice of Breach of Lease: This form should be used to notify a party to a lease of the violation of a term of the lease or of an instance of failure to perform a required duty under the lease, other than the failure to pay rent. Such violation might be having a pet if the lease prohibits this, or perhaps having too many people living in the rental property, or any other violation of the terms of the lease. This notice provides for a description of the alleged violation of the lease and for a time period in which the party is instructed to cure the breach of the lease. If the breach is not taken care of within the time period allowed, you may send the tenant a Final Notice Before Legal Action. In any event, a lawyer should be consulted for further action, which may entail a lawsuit to enforce the lease terms. A copy of the original lease should be attached to this form.

To complete this form, fill in the following information:

① Date of notice
② Name of tenant
③ Address of tenant
④ Name of tenat
⑤ Description of lease (address of property, dates covered, etc.)
⑥ Date of this notice
⑦ Exact description of breach of lease
⑧ Number of days allowed to correct the breach
⑨ Signature of landlord
⑩ Printed Name of landlord

Notice to Pay Rent or Vacate: This form allows for notice to be given to a tenant who is in default of the payment of rent. It provides for the amount of the defaulted payments to be specified and for a time limit to be placed on payment before further action is taken. It provides notice to either pay the rent or to vacate the property by a certain date. If the defaulted rent is not paid or the property is not vacated by the tenant within the time period allowed, a Landlord's Notice to Terminate Lease may be delivered to the tenant which demands that possession of the property be relinquished. Most states have laws relating to the time limits that must be allowed to a tenant to pay the late rent after the landlord's notice of a rent default. You should check your state's listing in the Appendix of this book for the time limit that you should use in this form. A lawyer should be consulted for further action, which may involve a lawsuit to enforce the lease terms, a lawsuit for collection of the past due rent, or legal proceedings for eviction of the tenant. A copy of the original lease should be attached to this form.

To complete this form, fill in the following information:

① Date of notice
② Name of tenant
③ Address of tenant
④ Name of tenant

⑤ Description of lease (address of property, dates covered, etc.)
⑥ Date of this notice
⑦ Exact amount of rent past due
⑧ Date on which tenant must pay rent or vacate the property (Check state's listing in the Appendix)
⑨ Signature of landlord
⑩ Printed Name of landlord

Landlord's Notice to Terminate Lease: By this notice, a landlord may inform a tenant of the termination of a lease for breach of the lease. This action may be taken under a lease, provided that there are specific lease provisions that allow this action and the tenant has agreed to these provisions by signing the lease. This notice is generally sent to a tenant after the tenant has first been notified that the rent is past due or that the lease has been breached for other reasons and the tenant has been given a time period in which to pay. This notice is not an eviction notice. It is a notice to demand that the tenant surrender possession of the property back to the landlord. Some states have time limits that must be complied with before a lease can be terminated and you should check your state's listing in the Appendix to determine if your state has such requirements. A lawyer should be consulted for further action, which may involve a lawsuit to enforce the lease terms, a lawsuit for collection of the past-due rent, or legal proceedings for eviction of the tenant. A copy of the original lease should be attached to this form. This form should be delivered to the tenant by certified first-class mail and the Proof of Service portion of this form should be completed by the person actually mailing the notice.

To complete this form, fill in the following information:

① Date of notice
② Name and address of tenant
③ Name of tenant
④ Description of lease (address of property, dates covered, etc.)
⑤ Date of this Notice
⑥ Exact nature of breach of lease (amount rent past due, etc.)
⑦ Date of the original Notice to Pay Rent or Vacate or Notice of Breach of Lease
⑧ Number of days allowed in original Notice to Pay Rent or Vacate or Notice of Breach of Lease
⑨ Date on which possession of property is demanded
⑩ Signature of landlord
⑪ Printed Name of landlord
⑫ Address of landlord
⑬ City, state, and zip code of landlord
⑭ Date of mailing of Notice
⑮ Date of signature on Proof of Service
⑯ Signature of person mailing Notice
⑰ Name of person mailing Notice

Final Notice Before Legal Action: This form allows for a final notice to be given to a person who is in default with a rent payment or other breach of a lease. It provides for the amount of the defaulted payments to be specified and for a time limit to be placed on payment before immediate legal action is taken. If the defaulted amount is not paid within the time period allowed, a lawyer should be consulted for further action, Further action may involve a lawsuit for collection of the past due amount, a lawsuit for possession of any collateral (if involved) or other legal proceedings. A copy of the original account statement or invoice should be attached to this form.

To complete this form, fill in the following information:
1. Date of notice
2. Name of person in default
3. Address of person in default
4. Description of lease which has been breached
5. Date of this notice
6. Exact amount of past due rent
7. Date on which payment must be made
8. Date of this notice
9. Signature of landlord
10. Printed name of landlord
11. Address of landlord
12. City, state, and zip code of landlord

Notice of Lease: This document should be used to record notice that a parcel of real estate has a current lease in effect on it. This may be necessary if the property is on the market for sale or it may be required by a bank or mortgage company at the closing of a real estate sale in order for the seller to verify to the buyer the existence of a lease covering the property. This form should be notarized.

In order to complete this document, the following information is required:

1. Description of lease
2. Name of landlord
3. Address of landlord
4. Name of tenant
5. Address of tenant
6. Description of property leased
7. Term of lease
8. Any extensions of lease
9. Signature of landlord
10. Printed name of landlord
11. The following should be completed by a notary public
Note: California residents must use the California Notary box available on the Forms-on-CD

Receipt for Lease Security Deposit: This form is to be used for receipt of a lease security deposit. To complete this form, insert the following information:.

① Amount of security deposit paid
② Description of lease
③ Date of receipt
④ Signature of landlord
⑤ Printed name of landlord

Rent Receipt: This form may be used as a receipt for the periodic payment of rent. To complete this form, insert the following information:

① Amount of rent paid
② Name of Tenant
③ Time period
④ Description of property for which rent is due
⑤ Date of receipt
⑥ Signature of landlord
⑦ Printed Name of landlord

CREDIT/RENTAL APPLICATION

Name ①
Address
City
State   Zip
Phone
Fax
e-mail Address

CREDIT REFERENCES

Creditor Name ②
Account Number
Phone
Address
City
State   Zip

Creditor Name ③
Account Number
Phone
Address
City
State   Zip

BANK REFERENCES

Bank Name ④
Account Number
Phone
Address
City
State   Zip

Bank Name ⑤
Account Number
Phone
Address
City
State   Zip

PERSONAL REFERENCES

Name ⑥
Relationship
Phone
Address
City
State   Zip

Name ⑦
Relationship
Phone
Address
City
State   Zip

OTHER INFORMATION ⑧

Have you ever filed for bankruptcy?

Have you ever been convicted of a felony?

Have you ever been evicted from or asked to leave a property you were renting?

Have you ever intentionally refused to pay rent when due?

How were you referred to us?

Driver's License Number: ⑨   State:

The Applicant accepts the above terms and states that all information contained in this application is true and correct. Applicant authorizes creditor to contact all references, inquire as to credit information, and receive any confidential information relevant to approving credit.

Dated: ⑩_____

⑪_____
Signature of Applicant

⑫_____
Printed Name of Applicant

FOR OFFICE USE ONLY

References Contacted	Person Contacted	Remarks
Creditor #1	⑬	⑭
Creditor #2	⑮	⑯
Bank #1	⑰	⑱
Bank #2	⑲	⑳
Personal #1	㉑	㉒
Personal #2	㉓	㉔

References Contacted by: ㉕
Date References Contacted: ㉖

Applicant Approved: ㉗

Approval by: ㉘
Date Approved: ㉙

Move-in/Move-out Checklist and Acknowledgment

Landlord Name: ①

Tenant Name: ②

Address of leased property: ③

Term of Lease: ④

Date of Move-in: ⑤

Date of Move-out: ⑥

This form is to catalog and note the condition of all of the furniture, furnishing, appliances, and personal property that is present at the leased property. The tenant is responsible for returning all of the following property upon moving out in as good a condition as is noted on the Move-in section of this form, except for normal wear and tear. Landlord should complete this form prior to move-in and Tenant should check this form upon move-in, noting any disagreements with landlord's assessment.

Item Description	Move-in Condition	Landlord Comments	Tenant Comments	Move-out Condition	Landlord Comments	Tenant Comments
⑦						

Move-in Acknowledgment

Landlord has reviewed this document and agrees with the items listed and their condition on the date of the Tenant's moving into the leased property.

Date: ⑧_____

⑨_____
Landlord Signature

Tenant has inspected all of the listed items and found them to be present on the leased property and to be in the condition indicated on the date of the Tenant's moving in to the leased property (or else has noted any discrepancy on this form). Tenant agrees to return all of the listed property on the date of moving out of the leased property in the same condition as indicated on this form, except for normal wear and tear. By signing this form, Tenant agrees with Landlord's assessment or notes his or her disagreement with the Landlord.

Date: ⑩_____

⑪_____
Tenant Signature

Move-out Acknowledgment

Landlord has inspected the listed items and compared them to the move-in condition. If any property differs from its move-in condition, other than normal wear and tear, any differences have been listed on this form.

Date: ⑫_____

⑬_____
Landlord Signature

Tenant has inspected the listed items and compared them to the move-in condition. If any property differs from its move-in condition, other than normal wear and tear, any differences have been listed on this form. If Tenant disagrees with Landlord's assessment of any differences in condition upon moving out, those discrepancies have been listed on this form. By signing this form, Tenant agrees with Landlord's assessment or notes his or her disagreement with the Landlord.

Date: ⑭_____

⑮_____
Tenant Signature

RESIDENTIAL LEASE

This lease is made on ① _____ , 20 _____ , between
② _____ , landlord,
address:③ _____

and ④ _____ , tenant,
address:⑤ _____

1. The landlord agrees to rent to the tenant and the tenant agrees to rent from the landlord the following residence:
   ⑥

2. The term of this lease will be from ⑦ _____ , 20 _____ , until
   ⑧ _____ , 20 _____ .

3. The rental payments will be $ ⑨ _____ per ⑩ _____ and will be payable by the tenant to
   the landlord on the ⑪ _____ day of each month, beginning on _____ , 20 _____ .

4. The tenant has paid the landlord a security deposit of $ ⑫ _____ . This security deposit will be held
   as security for the repair of any damages to the residence by the tenant. This deposit will be returned to the tenant
   within ten (10) days of the termination of this lease, minus any amounts needed to repair the residence, but without
   interest, except as required by law in the State of ⑬ _____ .

5. The Tenant has paid the Landlord an additional month's rent in the amount of $ ⑭ _____ . This rent
   deposit will be held as security for the payment of rent by the tenant. This rent payment deposit will be returned to the
   tenant within ten (10) days of the termination of this lease, minus any rent still due upon termination but without interest, except as required by law in the State of ⑮ _____ .

6. Tenant agrees to maintain the residence in a clean and sanitary manner and not to make any alterations to the
   residence without the landlord's written consent. Tenant also agrees not to conduct any business in the residence. At
   the termination of this lease, the tenant agrees to leave the residence in the same condition as when it was received,
   except for normal wear and tear.

7. Tenant also agrees not to conduct any type of business in the residence, nor store or use any dangerous or hazardous materials. Tenant agrees that the residence is to be used only as a single family residence, with a maximum of
   ⑯ _____ tenants. Tenant also agrees to comply with all rules, laws, and ordinances affecting the residence, including
   all laws of the State of ⑰ _____ . Tenant agrees that no pets or other animals are allowed in the residence without the written permission of the Landlord.

8. The landlord agrees to supply the following utilities to the tenant:⑱

9. The tenant agrees to obtain and pay for the following utilities:⑲

10. Tenant agrees not to sublet the residence or assign this lease without the landlord's written consent. Tenant agrees to allow
    the landlord reasonable access to the residence for inspection and repair. Landlord agrees to enter the residence only after
    notifying the tenant in advance, except in an emergency, and according to the laws of the State of ⑳ _____ .

11. The tenant has inspected the residence and has found it satisfactory.

12. If the tenant fails to pay the rent on time or violates any other terms of this lease, the landlord will have the right to terminate
    this lease in accordance with state law. The landlord will also have the right to re-enter the residence and take possession
    of it and to take advantage of any other legal remedies available under the laws of the State of ㉑ _____ .

13. If the Tenant remains as tenant after the expiration of this lease without signing a new lease, a month-to-month tenancy will be created with the same terms and conditions as this lease, except that such new tenancy may be terminated by thirty (30) days written notice from either the Tenant or the Landlord.

14. As required by law, the landlord makes the following statement: "Radon gas is a naturally occurring radioactive gas that, when accumulated in sufficient quantities in a building, may present health risks to persons exposed to it. Levels of radon gas that exceed federal and state guidelines have been found in buildings in this state. Additional information regarding radon gas and radon gas testing may be obtained from your county health department."

15. As required by law, the landlord makes the following LEAD WARNING STATEMENT:
"Every purchaser or lessee of any interest in residential real property on which a residential dwelling was built prior to 1978 is notified that such property may present exposure to lead from lead-based paint that may place young children at risk of developing lead poisoning. Lead poisoning in young children may produce permanent neurological damage, including learning disabilities, reduced intelligence quotient, behavioral problems, and impaired memory. Lead poisoning also poses a particular threat to pregnant women. The seller or lessor of any interest in residential real estate is required to provide the buyer with any information on lead-based paint hazards from risk assessments or inspection in the seller's or lessor's possession and notify the buyer or lessee of any known lead-based paint hazards. A risk assessment or inspection for possible lead-based paint hazards is recommended prior to purchase."

Landlord's Disclosure

Presence of lead-based paint and/or lead-based paint hazards: (Landlord to initial one).㉒

_____ Known lead-based paint and/or lead-based paint hazards are present in building (explain):

_____ Landlord has no knowledge of lead-based paint and/or lead-based paint hazards in building.

Records and reports available to landlord: (Landlord to initial one).
_____ Landlord has provided tenant with all available records and reports pertaining to lead-based paint and/or lead-based paint hazards are present in building (list documents):

_____ Landlord has no records and reports pertaining to lead-based paint and/or lead-based paint hazards in building.

Tenant's Acknowledgment

(Tenant to initial all applicable).㉓

_____ Tenant has received copies of all information listed above.

_____ Tenant has received the pamphlet "Protect Your Family from Lead in Your Home."

_____ Tenant has received a ten (10)-day opportunity (or mutually agreed on period) to conduct a risk assessment or inspection for the presence of lead-based paint and/or lead-based paint hazards in building.

_____ Tenant has waived the opportunity to conduct a risk assessment or inspection for the presence of lead-based paint and/or lead-based paint hazards in building.

The landlord and tenant have reviewed the information above and certify, by their signatures at the end of this lease, to the best of their knowledge, that the information they have provided is true and accurate.

16. The following are additional terms of this lease: ㉔

17. The parties agree that this lease is the entire agreement between them. This lease binds and benefits both the landlord and tenant and any successors. This Lease is governed by the laws of the State of ㉕_____ .

㉖_____
Signature of Landlord

㉘_____
Signature of Tenant

㉗_____
Printed Name of Landlord

㉙_____
Printed Name of Tenant

MONTH TO MONTH RENTAL AGREEMENT

This Agreement is made on ①_____ , 20 _____ , between
②_____ , landlord,
address:③_____

and④ _____ , tenant,
address:⑤_____

1. The Landlord agrees to rent to the Tenant and the Tenant agrees to rent from the Landlord on a month-to-month ba-
    sis, the following residence: ⑥

2. This Agreement will begin on ⑦_____ and will continue on a month-to-month basis until
   terminated. This agreement may only be terminated by ⑧_____ days written notice from either party.

3. The rental payments will be $ ⑨_____ per ⑩_____ and will be payable by the tenant to
    the landlord on the ⑪_____ day of each month, beginning on _____ , 20 _____ .

4. The tenant has paid the landlord a security deposit of $ ⑫_____ . This security deposit will be held
    as security for the repair of any damages to the residence by the tenant. This deposit will be returned to the tenant
    within ten (10) days of the termination of this agreement, minus any amounts needed to repair the residence, but with-
    out interest, except as required by law in the State of ⑬_____.

5. The Tenant has paid the Landlord an additional month's rent in the amount of $ ⑭_____ . This rent
    deposit will be held as security for the payment of rent by the tenant. This rent payment deposit will be returned to the
    tenant within ten (10) days of the termination of this agreement, minus any rent still due upon termination but without
    interest, except as required by law in the State of ⑮_____.

6. Tenant agrees to maintain the residence in a clean and sanitary manner and not to make any alterations to the
    residence without the landlord's written consent. Tenant also agrees not to conduct any business in the residence.
    At the termination of this agreement, the tenant agrees to leave the residence in the same condition as when it was
    received, except for normal wear and tear.

7. Tenant also agrees not to conduct any type of business in the residence, nor store or use any dangerous or hazardous
    materials. Tenant agrees that the residence is to be used only as a single family residence, with a maximum of
    ⑯_____ tenants. Tenant also agrees to comply with all rules, laws, and ordinances affecting the residence, in-
    cluding all the laws of the State of ⑰_____ . Tenant agrees that no pets or other animals are allowed
    in the residence without the written permission of the Landlord.

8. The landlord agrees to supply the following utilities to the tenant:⑱

9. The tenant agrees to obtain and pay for the following utilities:⑲

10. Tenant agrees not to sublet the residence or assign this agreement without the landlord's written consent. Tenant
    agrees to allow the landlord reasonable access to the residence for inspection and repair. Landlord agrees to enter
    the residence only after notifying the tenant in advance, except in an emergency, and according to the laws of the
    State of ⑳_____.

11. The tenant has inspected the residence and has found it satisfactory.

12. If the tenant fails to pay the rent on time or violates any other terms of this agreement, the landlord will have the right
    to terminate this agreement in accordance with state law. The landlord will also have the right to re-enter the resi-
    dence and take possession of it and to take advantage of any other legal remedies available.

13. As required by law, the landlord makes the following statement: "Radon gas is a naturally occurring radioactive gas that, when accumulated in sufficient quantities in a building, may present health risks to persons exposed to it. Levels of radon gas that exceed federal and state guidelines have been found in buildings in this state. Additional information regarding radon gas and radon gas testing may be obtained from your county health department."

14. As required by law, the landlord makes the following LEAD WARNING STATEMENT: "Every purchaser or lessee of any interest in residential real property on which a residential dwelling was built prior to 1978 is notified that such property may present exposure to lead from lead-based paint that may place young children at risk of developing lead poisoning. Lead poisoning in young children may produce permanent neurological damage, including learning disabilities, reduced intelligence quotient, behavioral problems, and impaired memory. Lead poisoning also poses a particular threat to pregnant women. The seller or lessor of any interest in residential real estate is required to provide the buyer or lessee with any information on lead-based paint hazards from risk assessments or inspection in the seller's or lessor's possession and notify the buyer or lessee of any known lead-based paint hazards. A risk assessment or inspection for possible lead-based paint hazards is recommended prior to purchase."

Landlord's Disclosure

Presence of lead-based paint and/or lead-based paint hazards: (Landlord to initial one). ㉑

_____ Known lead-based paint and/or lead-based paint hazards are present in building (explain):
_____ Landlord has no knowledge of lead-based paint and/or lead-based paint hazards in building.

Records and reports available to landlord: (Landlord to initial one).

_____ Landlord has provided tenant with all available records and reports pertaining to lead-based paint and/or lead-based paint hazards are present in building (list documents):
_____ Landlord has no records and reports pertaining to lead-based paint and/or lead-based paint hazards in building.

Tenant's Acknowledgment

(Tenant to initial all applicable). ㉒

_____ Tenant has received copies of all information listed above.
_____ Tenant has received the pamphlet "Protect Your Family from Lead in Your Home."
_____ Tenant has received a ten (10)-day opportunity (or mutually agreed on period) to conduct a risk assessment or inspection for the presence of lead-based paint and/or lead-based paint hazards in building.
_____ Tenant has waived the opportunity to conduct a risk assessment or inspection for the presence of lead-based paint and/or lead-based paint hazards in building.

The landlord and tenant have reviewed the information above and certify, by their signatures at the end of this agreement, to the best of their knowledge, that the information they have provided is true and accurate.

15. The following are additional terms of this agreement: ㉓

16. The parties agree that this agreement is the entire agreement between them. This Agreement binds and benefits both the landlord and tenant and any successors. This Agreement is governed by the laws of the State of ㉔ _____ .

㉕_____   ㉗_____
Signature of Landlord   Signature of Tenant

㉖_____   ㉘_____
Printed Name of Landlord   Printed Name of Tenant

COMMERCIAL LEASE

This lease is made on ①_____ , 20 _____ , between
②_____ , landlord,
address:③④⑤

and ⑥_____ , tenant,
address:⑦⑧⑨

1. The Landlord agrees to rent to the Tenant and the Tenant agrees to rent from the Landlord the following property: ⑩

2. The rental payments will be $ ⑪ _____ per month and will be payable by the Tenant to the Landlord on the ⑫_____ day of each month, beginning on _____. If any rental payment is not paid within 5 (five) days of its due date, the Tenant agrees to pay an additional late charge of 5% (five percent) of the rental due.

3. The term of this Lease will be from⑬ _____, until ⑭_____ _____. If Tenant is in full compliance with all of the terms of this Lease at the expiration of this term, Tenant shall have the option to renew this Lease for an additional term of ⑮ _____, with all terms and conditions of this Lease remaining the same, except that the rent shall be $⑯_____ If the Tenant remains as tenant after the expiration of this Lease with the consent of the Landlord but without signing a new lease, a month-to-month tenancy will be created with the same terms and conditions as this Lease, except that such new tenancy may be terminated by ninety (90) days written notice from either the Tenant or the Landlord, and that the rent shall be $ ⑰_____ .

4. The Tenant has paid the Landlord a security deposit of $⑱ _____ . This security deposit will be held as security for the repair of any damages to the property by the Tenant. This deposit will be returned to the Tenant within 10 (ten) days of the termination of this Lease, minus any amounts needed to repair the property, but without interest., unless required by state law.

5. The Tenant has paid the Landlord an additional month's rent in the amount of $⑲_____ . This rent deposit will be held as security for the payment of rent by the Tenant. This rent payment deposit will be returned to the Tenant within 10 (ten) days of the termination of this Lease, minus any rent still due upon termination, but without interest, unless required by state law.

6. The Tenant agrees to use the property only for the purpose of carrying on the following lawful business: ⑳

7. The Landlord agrees that the Tenant may install the following equipment and fixtures for the purpose of operating the Tenant's business and that such equipment and fixtures shall remain the property of the Tenant: ㉑

8. The Tenant has inspected the property and has found it satisfactory for its intended purposes. The Landlord shall be responsible for the repair and upkeep of the exterior of the property, including the roof, exterior walls, parking areas, landscaping, and building foundation. The Tenant shall be responsible for the repair and upkeep of the interior of the property, including all electrical, mechanical, plumbing, heating, cooling, or any other system or equipment on the property. Tenant agrees to maintain the interior of the property and the surrounding outside area in a clean, safe, and sanitary manner and not to make any alterations to the property without the Landlord's written consent. At the termination of this Lease, the Tenant agrees to leave the property in the same condition as when it was received, except for normal wear and tear. Tenant also agrees to comply with all rules, laws, regulations, and ordinances affecting the property or the business activities of the Tenant.

9. The Tenant agrees to obtain and pay for all necessary utilities for the property.

10. The Tenant agrees not to sub-let the property or assign this Lease without the Landlord's written consent, which shall not be unreasonably withheld. Tenant agrees to allow the Landlord reasonable access to the property for inspection and repair. Landlord agrees to enter the property only after notifying the Tenant in advance, except in an emergency.

11. If the Tenant fails to pay the rent on time or violates any other terms of this Lease, the Landlord will provide written notice of the violation or default, allowing ㉓ _____ days to correct the violation or default. If the violation or default is not completely corrected within the time prescribed, the Landlord will have the right to terminate this Lease with ㉔ _____ days notice and in accordance with state law. Upon termination of this Lease, the Tenant agrees to surrender possession of the property. The Landlord will also have the right to re-enter the property and take possession of it, remove Tenant and any equipment or possessions of Tenant, and to take advantage of any other legal remedies available.

12. The Landlord agrees to carry fire and casualty insurance on the property, but shall have no liability for the operation of the Tenant's business. The Tenant agrees not to do anything that will increase the Landlord's insurance premiums and, further agrees to indemnify and hold the Landlord harmless from any liability or damage, whether caused by Tenant's operations or otherwise. The Tenant agrees to carry and pay all premiums for casualty insurance on any equipment or fixtures that Tenant installs at the property. In addition, the Tenant agrees to carry business liability insurance, including bodily injury and property damage coverage, covering all Tenant's business operations in the amount of $ ㉕ _____ with the Landlord named as a co-insured party. Tenant agrees to furnish Landlord copies of the insurance policies and to not cancel the policies without notifying the Landlord in advance. Tenant agrees to provide Landlord with a Certificate of Insurance which indicates that Landlord is a co-insured party and that Landlord shall be provided with a minimum of ten (10) days written notice prior to cancellation or change of coverage.

13. This Lease is subject to any mortgage or deed of trust currently on the property or which may be made against the property at any time in the future. The Tenant agrees to sign any documents necessary to subordinate this Lease to a mortgage or deed of trust for the Landlord.

14. This Lease may only be terminated by ㉖ _____ days written notice from either party, except in the event of a violation of any terms or default of any payments or responsibilities due under this Lease, which are governed by the terms in Paragraph 11 of this Lease.

15. Tenant agrees that if any legal action is necessary to recover the property, collect any amounts due under this Lease, or correct a violation of any term of this Lease, Tenant shall be responsible for all costs incurred by Landlord in connection with such action, including any reasonable attorney's fees.

16. As required by law, the Landlord makes the following statement: "Radon gas is a naturally-occurring radioactive gas that, when accumulated in sufficient quantities in a building, may present health risks to persons exposed to it. Levels of radon gas that exceed federal and state guidelines have been found in buildings in this state. Additional information regarding radon gas and radon gas testing may be obtained from your county health department."

17. The following are additional terms of this Lease: ㉗

18. The parties agree that this Lease, including the following attachments: ㉘

is the entire agreement between them and that no terms of this Lease may be changed except by written agreement of both parties. This Lease is intended to comply with any and all applicable laws relating to landlord and tenant relationships in this state. This Lease binds and benefits both the Landlord and Tenant and any heirs, successors, representatives, or assigns. This Lease is governed by the laws of the State of ㉙ _____ .

㉚ _____
Signature of Landlord

㉛ _____
Printed Name of Landlord

㉜ _____
Signature of Tenant

㉝ _____
Printed Name of Tenant

LEASE WITH PURCHASE OPTION

This lease is made on ①_____ , 20 _____ , between
②_____ , landlord,
address:③④⑤

and ⑥_____ , tenant,
address:⑦⑧⑨

1. The Landlord agrees to rent to the Tenant and the Tenant agrees to rent from the Landlord the following residence: ⑩

2. The term of this lease will be from ⑪_____ , until ⑫_____ .

3. The rental payments will be $ ⑬_____ per ⑭_____ and will be payable by the Tenant to the
   Landlord on the ⑮_____ day of each month, beginning on ⑯_____ .

4. The Landlord agrees to give the Tenant an exclusive option to buy this property for the following price and terms:

   A. ⑰_____ percent of the amount that the Tenant pays the Landlord as rent under this Lease will
   be held as a deposit and credited against the purchase price of this property if this option is exercised by the Tenant. If
   the option is not exercised, the Seller will retain all of these payments as rent under this Lease.

   B. The option period will be from the beginning date of this Lease until ⑱_____ , at which
   time it will expire unless exercised.

   C. During this period, the Tenant has the exclusive option and right to buy the leased property for the purchase price of
   $ ⑲_____ . The Tenant must notify the Landlord, in writing, of the decision to exercise this option.
   The purchase price will be paid as follows:

   Rental payment deposit, to be held in trust by Landlord $ ⑳_____
   Other deposit: ㉑_____ $ ㉒_____
   Cash or certified check for balance on closing $ ㉓_____
   (subject to any adjustments or prorations on closing)
   Total Purchase Price $ ㉔_____

   D. Should the Tenant exercise this Option in writing, Landlord and Tenant agree to enter into a standard Agreement for
   the Sale of Real Estate. The Agreement will be conditional upon the Tenant being able to arrange suitable financing
   on the following terms at least thirty (30) days prior to the closing date specified in the Agreement for the Sale of Real
   Estate: a mortgage in the amount of ㉕_____ , payable in ㉖_____ monthly payments, with
   an annual interest rate of ㉗_____ percent.

5. The Tenant has paid the Landlord a security deposit of $ ㉘_____ . This security deposit will be held as
   security for the repair of any damages to the residence by the Tenant. This deposit will be returned to the Tenant within
   ten (10) days of the termination of this lease, minus any amounts needed to repair the residence, but without interest,
   unless required by state law.

6. The Tenant has paid the Landlord an additional month's rent in the amount of $ ㉙_____ . This
   rent deposit will be held as security for the payment of rent by the Tenant. This rent payment deposit will be returned
   to the Tenant within ten (10) days of the termination of this lease, minus any rent still due upon termination, but without
   interest unless required by state law.

7. The Tenant has inspected the residence and has found it satisfactory. Tenant agrees to maintain the residence and the
   surrounding outside area in a clean and sanitary manner and not to make any alterations to the residence without
   the Landlord's written consent. At the termination of this lease, the Tenant agrees to leave the residence in the same
   condition as when it was received, except for normal wear and tear.

8. Tenant also agrees not to conduct any type of business in the residence, nor store or use any dangerous or hazardous materials. Tenant agrees that the residence is to be used only as a single family residence, with a maximum of _____ ___㉚____ tenants. Tenant also agrees to comply with all rules, laws, and ordinances affecting the residence. Tenant agrees that no pets or other animals are allowed in the residence without the written permission of the Landlord.

9. The Landlord agrees to supply the following utilities to the Tenant: ㉛

10. The Tenant agrees to obtain and pay for the following utilities: ㉜

11. Tenant agrees not to sub-let the residence or assign this lease without the Landlord's written consent. Tenant agrees to allow the Landlord reasonable access to the residence for inspection and repair. Landlord agrees to enter the residence only after notifying the Tenant in advance, except in an emergency.

12. If the Tenant fails to pay the rent on time or violates any other terms of this lease, the Landlord will provide written notice of the violation or default. If the violation or default is not corrected, the Landlord will have the right to terminate this lease in accordance with state law. The Landlord will also have the right to re-enter the residence and take possession of it and to take advantage of any other legal remedies available.

13. If the Tenant remains as tenant after the expiration of this lease without signing a new lease, a month-to-month tenancy will be created with the same terms and conditions as this lease, except that such new tenancy may be terminated by thirty (30) days written notice from either the Tenant or the Landlord.

14. As required by law, the Landlord makes the following statement: "Radon gas is a naturally-occurring radioactive gas that, when accumulated in sufficient quantities in a building, may present health risks to persons exposed to it. Levels of radon gas that exceed federal and state guidelines have been found in buildings in this state. Additional information regarding radon gas and radon gas testing may be obtained from your county health department."

15. As required by law, the Landlord makes the following LEAD WARNING STATEMENT: "Every purchaser or lessee of any interest in residential real property on which a residential dwelling was built prior to 1978 is notified that such property may present exposure to lead from lead-based paint that may place young children at risk of developing lead poisoning. Lead poisoning in young children may produce permanent neurological damage, including learning disabilities, reduced intelligence quotient, behavioral problems, and impaired memory. Lead poisoning also poses a particular threat to pregnant women. The seller of any interest in residential real estate is required to provide the buyer with any information on lead-based paint hazards from risk assessments or inspection in the seller's possession and notify the buyer of any known lead-based paint hazards. A risk assessment or inspection for possible lead-based paint hazards is recommended prior to purchase."

LANDLORD'S DISCLOSURE
Presence of lead-based paint and/or lead-based paint hazards: (Landlord to initial one). ㉝
_____ Known lead-based paint and/or lead-based paint hazards are present in building (explain).
_____ Landlord has no knowledge of lead-based paint and/or lead-based paint hazards in building.

RECORDS AND REPORTS AVAILABLE TO LANDLORD: (Landlord to initial one). ㉞
_____ Landlord has provided Tenant with all available records and reports pertaining to lead-based paint and/or lead-based paint hazards are present in building (list documents).
_____ Landlord has no records and reports pertaining to lead-based paint and/or lead-based paint hazards in building.

TENANT'S ACKNOWLEDGMENT (Tenant to initial all applicable). ㉟
_____ Tenant has received copies of all information listed above.
_____ Tenant has received the pamphlet "Protect Your Family from Lead in Your Home."
_____ Tenant has received a 10-day opportunity (or mutually-agreed on period) to conduct a risk assessment or inspection for the presence of lead-based paint and/or lead-based paint hazards in building.
_____ Tenant has waived the opportunity to conduct a risk assessment or inspection for the presence of lead-based paint and/or lead-based paint hazards in building.

The Landlord and Tenant have reviewed the information above and certify, by their signatures at the end of this Lease, to the best of their knowledge, that the information they have provided is true and accurate.

16. The following are additional terms of this Lease: ㊱

17. The parties agree that this Lease with Option is the entire agreement between them and that no terms of this Lease with Option may be changed except by written agreement of both parties. This Lease is intended to comply with any and all applicable laws relating to landlord and tenant relationships in this state. This Lease binds and benefits both the Landlord and Tenant and any successors, representatives, or assigns. Time is of the essence of this agreement. This Lease is governed by the laws of the State of ㊲_____ .

㊳_____
Signature of Landlord

㊴_____
Printed Name of Landlord

㊵_____
Signature of Tenant

㊶_____
Printed Name of Tenant

AMENDMENT OF LEASE

This amendment of lease is made on ①_____ , 20 _____ , between
②_____ , landlord,
address:

and ③_____ , tenant,
address:

For valuable consideration, the parties agree as follows:

1.   The following described lease is attached to this amendment and is made a part of this amendment: ④

2.   The parties agree to amend this lease as follows:⑤

3.   All other terms and conditions of the original lease remain in effect without modification. This amendment binds and benefits both parties and any successors. This document, including the attached lease, is the entire agreement between the parties.

The parties have signed this amendment on the date specified at the beginning of this amendment.

⑥_____   ⑧_____
Signature of Landlord   Signature of Tenant

⑦_____   ⑨_____
Printed Name of Landlord   Printed Name of Tenant

EXTENSION OF LEASE

This extension of lease is made on ①_____ , 20 _____ , between
②_____ , landlord,
address:

and ③_____ , tenant,
address:

For valuable consideration, the parties agree as follows:④

1. The following described lease will end on ⑤_____ , 20 _____ :

This lease is attached to this extension and is a part of this extension.

2. The parties agree to extend this lease for an additional period, which will begin
    immediately on the expiration of the original time period and will end on
    ⑥_____ , 20 _____ .

3. The extension of this lease will be on the same terms and conditions as the original lease. This extension binds and
    benefits both parties and any successors. This document, including the attached lease, is the entire agreement between
    the parties.

The parties have signed this extension on the date specified at the beginning of this extension.

⑦_____   ⑨_____
Signature of Landlord   Signature of Tenant

⑧_____   ⑩_____
Printed Name of Landlord   Printed Name of Tenant

MUTUAL TERMINATION OF LEASE

This termination of lease is made on ①_____ , 20 _____ , between
②_____ , landlord,
address:

and ③_____ , tenant,
address:

For valuable consideration, the parties agree as follows:

1. The parties are currently bound under the terms of the following described lease: ④

2. They agree to mutually terminate and cancel this lease effective on this date. This termination agreement will act as a mutual release of all obligations under this lease for both parties, as if the lease has not been entered into in the first place. Landlord agrees that all rent due has been paid and that the possession of the property has been returned in satisfactory condition.

3. This termination binds and benefits both parties and any successors. This document, including the attached lease being terminated, is the entire agreement between the parties.

The parties have signed this termination on the date specified at the beginning of this termination.

⑤_____   ⑦_____
Signature of Landlord   Signature of Tenant

⑥_____   ⑧_____
Printed Name of Landlord   Printed Name of Tenant

ASSIGNMENT OF LEASE

This assignment is made on ①_____ , 20 _____ , between

②_____ , assignor,

address: ③

and ④_____ , assignee,

address: ⑤

For valuable consideration, the parties agree to the following terms and conditions:

1. The assignor assigns all interest, burdens, and benefits in the following described lease to the assignee: ⑥

    This lease is attached to this assignment and is a part of this assignment.

2. The assignor warrants that this lease is in effect, has not been modified, and is fully assignable. If the consent of the landlord is necessary for this assignment to be effective, such consent is attached to this assignment and is a part of this assignment. Assignor agrees to indemnify and hold the assignee harmless from any claim which may result from the assignor's failure to perform under this lease prior to the date of this assignment.

3. The assignee agrees to perform all of the obligations of the assignor and receive all of the benefits of the assignor under this lease. Assignee agrees to indemnify and hold the assignor harmless from anyclaim which may result from the assignee's failure to perform under this lease after the date of this assignment.

4. This assignment binds and benefits both parties and any successors. This document, including any attachments, is the entire agreement between the parties.

⑦_____   ⑨_____
Signature of Assignor   Signature of Assignee

⑧_____   ⑩_____
Printed Name of Assignor   Printed Name of Assignee

CONSENT TO ASSIGNMENT OF LEASE

Date: ①_____ , 20 _____

To: ② ③

RE: Assignment of Lease

Dear ④_____ :

I am the landlord under the following described lease: ⑤

This lease is the subject of the attached assignment of lease.

I consent to the assignment of this lease as described in the attached assignment, which provides that the assignee is fully substituted for the assignor.

⑥_____
Signature of Landlord

⑦_____
Printed Name of Landlord

SUBLEASE

This sublease is made on ①_____ , 20 _____ , between
②_____ , tenant,
address:③

and ④_____ , subtenant,
address:⑤

For valuable consideration, the parties agree to the following terms and conditions:

1. The tenant subleases to the subtenant the following described property: ⑥

2. This property is currently leased to the tenant under the terms of the following described lease: ⑦

    This lease is attached to this sublease and is a part of this sublease.

3. This sublease will be for the period from ⑧_____ , 20 _____ , to
    ⑨_____ , 20 _____ .

4. The subrental payments will be $ ⑩_____ per ⑪_____ and will be payable by the subtenant
    to the landlord on the ⑫_____ day of each month, beginning on ⑬ _____ , 20 _____ .

5. The tenant warrants that the underlying lease is in effect, has not been modified, and that the property may be sublet. If
    the consent of the landlord is necessary for his sublease to be effective, such consent is attached to this sublease and
    is a part of this sublease. Tenant agrees to indemnify and hold the subtenant harmless from any claim which may result
    from the tenant's failure to perform under this lease prior to the date of this sublease.

6. The subtenant agrees to perform all of the obligations of the tenant under the original lease and receive all of the benefits
    of the tenant under this lease. Subtenant agrees to indemnify and hold the tenant harmless from any claim which may
    result from the subtenant's failure to perform under this lease after the date of this sublease.

7. The tenant agrees to remain primarily liable to the landlord for the obligations under the lease.

8. The parties agree to the following additional terms:⑭

9. This sublease binds and benefits both parties and any successors. This document, including any attachments, is the en-
    tire agreement between the parties. This sublease is subject to the laws of the State of ⑮_____ .

⑯_____
Signature of Tenant

⑱_____
Signature of Subtenant

⑰_____
Printed Name of Tenant

⑲_____
Printed Name of Subtenant

CONSENT TO SUBLEASE

Date: ①_____ , 20 _____

To ②③

RE: Sublease of Lease

Dear ④_____ :

I am the landlord under the following described lease: ⑤

This lease is the subject of the attached sublease.

I consent to the sublease of this lease as described in the attached sublease, which provides that the subtenant is substituted for the tenant for the period indicated in the sublease. This consent does not release the tenant from any obligations under the lease and the tenant remains fully bound under the lease.

⑥_____
Signature of Landlord

⑦_____
Printed Name of Landlord

NOTICE OF RENT DEFAULT

Date: ① _____ , 20 _____

To: ② ③

RE: Notice of Rent Default

Dear ④ _____ :

This notice is in reference to the following described lease: ⑤

Please be advised that as of ⑥ _____ , 20 _____ , you are in
DEFAULT IN YOUR PAYMENT OF RENT in the amount of $⑦ _____ .

If this breach of lease is not corrected within ⑧ _____ days of this notice, we will take further action to
protect our rights, which may include termination of this lease and collection proceedings. This notice is made under all
applicable laws. All of our rights are reserved under this notice.

⑨ _____
Signature of Landlord

⑩ _____
Printed Name of Landlord

NOTICE OF BREACH OF LEASE

Date: ①_____ , 20 _____

To:②③

RE: Breach of Lease

Dear ④_____ :

This notice is in reference to the following described lease: ⑤

Please be advised that as of ⑥_____ , 20 _____ , we are holding you in BREACH OF LEASE for the following reasons:⑦

If this breach of lease is not corrected within ⑧_____ days of this notice, we will take further action to protect our rights, which may include termination of this lease. This notice is made under all applicable laws. All of our rights are reserved under this notice.

⑨_____
Signature of Landlord

⑩_____
Printed Name of Landlord

NOTICE TO PAY RENT OR VACATE

Date: ①_____ , 20 _____

To: ②③

RE: Notice to Vacate Property

Dear ④_____ :

This notice is in reference to the following described lease: ⑤

Please be advised that as of ⑥_____ , you are in DEFAULT OF YOUR PAYMENT OF RENT in the amount of $ ⑦_____ , which is immediately payable.

THEREFORE, YOU ARE HEREBY GIVEN NOTICE:

To immediately pay the amount of rent that is in default as noted above or to immediately vacate the property and deliver possession to the Landlord on or before ⑧_____ . If you fail to pay the rent in default or vacate the property by this date, we will take further action to protect our rights, which may include termination of this lease, collection, and eviction proceedings. Be also advised that any legal costs involved in the collection of rent in default or in obtaining possession of this property will also be recovered from you as may be allowed by law. This notice is made under all applicable laws of this state. All of our rights are reserved under this notice. Regardless of your vacating the property, you are still responsible for all rent due under the lease.

THIS IS NOT AN EVICTION NOTICE.

⑨_____
Signature of Landlord

⑩_____
Printed Name of Landlord

LANDLORD'S NOTICE TO TERMINATE LEASE

Date: ① _____ , 20 _____

To:②

RE: Notice to Terminate Lease

Dear ③ _____ :

This notice is in reference to the following described lease: ④

Please be advised that as of ⑤ _____ , 20 _____ , you have been in BREACH OF LEASE for the following reasons:⑥

You were previously notified of this breach in the NOTICE dated ⑦ _____ , 20 _____ . At that time you were given ⑧ _____ days to correct the breach of the lease and you have not complied.

THEREFORE, YOU ARE HEREBY GIVEN NOTICE:

The lease is immediately terminated and you are directed to deliver possession of the property to the landlord on or before ⑨ _____ , 20 _____ . If you fail to deliver the property by this date, legal action to evict you from the property will be taken. Regardless of your deliverance of the property, you are still responsible for all rent due under the lease.

⑩ _____
Signature of Landlord

⑪ _____
Printed Name of Landlord

⑫ _____
Address of Landlord

⑬ _____
City, State, Zip code of Landlord

PROOF OF SERVICE

I, the undersigned, being of legal age, declare under penalty of perjury that I served the above Notice to Terminate Lease on the above-named tenant by mailing an exact copy to the tenant by certified mail on ⑭ _____ .

Signed on: ⑮ _____

By: ⑯ _____
Signature of person mailing notice

⑰ _____
Printed name of person mailing notice

FINAL NOTICE BEFORE LEGAL ACTION

Date: ①_____ , 20 _____

To: ②③

This notice is in reference to the following Lease: ④

Please be advised that as of ⑤_____ , you are in DEFAULT ON THIS LEASE in the amount of $ ⑥_____ , which is immediately due and payable. You have previously been repeatedly notified of your delinquency regarding this Lease.

THEREFORE, YOU ARE HEREBY GIVEN FINAL NOTICE:

That you must immediately pay the full amount that is in default as noted above on or before ⑦_____ . If you fail to pay the full amount in default by this date, we will take immediate action to protect our rights by proceeding with legal action. Be also advised that any and all legal costs associated with such legal action will also be recovered from you to the fullest extent allowed by law and that such legal proceedings may impair your credit rating. This notice is made under all applicable laws of this state. All of our rights are reserved under this notice.

THIS IS YOUR FINAL OPPORTUNITY TO RESOLVE MATTERS WITHOUT THE EXPENSE OF COURT PROCEED-INGS.

Dated: ⑧ _____

⑨_____
Signature

⑩_____
Printed Name

⑪_____
Address

⑫_____
City, State, Zip Code

NOTICE OF LEASE

NOTICE is given of the existence of the following lease:①

Name of landlord:②
Address:③

Name of tenant:④
Address:⑤

Description of property leased:⑥

Term of lease: From ⑦_____ , 20 _____ , to _____ , 20 _____ .

Any options to extend lease:⑧

⑨_____   ⑩_____
Signature   Printed Name

⑪
State of _____
County of _____

On _____ , 20 _____ , _____
personally came before me and, being duly sworn, did state that he or she is the person described in the above document
and that he or she signed the above document in my presence.

_____
Signature of Notary Public

Notary Public, In and for the County of _____
State of _____

My commission expires: _____ Notary Seal

RECEIPT FOR LEASE SECURITY DEPOSIT

The landlord acknowledges receipt of the sum of $ ① _____ paid by the tenant under the following described lease: ②

This security deposit payment will be held by the landlord under the terms of this lease, and unless required by law, will not bear any interest. This security deposit will be repaid when due under the terms of the lease.

Dated: ③ _____ , 20 _____

④ _____
Signature of Landlord

⑤ _____
Printed Name of Landlord

RENT RECEIPT

The landlord acknowledges receipt of the sum of $ ① _____ paid by
② _____ , the tenant, for rent during the time period of ③ _____ to
_____ for the property located at: ④ _____ .

Dated: ⑤ _____ , 20 _____

⑥ _____
Signature of Landlord

⑦ _____
Printed Name of Landlord

Chapter 7

Sale of Personal Property

The forms in this chapter are for use when selling personal property as part of a real estate transaction. A *bill of sale* provides a receipt for both parties that the sale has been consummated and the delivery of the item in question has taken place. Bills of sale are often utilized to document the sale of personal property that is part of a real estate transaction when the actual terms of the sale are part of the real estate sales contract.

Instructions for Sale of Personal Property

Contract for Sale of Personal Property: This form may be used for documenting the sale of any type of personal property. It may be used for vehicles, business assets, or any other personal property. The information necessary to complete this form are the names and addresses of the seller and the buyer, a complete description of the property being sold, the total purchase price, and the terms of the payment of this price.

To prepare this form, fill in the following information:

① Date of Contract
② Name of Seller
③ Address of Seller
④ Name of Buyer
⑤ Address of Buyer
⑥ Describe personal property being sold
⑦ Amount personal property being sold for
⑧ Payment description
⑨ The date that the buyer takes ownership of property
⑩ State where transaction occurs

⑪ Signature of Seller
⑫ Printed name of Seller
⑬ Signature of Buyer
⑭ Printed name of Buyer

Bill of Sale, with Warranties: This document is used as a receipt of the sale of personal property. It is, in many respects, often used to operate as a *title* (or ownership document) to items of personal property. It verifies that the person noted in the bill of sale has obtained legal title to the property from the previous owner. This particular version also provides that the seller *warrants* (or guarantees) that he or she has the authority to transfer legal title to the buyer and that there are no outstanding debts or liabilities for the property. In addition, this form provides that the seller warrants that the property is in good working condition on the date of the sale. To complete this form, simply fill in the names and addresses of the seller and buyer, the purchase price of the item, and a description of the property.

To prepare this form, fill in the following information:

① Date of Bill of Sale
② Name of Seller
③ Address of Seller
④ Name of Buyer
⑤ Address of Buyer
⑥ Amount received for property
⑦ Describe property being purchased
⑧ Signature of Seller
⑨ Printed name of Seller

Bill of Sale, without Warranties: This form also provides a receipt to the buyer for the purchase of an item of personal property. However, in this form, the seller makes no warranties at all, either regarding the authority to sell the item or the condition of the item. It is sold to the buyer in "as is" condition. The buyer takes it regardless of any defects. To complete this form, fill in the names and addresses of the seller and buyer, the purchase price of the item, and a description of the property.

To prepare this form, fill in the following information:

① Date of Bill of Sale
② Name of Seller
③ Address of Seller
④ Name of Buyer
⑤ Address of Buyer
⑥ Amount received for property
⑦ Describe property being purchased

⑧ Signature of Seller
⑨ Printed name of Seller

Bill of Sale, Subject to Debt: This form also provides a receipt to the buyer for the purchase of an item of personal property. This form, however, provides that the property sold is subject to a certain prior debt. It verifies that the seller has obtained legal title to the property from the previous owner, but that the seller specifies that the property is sold subject to a certain debt which the buyer is to pay off. In addition, the buyer agrees to indemnify the seller regarding any liability on the debt. This particular bill of sale version also provides that the seller warrants that he or she has authority to transfer legal title to the buyer. In addition, this form provides that the owner warrants that the property is in good working condition on the date of the sale. To complete this form, fill in the names and addresses of the seller and buyer, the purchase price of the item, a description of the property, and a description of the debt.

To prepare this form, fill in the following information:

① Date of Bill of Sale
② Name of Seller
③ Address of Seller
④ Name of Buyer
⑤ Address of Buyer
⑥ Amount received for property
⑦ Describe property being purchased
⑧ Describe debt
⑨ Signature of Seller
⑩ Printed name of Seller
⑪ Signature of Buyer
⑫ Printed name of Buyer

CONTRACT FOR SALE OF PERSONAL PROPERTY

This Contract is made on ① _____ , 20 _____ , between
② _____ , Seller,
address: ③

and ④ _____ , Buyer,
address: ⑤

1. The Seller agrees to sell to the Buyer, and the Buyer agrees to buy the following personal property: ⑥

2. The Buyer agrees to pay the Seller $ ⑦ _____ for the property. The Buyer agrees to pay this purchase price in the following manner: ⑧

3. The Buyer will be entitled to possession of this property on
   ⑨ _____ , 20 _____ .

4. The Seller represents that it has legal title to the property and full authority to sell the property. Seller also represents that the property is sold free and clear of all liens, indebtedness, or liabilities. Seller agrees to provide Buyer with a Bill of Sale for the property.

5. This Contract binds and benefits both the Buyer and Seller and any successors. This document, including any attachments, is the entire agreement between the Buyer and Seller. This agreement is governed by the laws of the State of
   ⑩ _____ .

⑪ _____
Signature of Seller

⑬ _____
Signature of Buyer

⑫ _____
Printed Name of Seller

⑭ _____
Printed Name of Buyer

BILL OF SALE, WITH WARRANTIES

This Bill of Sale is made on ①_____ , 20 _____ , between

②_____ , Seller,

address:③

and ④_____ , Buyer,

address:⑤

In exchange for the payment of $ ⑥_____ , received from the Buyer, the Seller sells and transfers possession of the following property to the Buyer:⑦

The Seller warrants that it owns this property and that it has the authority to sell the property to the Buyer. Seller also warrants that the property is sold free and clear of all liens, indebtedness, or liabilities.

The Seller also warrants that the property is in good working condition as of this date.

Signed and delivered to the Buyer on the above date.

⑧_____

Signature of Seller

⑨_____

Printed Name of Seller

BILL OF SALE, WITHOUT WARRANTIES

This Bill of Sale is made on ① _____ , 20 _____ , between
② _____ , Seller,
address:③

and ④ _____ , Buyer,
address:⑤

In exchange for the payment of $ ⑥ _____ , received from the Buyer, the Seller sells and transfers possession of the following property to the Buyer:⑦

The Seller disclaims any implied warranty of merchantability or fitness and the property is sold in its present condition, "as is."

Signed and delivered to the Buyer on the above date.

⑧ _____
Signature of Seller

⑨ _____
Printed Name of Seller

BILL OF SALE, SUBJECT TO DEBT

This Bill of Sale is made on ① _____ , 20 _____ , between
② _____ , Seller,
address:③

and ④ _____ , Buyer,
address:⑤

In exchange for the payment of $ ⑥ _____ , received from the Buyer, the Seller sells and transfers possession of the
following property to the Buyer:⑦

The Seller warrants that it owns this property and that it has the authority to sell the property to the Buyer. Seller also states
that the property is sold subject to the following debt:⑧

The Buyer buys the property subject to the above debt and agrees to pay the debt. Buyer also agrees to indemnify and hold
the Seller harmless from any claim based on failure to pay off this debt.

The Seller also warrants that the property is in good working condition as of this date.

Signed and delivered to the Buyer on the above date.

⑨ _____ ⑪ _____
Signature of Seller   Signature of Buyer

⑩ _____ ⑫ _____
Printed Name of Seller   Printed Name of Buyer

Chapter 8

Real Estate Contract Modification Forms

The following documents are included for use in situations requiring the modification of a basic real estate agreement or contract. There are documents included for adding items to a contract, assigning, modifying, extending, and terminating a basic contract.

Addendum to Contract: This form may be used to include additional terms or conditions to an Agreement to Sell Real Estate or Contract for Deed (or any other contract). The included Agreement to Sell Real Estate and the Contract for Deed both have space to add additional information or terms. This form will allow for the inclusion of any additional terms and conditions that the Seller and Buyer mutually agree upon. If this form is used, the following statement should be included in the the original Agreement to Sell Real Estate or Contract for Deed: "The attached Addendum to Contract is made part of this Agreement." The Addendum should then be stapled to the original Agreement or Contract after the last page of the Agreement or Contract. In order to prepare this Addendum, please fill in the following information:

① Date of Addendum to Contract
② Name of seller
③ Address of seller
④ Name of buyer
⑤ Address of buyer
⑥ Date of original Agreement to Sell Real Estate or Contract for Deed
⑦ Any additional terms or conditions to be included
⑧ Signature of seller
⑨ Printed name of seller
⑩ Signature of buyer
⑪ Printed name of buyer

Extension of Contract: This document should be used to extend the effective time period during which a contract is in force. The use of this form allows the time limit to be extended without having to entirely re-draft the contract. Under this document, all of the other terms of the contract will remain the same, with only the expiration date changing. You will need to fill in the original expiration date and the new expiration date. Other information necessary will be the names and addresses of the parties to the contract and a description of the contract. A copy of the original contract should be attached to this form. To complete this document, fill in the following information:

① Date of Extension to Contract
② Name of seller
③ Address of seller
④ Name of buyer
⑤ Address of buyer
⑥ Date ending of original contract
⑦ Description of original contract
⑧ New ending date of contract
⑨ Signature of seller
⑩ Printed name of seller
⑪ Signature of buyer
⑫ Printed name of buyer

Modification of Contract: Use this form to modify any other terms of an Agreement to Sell Real Estate or Contract for Deed after the date of the original signing of the Agreement or Contract. It can be used to change any portion of the agreement. Simply note what changes are being made in the appropriate place on this form. If a portion of the agreement is being deleted, make note of the deletion. If certain language is being substituted, state the substitution clearly. If additional language is being added, make this clear. A copy of the original agreement should be attached to this form. For example, you may wish to use language as follows:

"Paragraph _____ is deleted from this agreement."

"Paragraph _____ is deleted from this agreement and the following para graph   is substituted in its place:"

"The following new paragraph is added to this agreement:"

In order to prepare this Modification, please fill in the following information:

① Date of modification agreement
② Name and address of seller
③ Name and address of buyer

④ Description of original Agreement to Sell Real Estate or Contract for Deed (including date of agreement and description of property involved)
⑤ Terms of modification
⑥ Signature of seller
⑦ Printed name of seller
⑧ Signature of buyer
⑨ Printed name of buyer

Termination of Contract: This document is intended to be used when both parties to a contract mutually desire to end a contract prior to its original expiration date. Under this form, both parties agree to release each other from any claims against each other based on anything in the contract. This document effectively ends any contractual arrangement between two parties. Please note that this Termination of Contract should *not* be used to terminate a Contract for Deed. This Termination states that after the termination, both parties are returned to their respective positions, as if there had been no contract in the first place. This is different than if the seller under a Contract for Deed desires to terminate the contract because of a default by the buyer. The terms of the Contract for Deed in this book provide for a buyer in default to forfeit to the seller any monies paid. To terminate a Contract for Deed, you should use the Declaration of Intention to Forfeit and Terminate Contract for Deed (contained in Chapter3).

In order to prepare this document, please insert the following information:

① Date of termination agreement
② Name and address of seller
③ Name and address of buyer
④ Description of original Agreement to Sell Real Estate or other contract (including date of agreement and description of property involved
⑤ Signature of seller
⑥ Printed name of seller
⑦ Signature of buyer
⑧ Printed name of buyer

Assignment of Contract: This form is for use if one party to a contract is assigning its full interest in the contract to another party. This effectively substitutes one party for another under a contract. This particular assignment form has both of the parties agreeing to indemnify and hold each other harmless for any failures to perform under the contract while they were the party liable under it. This *indemnify and hold harmless* clause simply means that if a claim arises for failure to perform, each party agrees to be responsible for the period of their own performance obligations. Note that the *assignor* is the party who is assigning the contract and the *assignee* is the party to whom the contract is being assigned. A copy of the original contract should be attached to this form. A copy of a Consent to Assignment of Contract should also be attached, if necessary.

① Date of assignment of contract
② Name and address of assignor
③ Name and address of assignee
④ Description of original Agreement to Sell Real Estate, Contract for Deed, or other contract (including date of agreement and description of property involved)
⑤ Signature of assignor
⑥ Printed name of assignor
⑦ Signature of assignee
⑧ Printed name of assignee

Consent to Assignment of Contract: This form is used if the original contract states that the consent of one of the parties is necessary for the assignment of the contract to be valid. A description of the contract and the name and signature of the person giving the consent are all that is necessary for completing this form. A copy of the original contract should be attached to this form.

① Date of consent to assignement of contract
② Name and address of person to whom consent is given
③ Description of original Agreement to Sell Real Estate, Contract for Deed, or other contract (including date of agreement and description of property involved)
④ Signature of person giving consent
⑤ Printed name of person giving consent

Notice of Assignment of Contract: If a third party is involved in any of the contractual obligations or benefits of an assigned contract, that party should be notified of the assignment in writing. This alerts the third party to look to the new party for satisfaction of any obligations under the contract or to make any payments under the contract directly to the new party. A copy of a Consent to Assignment of Contract should also be attached, if necessary.

① Date of notice of assignement of contract
② Name and address of person to whom notice is given
③ Name of person receiving notice
④ Description of original Agreement to Sell Real Estate, Contract for Deed, or other contract (including date of agreement and description of property involved
⑤ Date of Assignment of Contract
⑥ Name and address of assignor
⑦ Name and address of assignee
⑧ Signature
⑨ Printed name

Notice of Breach of Contract: This form should be used to notify a party to a contract of the violation of a term of the contract or of an instance of failure to perform a required duty under the contract. It provides for a description of the alleged violation of the contract and for a time period in which the party is instructed to cure the breach of the contract. If the breach is not taken care of within the time period allowed, a lawyer should be consulted for further action, which may entail a lawsuit to enforce the contract terms. A copy of the original contract should be attached to this form.
To complete this form, please fill in the following information:

1. Date of notice of breach of contract
2. Name and address of person receiving notice
3. Name of person receiving notice
4. Description of original Agreement to Sell Real Estate or Contract for Deed (including date of agreement and description of property involved
5. Date of breach of contract
6. Cause of breach of contract
7. Number of days allowed to correct breach of contract
8. Signature
9. Printed name

Addendum to Contract

This Addendum to Contract is made on ①_____ , 20 ___ , between ②_____ , seller
address:③

and ④_____ , buyer
address:

For valuable consideration, the parties agree as follows:⑤

1. This Addendum is added to the following described contract, dated ⑥_____, which is attached, and this Addendum is made a part of that contract:

2. The parties agree to add to this contract as follows:⑦

3. All other terms and conditions of the original contract remain in effect without further modification. This Addendum binds and benefits both parties and any successors. This document, including the attached contract, is the entire agreement between the parties.

The parties have signed this Addendum on the date specified at the beginning of this Addendum of Contract.

⑧_____
Signature of seller

⑩_____
Signature of buyer

⑨_____
Printed name of seller

⑪_____
Printed name of buyer

Extension of Contract

This extension of contract is made on ① _____ , 20 _____ , between ② _____ , seller
address: ③ _____

and ④ _____ , buyer
address: ⑤ _____

For valuable consideration, the parties agree as follows:

1. The following described original contract will end on ⑥ _____ , 20 _____ : ⑦

   This contract is attached to this extension and is a part of this extension.

2. The parties agree to extend this contract for an additional period, which will begin
   immediately on the expiration of the original time period and will end on
   ⑧ _____ , 20 _____ .

3. The extension of this contract will be on the same terms and conditions as the original contract.
   This extension binds and benefits both parties and any successors. This document, including
   the attached original contract, is the entire agreement between the parties.

The parties have signed this extension on the date specified at the beginning of this extension
of contract.

⑨ _____
Signature of seller

⑪ _____
Signature of buyer

⑩ _____
Printed name of seller

⑫ _____
Printed name of buyer

Modification of Contract

This modification of contract is made on ①_____ , 20 _____ ,
between ②_____ , seller
address:

and ③_____ , buyer
address:

For valuable consideration, the parties agree as follows:

1. The following described contract is attached to this modification and is made a part of this
   modification:④

2. The parties agree to modify this contract as follows:⑤

3. All other terms and conditions of the original contract remain in effect without modification. This
   modification binds and benefits both parties and any successors. This document, including the
   attached contract, is the entire agreement between the parties.

The parties have signed this modification on the date specified at the beginning of this modification of contract.

⑥_____   ⑧_____
Signature of seller   Signature of buyer

⑦_____   ⑨_____
Printed name of seller   Printed name of buyer

Termination of Contract

This termination of contract is made on ①_____ , 20 _____ ,
between ②_____ , seller
address:

and ③_____ , buyer
address:

For valuable consideration, the parties agree as follows:

1. The parties are currently bound under the terms of the following described contract, which is attached and is part of this termination: ④

2. They agree to mutually terminate and cancel this contract effective on this date. This termination agreement will act as a mutual release of all obligations under this contract for both parties, as if the contract has not been entered into in the first place.

3. This termination binds and benefits both parties and any successors. This document, including the attached contract being terminated, is the entire agreement between the parties.

The parties have signed this termination on the date specified at the beginning of this termination of contract.

⑤_____   ⑦_____
Signature of seller   Signature of buyer

⑥_____   ⑧_____
Printed name of seller   Printed name of buyer

Assignment of Contract

This assignment of contract is made on ① _____ , 20 _____ , between ② _____ , assignor address:

and ③ _____ , assignee address:

For valuable consideration, the parties agree to the following terms and conditions:

1. The assignor assigns all interest, burdens, and benefits in the following described contract to the assignee: ④

   This contract is attached to this assignment and is a part of this assignment.

2. The assignor warrants that this contract is in effect, has not been modified, and is fully assignable. If the consent of a third party is necessary for this assignment to be effective, such consent is attached to this assignment and is a part of this assignment. Assignor agrees to indemnify and hold the assignee harmless from any claim which may result from the assignor's failure to perform under this contract prior to the date of this assignment.

3. The assignee agrees to perform all obligations of the assignor and receive all of the benefits of the assignor under this contract. Assignee agrees to indemnify and hold the assignor harmless from any claim which may result from the assignee's failure to perform under this contract after the date of this assignment.

4. This assignment binds and benefits both parties and any successors. This document, including any attachments, is the entire agreement between the parties.

The parties have signed this assignment on the date specified at the beginning of this assignment of contract.

⑤ _____
Signature of Assignor
⑥ _____
Printed Name of Assignor

⑦ _____
Signature of Assignee
⑧ _____
Printed Name of Assignee

Consent to Assignment of Contract

Date: ①_____ , 20 _____

To:②

I am a party to the following described contract:③

This contract is the subject of the attached assignment of contract.

I consent to the assignment of this contract as described in the attached assignment, which provides that the assignee is substituted for the assignor.

④_____
Signature

⑤_____
Printed Name

Notice of Assignment of Contract

Date: ① _____ , 20 _____

To: ②

RE: Assignment of Contract

Dear ③ _____ :

This notice is in reference to the following described contract: ④

Please be advised that as of ⑤ _____ , 20 _____ , all interest and rights under this contract which were formerly owned by ⑥ _____ , assignor whose address is _____ , have been permanently assigned to ⑦ _____ . assignee, whose address is _____ .

Please be advised that all of the obligations and rights of the former party to this contract are now the responsibility of the new party to this contract.

⑧ _____
Signature

⑨ _____
Printed Name

Notice of Breach of Contract

Date: ①_____ , 20 _____

To: ②

RE: Breach of Contract

Dear ③_____:

This notice is in reference to the following described contract:④

Please be advised that as of ⑤_____ , 20 _____ , we are holding you in
BREACH OF CONTRACT for the following reasons:⑥

If this breach of contract is not corrected within ⑦_____ days of this notice, we will take further
action to protect our rights, which may include the right to obtain a substitute service and charge
you for any additional costs. This notice is made under the Uniform Commercial Code and any
other applicable laws. All of our rights are reserved under this notice.

⑧_____
Signature

⑨_____
Printed Name

Chapter 9

Signatures and Notary Acknowledgments

Signatures and notary acknowledgments for legal forms serve similar but slightly different purposes. Both are used to document the formal signing of a legal instrument, but the notarized acknowledgment also serves as a method of providing a neutral witness to the signature, and so, authenticates the signature. In addition, a notarized acknowledgment can serve an additional purpose of providing a statement under oath. For example, a notarized acknowledgment can be used to assert that a person states, under oath, that he has read the document that she or he is signing and believes that what it contains is the truth.

The use of a notary acknowledgment is not required for all legal forms. The notary acknowledgments contained in this chapter are to be used only for the purpose of providing a notarization required for recording a document. Generally, notarization is only necessary if the document is intended to be recorded with an official government office in some manner. For example, all documents which intend to convey real estate should be recorded in the county recorder's office or register of deeds office in the county (or parish) where the property is located. In virtually all jurisdictions, such documents must be notarized before they will be recorded. Similarly, some states require automobile titles and similar documents to be notarized. Check with your local county clerk to determine the requirements in your locale.

Another unofficial purpose of notarization of legal documents is to make the document seem more important to the parties. By formally having their signatures witnessed by a notary public, they are attesting to the fact that they ascribe a powerful purpose to the document. Although this type of notarization carries with it no legal value, it does serve a valid purpose in solemnizing the signing of an important business document.

For all of the notary acknowledgment forms contained in this chapter, the following information is necessary:

- The name of the state in which the document is signed
- The name of the county in which the document is signed
- The date on which the document is signed
- The name of the person who is signing the document
- The entity on whose behalf the person is signing (for example: a corporation, partnership, etc.)
- The name of the notary public (or similar official)
- The county in which the notary is registered to act
- The state in which the notary is authorized to perform
- The date on which the notary's commission will expire

NOTE for residents of California: The state of California requires a different notary block than other states. If you intend any of the notarized forms in this book to be valid in California, you will need to use the California notary block that is provided on the accompanying Forms-on-CD.

In addition, many states require that the notary place an embossed seal on the document to authenticate the notarization process. The notary who completes the acknowledgment will know the correct procedure for your state.

A simple signature line merely serves to provide a place for a party to a document to sign his or her name. However, care must be taken to be sure that the type of signature line used corresponds exactly with the person or business entity who is joining in the signing of a document. If the entity is a partnership, the signature must be set up for a partner to sign and clearly state that the signature is for the partnership. The same holds true for the signature of a corporate officer.

Instructions

The following notary acknowledgments and signature lines are intended to be used for the specific purposes outlined below. When preparing a legal document, choose the correct version of these additions carefully. You may need to use the 'text' versions of a particular form in order to add the correct notary acknowledgment and/or signature lines to the document. The following are contained in this chapter:

Corporate Acknowledgment: This clause should be used on documents where a corporation is one of the parties who is to sign the document and the document needs to be notarized. The person signing the document on behalf of the corporation must be either an officer of the corporation or be specifically authorized by a resolution of the Board of Directors of the corporation to act on its behalf.

Corporate Signature Line: This line should be inserted on all documents where a party that will sign the document is a corporation. This may be used regardless of whether the corporation is a corporation, an S-corporation, or a not-for-profit corporation. The person signing must have authority to bind the corporation. Again, it must either be an officer of the corporation or a person specifically authorized by a resolution of the Board of Directors of the corporation to act on its behalf. The state in which the corporation is registered to do business should be noted.

Partnership Acknowledgment: This clause should be used on documents where one of the parties who is to sign the document is a standard partnership and the document needs to be notarized. Any partner in a partnership may have authority to act on behalf of the corporation. However, it may be wise to request a copy of the partnership agreement which authorizes the partner to bind the partnership.

Partnership Signature Line: This line should be inserted on all documents where one of the parties that will sign the document is a partnership. This may be used if the entity is a partnership. Any partner may bind the partnership if authorized by the partnership agreement. The state in which the partnership is doing business should be noted.

Limited Liability Company Acknowledgment: This clause should be used on documents where a limited liability company is one of the parties who is to sign the document and the document needs to be notarized. Any member of a limited liability company has authority to bind the limited liability company.

Limited Liability Company Signature Line: This line should be inserted on all documents where one of the parties who will sign the document is a limited liability company. Any member may sign on behalf of a limited liability company. The state in which the limited liability company is doing business should be noted.

Sole Proprietorship Acknowledgment: This clause should be used on documents where an individual who owns a sole proprietorship is one of the parties who is to sign the document and the document needs to be notarized. Many sole proprietorships are designated as persons "doing business as." This is abbreviated as "DBA." For example: "John Washington, DBA Washington's Restaurant" indicates that John Washington is operating Washington's Restaurant as a sole proprietorship. The owner of the sole proprietorship is the person who should sign all documents for this type of business.

Sole Proprietorship Signature Line: This line should be inserted on all documents where a party that will sign the document is an individual that owns a sole proprietorship. Only the owner of a sole proprietorship has authority to bind such a business. The state in which the sole proprietorship is doing business should be noted.

Power of Attorney Acknowledgment: This clause should be used on documents where an individual acting under a power of attorney is one of the parties who is to sign the document and the document needs to be notarized. As noted in Chapter 10, an attorney-in-fact is a person who is authorized to act for another person by virtue of a document entitled a "power of attorney," also found in Chapter 10.

Power of Attorney Signature Line: This line should be inserted on all documents where a party that will sign the document is an individual acting under a power of attorney. The person signing must have the specific authority to act for another person under some form of Power of Attorney. The date of the Power of Attorney form should be noted.

Individual Acknowledgment: This clause should be used on documents where an individual is one of the parties who is to sign the document and the document needs to be notarized. However, if the document is to be signed by a husband and wife together, use the appropriate acknowledgment form which follows.

Individual Signature Line: This line should be inserted on all documents where a party that will sign the document is an individual. Again, however, if the document is to be signed by a husband and wife together, use the appropriate signature line which follows.

Husband and Wife Acknowledgment: This clause should be used on documents where both a husband and wife are to sign the document and the document needs to be notarized.

Husband and Wife Signature Line: This line should be inserted on all documents where both a husband and wife are intended to sign the document.

Corporate Acknowledgment

State of _____
County of _____

On _____ , 20 _____ , _____ personally came before me and, being duly sworn, did state that he or she is the _____ of the corporation described in the above document; that he or she signed the above document in my presence on behalf of this corporation; and that he or she had full authority to do so.

_____
Signature of Notary Public

Notary Public, In and for the County of _____
State of _____
My commission expires: _____   Notary Seal

Corporate Signature Line

_____ (name of corporation), a(n) _____ (state of incorporation) corporation

By:

_____
Signature of Corporate Officer

_____
Printed Name of Corporate Officer

The _____ (*title of corporate officer*) of the corporation

Partnership Acknowledgment

State of _____
County of _____

On _____ , 20 _____ , _____ personally came
before me and, being duly sworn, did state that he or she is a partner of the partnership described
in the above document; that he or she signed the above document in my presence on behalf of
this partnership; and that he or she had full authority to do so.

_____
Signature of Notary Public

Notary Public, In and for the County of _____
State of _____

My commission expires: _____   Notary Seal

Partnership Signature Line

_____ (*name of partnership*), a(n)
_____ (*state of operation*) partnership

By:
_____
Signature of Partner

_____
Printed Name of Partner

A Partner of the Partnership

Limited Liability Company Acknowledgment

State of _____

County of _____

On _____ , 20 _____ , _____ personally came before me and, being duly sworn, did state that he or she is a member of the limited liability company described in the above document; that he or she signed the above document in my presence on behalf of this limited liability company; and that he or she had full authority to do so.

_____
Signature of Notary Public

Notary Public, In and for the County of _____
State of _____

My commission expires: _____   Notary Seal

Limited Liability Company Signature Line

_____ (*name of limited liability company*), a(n) _____
_____ (*state of operation*) limited liability company

By:

_____
Signature of Member

_____
Printed Name of Member

A Member of the Limited Liability Company

Sole Proprietorship Acknowledgment

State of _____

County of _____

On _____ , 20 _____ , _____ personally came before me and, being duly sworn, did state that he or she is the person who owns the sole proprietorship described in the above document and that he or she signed the above document in my presence on behalf of the sole proprietorship and on his or her own behalf.

_____

Signature of Notary Public

Notary Public, In and for the County of _____

State of _____

My commission expires: _____   Notary Seal

Sole Proprietorship Signature Line

_____

Signature of Sole Proprietor

_____

Printed Name of Sole Proprietor

DBA _____ (name of business), a(n) _____ (state of operation) sole proprietorship

Power of Attorney Acknowledgment

State of _____

County of _____

On _____ , 20 _____ , _____ personally came before me and, being duly sworn, did state that he or she is the attorney-in-fact of _____ _____ described in the above document; that he or she signed the above document in my presence as attorney-in-fact on behalf of this person; and that he or she had full authority to do so under Power of Attorney dated _____ , 20 _____ .

_____
Signature of Notary Public

Notary Public, In and for the County of _____
State of _____

My commission expires: _____   Notary Seal

Power of Attorney Signature Line

_____
Signature of Person Holding Power of Attorney

_____
Printed Name of Person Holding Power of Attorney

As attorney-in-fact for _____
(*name of person granting power of attorney*)

Under Power of Attorney dated _____ , 20 _____

Individual Acknowledgment

State of _____
County of _____

On _____ , 20 _____ , _____ personally came before me and, being duly sworn, did state that he or she is the person described in the above document and that he or she signed the above document in my presence as a free and voluntary act for the purposes stated.

_____
Signature of Notary Public

Notary Public, In and for the County of _____
State of _____

My commission expires: _____   Notary Seal

Individual Signature Line

_____
Signature

_____
Printed Name

Husband and Wife Acknowledgment

State of _____
County of _____

On _____ , 20 _____ , _____ and _____
_____ personally came before me and, being duly sworn, did state that
they are the husband and wife described in the above document and that they signed the above
document in my presence as a free and voluntary act for the purposes stated.

_____
Signature of Notary Public

Notary Public, In and for the County of _____
State of _____

My commission expires: _____   Notary Seal

Husband and Wife Signature Line

_____
Signature of Husband

_____
Printed Name of Husband

_____
Signature of Wife

_____
Printed Name of Wife

Chapter 10

Powers of Attorney

A power of attorney form is a document that is used to allow one person to give the authority to act on his or her behalf to another person. The person signing the power of attorney grants legal authority to another person to "stand in his or her shoes" and act legally for him or her. The person who receives the power of attorney is called an *attorney-in-fact*. However, this title and the power of attorney form does not mean that the person receiving the power has to be a lawyer.

Power of attorney forms are useful documents for many occasions. They can be used to authorize someone else to sign certain documents if you cannot be present when the signatures are necessary. For example, a real estate closing in another state can be completed without your presence by providing a power of attorney to a real estate agent (or even a friend) that authorizes him or her to sign the documents on your behalf. Similarly, if you must be away from your home on a trip, and certain actions must be made in your absence, a power of attorney can be granted to enable another person to legally perform on your behalf. The form can also be used to allow your accountant to negotiate with the Internal Revenue Service, allow your secretary to sign checks and temporarily operate your business, or for many other purposes.

Traditionally, property matters were the type of actions handled with powers of attorney. Increasingly, however, people are using a specific type of power of attorney to authorize other persons to act on their behalf in the event of disability. This broad type of power of attorney is called a *durable power of attorney*. A durable power of attorney is intended to remain in effect even if a person becomes disabled or incompetent. All states have passed legislation that specifically authorizes this type of power of attorney. Durable power of attorney forms are not, however, included in this book. *Note:* Powers of attorney are very powerful legal documents. They can be used to grant virtually unlimited legal power to another person. Even though you can revoke a power of attorney at any time, you are advised to proceed with caution when using any of these forms. If you have any questions regarding their use, please consult a competent attorney.

Unlimited Power of Attorney

An unlimited power of attorney should be used only in situations where you desire to authorize another person to act for you in *any and all* transactions. The grant of power under this document is unlimited. However, the powers you grant with this document cease to be effective should you become disabled or incompetent. This form gives the person whom you designate as your "attorney-in-fact" extremely broad powers to handle your property during your lifetime, which may include powers to mortgage, sell, or otherwise dispose of any real or personal property without advance notice to you or approval by you. This document does not authorize anyone to make medical or other health care decisions. You must execute a durable health care power of attorney to do this. The authority granted by this power of attorney may be revoked by you at any time and is automatically revoked if you die or become incapacitated or incompetent. If there is anything about this form that you do not understand, you should ask a lawyer to explain it to you. This power of attorney contains an important notice prior to the form itself.

When You Should Use an Unlimited Power of Attorney

An unlimited power of attorney authorizes your agent to handle *any and all* of your financial and business affairs, including all of the following possible matters:

> Real estate transactions; Personal property and goods and services transactions; Stock, bond, share and commodity transactions; Banking and financial institution transactions; Business operating transactions; Insurance and annuity transactions; Estate, trust, and other transactions where the principal is a beneficiary; Legal claims and litigation; Personal and family maintenance; Benefits from social security, medicare, medicaid, or civil or military service; Records, reports and statements; Retirement benefit transactions; Tax matters; Delegation of the agent's authority to others; and any and all other matters.

All of the above mentioned powers that are granted to your agent are spelled out in great detail in this particular power of attorney form. This is the most extensive and detailed power of attorney form that is provided. It should only be used if you are absolutely certain that the agent you choose is fully and totally trustworthy and able to exercise these broad powers in your best interest. The detailed powers that are listed in this form are taken from the Uniform Power of Attorney Act that has been legislatively adopted by many states. Please note that the "delegation of the agent's authority to others" provision in this document grants your chosen agent the power to delegate any of his or her powers to another person of his or her own choosing. If you do not wish your agent to have this authority, or you wish to limit your agent's power under any of the other powers which are enumerated in this document, you should use instead a *general power of attorney*. A general power of attorney will allow you to pick and choose which of these powers you wish to grant to your agent.

If you wish to provide a very limited power to your agent, you may wish to use a *limited power of attorney* instead of an unlimited power of attorney. A limited power of attorney allows you to limit the power granted to a specific action or a specific date range. An unlimited power of attorney is not valid if you become disabled or incapacitated. You must use a *'durable' power of attorney* for that purpose. In addition, an unlimited power of attorney also can *not* be used for health care decisions. You must use a *durable health care power of attorney* for that purpose.

To complete your unlimited power of attorney, please follow the instructions below. To use the form on the enclosed CD, simply fill in the required information in either the text or PDF versions of this form.

Instructions for Unlimited Power of Attorney

① Name and address of person granting power (principal)
② Name and address of person granted power (attorney-in-fact)
③ Name and address of successor to person originally granted power (successor attorney-in-fact) (optional-if not used, write N/A in this space)
④ Date
⑤ Printed name of principal, date of signing of power of attorney, and signature of principal (signed in front of notary public)
⑥ Printed names and signatures of witnesses (signed in front of notary public)
⑦ Notary acknowledgement should be completed by the notary public*
⑧ Printed name, date, and signature of attorney-in-fact (need not be witnessed or notarized)
⑨ Printed name, date, and signature of successor attorney-in-fact (optional-if not used, write N/A in this space) (need not be witnessed or notarized)
Note: California residents must use the California Notary box available on the Forms-on-CD

Limited Power of Attorney

This document provides for a *limited* grant of authority to another person. It should be used in those situations when you need to authorize another person to act for you in a specific transaction or transactions. The type of acts that you authorize the other person to perform should be spelled out in detail to avoid confusion (for example, to sign any necessary forms to open a bank account). If desired, the dates when the power of attorney will be valid may also be specified. The authority that you grant with a limited power of attorney may be revoked by you at any time and is automatically revoked if you die or become incapacitated or incompetent. This document does not authorize the appointed attorney-in-fact to make any decisions relating to medical or health care. If there is anything about these forms that you do not understand, you should ask a lawyer to explain it to you. These powers of attorney contain an important notice prior to the form itself.

When You Should Use a Limited Power of Attorney

A limited power of attorney allows you to select a specific power that you wish for your agent (attorney-in-fact) to have. This type of power of attorney can be used to authorize someone else to sign certain documents if you can not be present when the signatures are necessary. They can be used to authorize someone to handle any of the following possible matters:

Real estate transactions; goods and services transactions; stock, bond, share and commodity transactions; banking transactions; business operating transactions; insurance transactions; estate transactions; legal claims and litigation; personal relationships and affairs; benefits from military service; records, reports and statements; retirement benefit transactions; making gifts to a spouse, children, parents and other descendants; tax matters; and certain child care decisions, such as consent to emergency medical care.

A limited power of attorney is most useful if you wish to grant your agent only some, but not all of the possible powers available to an agent. If you wish to grant full and complete authority to your agent, you may wish to use an *unlimited power of attorney* instead. An unlimited power of attorney provides that your agent will have total authority to act on your behalf for all financial and/or business matters (but not for health care decisions). If you wish to provide a range of powers to your agent, you may wish to use a *general power of attorney* instead of a limited power of attorney. A limited power of attorney allows you to limit the power granted to a specific action or a specific date range. A limited power of attorney is not valid if you become disabled or incapacitated. You must use a *'durable' power of attorney* for that purpose (Note: you can prepare a *'durable' limited power of attorney*). In addition, a limited power of attorney also can *not* be used for health care decisions. You must use a *durable health care power of attorney* for that purpose.

To complete a limited power of attorney, please follow the instructions below. To use the form on the enclosed CD, simply fill in the required information in either the text or PDF versions of this form.

Instructions for Limited Power of Attorney

① Name and address of person granting power (principal)
② Name and address of person granted power (attorney-in-fact)
③ List specific acts that you want your attorney-in-fact to perform (be as detailed as possible)
④ Name and address of successor to person originally granted power (successor attorney-in-fact) (optional-if not used, write N/A in this space.)
⑤ Date
⑥ Printed name of principal, date of signing of power of attorney, and signature of principal (signed in front of notary public)

⑦ Printed names and signatures of witnesses (signed in front of notary public)
⑧ Notary acknowledgement should be completed by the notary public*
⑨ Printed name, date, and signature of attorney-in-fact (need not be witnessed or notarized)
⑩ Printed name, date, and signature of successor attorney-in-fact (optional-if not used, write N/A in this space) (need not be witnessed or notarized)
Note: California residents must use the California Notary box available on the Forms-on-CD

Revocation of Powers of Attorney

This document may be used with any of the previous power of attorney forms. The revocation is used to terminate the original authority that was granted to the other person in the first place. Some limited powers of attorney specifiy that the powers that are granted will end on a specific date. If that is the case, you will not need a revocation unless you wish the powers to end sooner than the date specified. If the grant of power was for a limited purpose and that purpose is complete but no date for the power to end was specified, this revocation should be used as soon after the transaction as possible. In any event, if you choose to revoke a power of attorney, a copy of this revocation should be provided to the person to whom the power was given. Copies should also be given to any party that may have had dealings with the attorney-in-fact before the revocation and to any party with whom the attorney-in-fact may be expected to attempt to deal with after the revocation. If you feel that it is important to verify the revocation of your power of attorney, you should have any third party that you supply with a copy of the revocation sign another copy for you to keep. If that is not possible, you should mail a copy of the revocation to that person or institution by first class mail, with a return receipt requested that requires a signature to verify delivery.

Although this revocation may be used to revoke a health care power of attorney, please also note that there are other acceptable methods to revoke a health care power of attorney.

To complete this document, fill in the following information:

① Printed name and address of person who originally granted power (principal)
② Date of original power of attorney
③ Printed name and address of person granted power (attorney-in-fact)
④ Date of revocation of power of attorney
⑤ Signature of person revoking power of attorney (principal) (signed in front of notary)
⑥ Notary to complete the notary acknowledgment*
Note: California residents must use the California Notary box available on the Forms-on-CD

Unlimited Power of Attorney

Notice: This is an important document. Before signing this document, you should know these important facts. By signing this document, you are not giving up any powers or rights to control your finances and property yourself. In addition to your own powers and rights, you are giving another person, your attorney-in-fact, broad powers to handle your finances and property. This unlimited power of attorney will give the person whom you designate (your "attorney-in-fact") broad powers to handle your finances and property, which includes powers to encumber, sell or otherwise dispose of any real or personal property without advance notice to you or approval by you. THE POWERS GRANTED WILL NOT EXIST AFTER YOU BECOME DISABLED, OR INCAPACITATED. This document does not authorize anyone to make medical or other health care decisions for you. If you own complex or special assets such as a business, or if there is anything about this form that you do not understand, you should ask a lawyer to explain this form to you before you sign it. If you wish to change your unlimited power of attorney, you must complete a new document and revoke this one. You may revoke this document at any time by destroying it, by directing another person to destroy it in your presence or by signing a written and dated statement expressing your intent to revoke this document. If you revoke this document, you should notify your attorney-in-fact and any other person to whom you have given a copy of the form. You also should notify all parties having custody of your assets. These parties have no responsibility to you unless you actually notify them of the revocation. If your attorney-in-fact is your spouse and your marriage is annulled, or you are divorced after signing this document, this document is invalid. Since some 3rd parties or some transactions may not permit use of this document, it is advisable to check in advance, if possible, for any special requirements that may be imposed. You should sign this form only if the attorney-in-fact you name is reliable, trustworthy and competent to manage your affairs. This form must be signed by the Principal (the person appointing the attorney-in-fact), witnessed by two persons other than the notary public, and acknowledged by a notary public.

①I, _____ (printed name), of (address)_____,

as principal, do grant an unlimited power of attorney to, and do hereby appoint:

② _____(printed name), of (address)_____,

my attorney-in-fact and do grant him or her unlimited power and authority to act in my name, place and stead in any way which I myself could do, if I were personally present, with respect to all of the following matters to the extent that I am permitted by law to act through an agent:

IN GENERAL, the principal authorizes the agent to: (1) demand, receive, and obtain by litigation or otherwise, money or other thing of value to which the principal is, may become, or claims to be entitled, and conserve, invest, disburse, or use anything so received for the purposes intended; (2) contract in any manner with any person, on terms agreeable to the agent, to accomplish a purpose of a transaction, and perform, rescind, reform, release, or modify the contract or another contract made by or on behalf of the principal; (3) execute, acknowledge, seal, and deliver a deed, revocation, mortgage, security agreement, lease, notice, check, promissory note, electronic funds transfer, release, or other instrument or communication the agent considers desirable to accomplish a purpose of a transaction, including creating a schedule of the principal's property and attaching it to the power of attorney; (4) prosecute, defend, submit to arbitration or mediation, settle, and propose or accept a compromise with respect to, a claim existing in favor of or against the principal or intervene in litigation relating to the claim; (5) seek on the principal's behalf the assistance of a court to carry out an act authorized by the principal in the power of attorney; (6) engage, compensate, and discharge an attorney, accountant, expert witness, or other assistant; (7) keep appropriate records of each transaction, including an accounting of receipts and disbursements; (8) prepare, execute, and file a record, report, or other document the agent considers desirable to safeguard or promote the principal's interest under a statute or governmental regulation; (9) reimburse the agent for expenditures properly made by the agent in exercising the powers granted by the power of attorney; and (10) in general, do any other lawful act with respect to the power and all property related to the power.

WITH RESPECT TO REAL PROPERTY, the principal authorizes the agent to: (1) accept as a gift or as security for an extension of credit, reject, demand, buy, lease, receive, or otherwise acquire, an interest in real property or a right incident to real property; (2) sell, exchange, convey with or without covenants, quitclaim, release, surrender, mortgage, retain title for security, encumber, partition, consent to partitioning, subdivide, apply for zoning, rezoning, or other governmental permits, plat or consent to platting, develop, grant options concerning, lease, sublease, or otherwise dispose of, an interest in real property or a right incident to real property; (3) release, assign, satisfy, or enforce by litigation or otherwise, a mortgage, deed of trust, conditional sale contract, encumbrance, lien, or other claim to real property which exists or is asserted; (4) manage or conserve an interest in real property or a right incident to real property, owned or claimed to be owned by the principal, including: (a) insuring against a casualty, liability, or loss; (b) obtaining or regaining possession, or protecting the interest or right, by litigation or otherwise; (c) paying, compromising, or contesting taxes or assessments, or applying for and receiving refunds in connection with them; and (d) purchasing supplies, hiring assistance or labor, and making repairs or alterations to the real property; (5) use, develop, alter, replace, remove, erect, or install structures or other improvements upon real property in or incident to which the principal has, or claims to have, an interest or right; (6) participate in a reorganization with respect to real property or a legal entity that owns an interest in or right incident to real property and receive and hold, directly or indirectly, shares of stock or obligations, or other evidences of ownership or debt, received in a plan of reorganization, and act with respect to them, including: (a) selling or otherwise disposing of them; (b) exercising or selling an option, conversion, or similar right with respect to them; and (c) voting them in person or by proxy; (7) change the form of title of an interest in or right incident to real property, and (8) dedicate to public use, with or without consideration, easements or other real property in which the principal has, or claims to have, an interest.

WITH RESPECT TO TANGIBLE PERSONAL PROPERTY, the principal authorizes the agent to: (1) accept as a gift or as security for an extension of credit, reject, demand, buy, receive, or otherwise acquire ownership or possession of tangible personal property or an interest in tangible personal property; (2) sell, exchange, convey with or without covenants, release, surrender, create a security interest in, grant options concerning, lease, sublease to others, or otherwise dispose of tangible personal property or an interest in tangible personal property; (3) release, assign, satisfy, or enforce by litigation or otherwise, a security interest, lien, or other claim on behalf of the principal, with respect to tangible personal property or an interest in tangible personal property; (4) manage or conserve tangible personal property or an interest in tangible personal property on behalf of the principal, including: (a) insuring against casualty, liability, or loss; (b) obtaining or regaining possession, or protecting the property or interest, by litigation or otherwise; (c) paying, compromising, or contesting taxes or assessments or applying for and receiving refunds in connection with taxes or assessments; (d) moving from place to place; (e) storing for hire or on a gratuitous bailment; and (f) using, altering, and making repairs or alterations; and (5) change the form of title of an interest in tangible personal property.

WITH RESPECT TO TRANSACTIONS CONCERNING STOCKS AND BONDS, the principal authorizes the agent to: (1) buy, sell, and exchange stocks, bonds, mutual funds, and all other types of securities and financial instruments, whether held directly or indirectly, except commodity futures contracts and call and put options on stocks and stock indexes, (2) receive certificates and other evidences of ownership with respect to securities, (3) exercise voting rights with respect to securities in person or by proxy, enter into voting trusts, and consent to limitations on the right to vote.

WITH RESPECT TO TRANSACTIONS CONCERNING COMMODITIES AND OPTIONS, the principal authorizes the agent to: (1) buy, sell, exchange, assign, settle, and exercise commodity futures contracts and call and put options on stocks and stock indexes traded on a regulated option exchange, and (2) establish, continue, modify, and terminate option accounts with a broker.

WITH RESPECT TO TRANSACTIONS CONCERNING BANKS AND OTHER FINANCIAL INSTITUTIONS, the principal authorizes the agent to: (1) continue, modify, and terminate an account or other banking arrangement made by or on behalf of the principal; (2) establish, modify, and terminate an account or other banking arrangement with a bank, trust company, savings and loan association, credit union, thrift company, brokerage firm, or other financial institution selected by the agent; (3) rent a safe deposit box or space in a vault; (4) contract for other services available from a financial institution as the agent considers desirable; (5) withdraw by check, order, or otherwise money or property of the principal deposited with or left in the custody of a financial institution; 6) receive bank statements, vouchers, notices, and similar documents from a financial institution and act with respect to them; (7) enter a safe deposit box or vault and withdraw or add to the contents; (8) borrow money at an interest rate agreeable to the agent and pledge as security personal property of the principal necessary in order to borrow, pay, renew, or extend the time of payment of a debt of the principal; (9) make, assign, draw, endorse, discount, guarantee, and negotiate promissory notes, checks, drafts, and other negotiable or nonnegotiable paper of the principal, or payable to the principal or the principal's order, transfer money, receive the cash or other proceeds of those transactions, accept a draft drawn by a person upon the principal, and pay it when due; (10) receive for the principal and act upon a sight draft, warehouse receipt, or other negotiable or nonnegotiable instrument; (11) apply for, receive, and use letters of credit, credit and debit cards, and traveler's checks from a financial institution and give an indemnity or other agreement in connection with letters of credit; and (12) consent to an extension of the time of payment with respect to commercial paper or a financial transaction with a financial institution.

WITH RESPECT TO OPERATING A BUSINESS, the principal authorizes the agent to: (1) operate, buy, sell, enlarge, reduce, and terminate a business interest; (2) act for a principal, subject to the terms of a partnership agreement or operating agreement, to: (a) perform a duty or discharge a liability and exercise a right, power, privilege, or option that the principal has, may have, or claims to have, under the partnership agreement or operating agreement, whether or not the principal is a partner in a partnership or member of a limited liability company; (b) enforce the terms of the partnership agreement or operating agreement by litigation or otherwise; and (c) defend, submit to arbitration, settle, or compromise litigation to which the principal is a party because of membership in a partnership or limited liability company; (3) exercise in person or by proxy, or enforce by litigation or otherwise, a right, power, privilege, or option the principal has or claims to have as the holder of a bond, share, or other instrument of similar character and defend, submit to arbitration or mediation, settle, or compromise litigation to which the principal is a party because of a bond, share, or similar instrument; (4) with respect to a business controlled by the principal: (a) continue, modify, renegotiate, extend, and terminate a contract made by or on behalf of the principal with respect to the business before execution of the power of attorney; (b) determine: (i) the location of its operation; (ii) the nature and extent of its business; (iii) the methods of manufacturing, selling, merchandising, financing, accounting, and advertising employed in its operation; (iv) the amount and types of insurance carried; and (v) the mode of engaging, compensating, and dealing with its accountants, attorneys, other agents, and employees; (c) change the name or form of organization under which the business is operated and enter into a partnership agreement or operating agreement with other persons or organize a corporation or other business entity to take over all or part of the operation of the business; and (d) demand and receive money due or claimed by the principal or on the principal's behalf in the operation of the business, and control and disburse the money in the operation of the business; (5) put additional capital into a business in which the principal has an interest; (6) join in a plan of reorganization, consolidation, or merger of the business; (7) sell or liquidate a business or part of it at the time and upon the terms the agent considers desirable; (8) establish the value of a business under a buy-out agreement to which the principal is a party; (9) prepare, sign, file, and deliver reports, compilations of information, returns, or other papers with respect to a business which are required by a governmental agency or instrumentality or which the agent considers desirable, and make related payments; and (10) pay, compromise, or contest taxes or assessments and perform any other act that the agent considers desirable to protect the principal from illegal or unnecessary taxation, fines, penalties, or assessments with respect to a business, including attempts to recover, in any manner permitted by law, money paid before or after the execution of the power of attorney.

WITH RESPECT TO INSURANCE AND ANNUITIES, the principal authorizes the agent to: (1) continue, pay the premium or assessment on, modify, rescind, release, or terminate a contract procured by or on behalf of the principal which insures or provides an annuity to either the principal or another person, whether or not the principal is a beneficiary under the contract; (2) procure new, different, and additional contracts of insurance and annuities for the principal and the principal's spouse, children, and other dependents, and select the amount, type of insurance or annuity, and mode of payment; (3) pay the premium or assessment on, modify, rescind, release, or terminate a contract of insurance or annuity procured by the agent; (4) apply for and receive a loan on the security of a contract of insurance or annuity; (5) surrender and receive the cash surrender value; (6)

exercise an election; (7) change the manner of paying premiums; (8) change or convert the type of insurance or annuity, with respect to which the principal has or claims to have a power described in this section; (9) apply for and procure government aid to guarantee or pay premiums of a contract of insurance on the life of the principal; (10) collect, sell, assign, hypothecate, borrow upon, or pledge the interest of the principal in a contract of insurance or annuity; and (11) pay from proceeds or otherwise, compromise or contest, and apply for refunds in connection with, a tax or assessment levied by a taxing authority with respect to a contract of insurance or annuity or its proceeds or liability accruing by reason of the tax or assessment.

WITH RESPECT TO ESTATES, TRUSTS, AND OTHER RELATIONSHIPS IN WHICH THE PRINCIPAL IS A BENEFICIARY, the principal authorizes the agent to act for the principal in all matters that affect a trust, probate estate, guardianship, conservatorship, escrow, custodianship, or other fund from which the principal is, may become, or claims to be entitled, as a beneficiary, to a share or payment, including to: (1) accept, reject, disclaim, receive, receipt for, sell, assign, release, pledge, exchange, or consent to a reduction in or modification of a share in or payment from the fund; (2) demand or obtain by litigation or otherwise money or other thing of value to which the principal is, may become, or claims to be entitled by reason of the fund; (3) initiate, participate in, and oppose litigation to ascertain the meaning, validity, or effect of a deed, will, declaration of trust, or other instrument or transaction affecting the interest of the principal; (4) initiate, participate in, and oppose litigation to remove, substitute, or surcharge a fiduciary; (5) conserve, invest, disburse, and use anything received for an authorized purpose; and (6) transfer an interest of the principal in real property, stocks, bonds, accounts with financial institutions or securities intermediaries, insurance, annuities, and other property, to the trustee of a revocable trust created by the principal as settlor.

WITH RESPECT TO CLAIMS AND LITIGATION, the principal authorizes the agent to: (1) assert and prosecute before a court or administrative agency a claim, a claim for relief, cause of action, counterclaim, offset, or defense against an individual, organization, or government, including actions to recover property or other thing of value, to recover damages sustained by the principal, to eliminate or modify tax liability, or to seek an injunction, specific performance, or other relief; (2) bring an action to determine adverse claims, intervene in litigation, and act as amicus curiae; (3) in connection with litigation, procure an attachment, garnishment, libel, order of arrest, or other preliminary, provisional, or intermediate relief and use an available procedure to effect or satisfy a judgment, order, or decree; (4) in connection with litigation, perform any lawful act, including acceptance of tender, offer of judgment, admission of facts, submission of a controversy on an agreed statement of facts, consent to examination before trial, and binding the principal in litigation; (5) submit to arbitration or mediation, settle, and propose or accept a compromise with respect to a claim or litigation; (6) waive the issuance and service of process upon the principal, accept service of process, appear for the principal, designate persons upon whom process directed to the principal may be served, execute and file or deliver stipulations on the principal's behalf, verify pleadings, seek appellate review, procure and give surety and indemnity bonds, contract and pay for the preparation and printing of records and briefs, receive and execute and file or deliver a consent, waiver, release, confession of judgment, satisfaction of judgment, notice, agreement, or other instrument in connection with the prosecution, settlement, or defense of a claim or litigation; (7) act for the principal with respect to bankruptcy or insolvency, whether voluntary or involuntary, concerning the principal or some other person, or with respect to a reorganization, receivership, or application for the appointment of a receiver or trustee which affects an interest of the principal in property or other thing of value; and (8) pay a judgment against the principal or a settlement made in connection with litigation and receive and conserve money or other thing of value paid in settlement of or as proceeds of a claim or litigation.

WITH RESPECT TO PERSONAL AND FAMILY MAINTENANCE, the principal authorizes the agent to: (1) perform the acts necessary to maintain the customary standard of living of the principal, the principal's spouse, children, and other individuals customarily or legally entitled to be supported by the principal, including providing living quarters by purchase, lease, or other contract, or paying the operating costs, including interest, amortization payments, repairs, and taxes, on premises owned by the principal and occupied by those individuals; (2) provide for the individuals described under (1) normal domestic help, usual vacations and travel expenses, and funds for shelter, clothing, food, appropriate education, and other current living costs; (3) pay on behalf of the individuals described under (1) expenses for necessary medical, dental, and surgical care, hospitalization, and custodial care; (4) act as the principal's personal representative pursuant to sections 1171 through 1179 of the Social Security Act, 42 U.S.C. Section 1320d (sections 262 and 264 of Public Law 104-191) [or successor provisions] and applicable regulations, in making decisions related to the past, present, or future payment for the provision of health care consented to by the principal or anyone authorized under the law of this state to consent to health care on behalf of the principal; (5) continue any provision made by the principal, for the individuals described under (1), for automobiles or other means of transportation, including registering, licensing, insuring, and replacing them; (6) maintain or open charge accounts for the convenience of the individuals described under (1) and open new accounts the agent considers desirable to accomplish a lawful purpose; and (7) continue payments incidental to the membership or affiliation of the principal in a church, club, society, order, or other organization or to continue contributions to those organizations.

WITH RESPECT TO BENEFITS FROM SOCIAL SECURITY, MEDICARE, MEDICAID, OTHER GOVERNMENTAL PROGRAMS, OR CIVIL OR MILITARY SERVICE, the principal authorizes the agent to: (1) execute vouchers in the name of the principal for allowances and reimbursements payable by the United States or a foreign government or by a state or subdivision of a state to the principal, including allowances and reimbursements for transportation of the individuals described in Section 212(1), and for shipment of their household effects; (2) take possession and order the removal and shipment of property of the principal from a post, warehouse, depot, dock, or other place of storage or safekeeping, either governmental or private, and execute and deliver a release, voucher, receipt, bill of lading, shipping ticket, certificate, or other instrument for that purpose; (3) prepare, file, and prosecute a claim of the principal to a benefit or assistance, financial or otherwise, to which the principal claims to be entitled under a statute or governmental regulation; (4) prosecute, defend, submit to arbitration or mediation, settle, and propose or accept a compromise with respect to any benefit or assistance the principal may be entitled to receive under a statute or governmental regulation; and (5) receive the financial proceeds of a claim of the type described in paragraph (3) and conserve, invest, disburse, or use anything so received for a lawful purpose.

WITH RESPECT TO RETIREMENT PLANS, the principal authorizes the agent to: (1) select a payment option under a retirement plan in which the principal participates, including a plan for a self-employed individual; (2) make voluntary contributions to those plans; (3) exercise the investment powers available under a self-directed retirement plan; (4) make a rollover of benefits into another retirement plan; (5) if authorized by the plan, borrow from, sell assets to, purchase assets from, or request distributions from the plan; and (6) waive the right of the principal to be a beneficiary of a joint or survivor annuity if the principal is a spouse who is not employed.

WITH RESPECT TO TAX MATTERS, the principal authorizes the agent to: (1) prepare, sign, and file federal, state, local, and foreign income, gift, payroll, Federal Insurance Contributions Act, and other tax returns, claims for refunds, requests for extension of time, petitions regarding tax matters, and any other tax-related documents, including receipts, offers, waivers, consents, including consents and agreements under the Internal Revenue Code, 26 U.S.C. Section 2032A [or successor provisions], closing agreements, and any power of attorney required by the Internal Revenue Service or other taxing authority with respect to a tax year upon which the statute of limitations has not run and the following 25 tax years; (2) pay taxes due, collect refunds, post bonds, receive confidential information, and contest deficiencies determined by the Internal Revenue Service or other taxing authority; (3) exercise any election available to the principal under federal, state, local, or foreign tax law; and (4) act for the principal in all tax matters for all periods before the Internal Revenue Service, and any other taxing authority.

WITH RESPECT TO GIFTS, the principal authorizes the agent to make gifts of any of the principal's property to individuals or organizations within the limits of the annual exclusion under the Internal Revenue Code, 26 U.S.C. Section 2503(b) [or successor provisions], as the agent determines to be in the principal's best interest based on all relevant factors, including: (1) the value and nature of the principal's property; (2) the principal's foreseeable obligations and need for maintenance; 3) minimization of income, estate, inheritance, generation-skipping transfer or gift taxes; (4) eligibility for public benefits or assistance under a statute or governmental regulation; and (5) the principal's personal history of making or joining in making gifts.

WITH RESPECT TO DELEGATION OF AGENCY AUTHORITY, the principal authorizes the agent to delegate revocably by writing or other record to one or more persons a power granted to the agent by the principal.

If the attorney-in-fact named above is unable or unwilling to serve, I appoint
③ _____ (printed name),
of (address) _____ ,
to be my attorney-in-fact for all purposes hereunder.

To induce any third party to rely upon this power of attorney, I agree that any third party receiving a signed copy or facsimile of this power of attorney may rely upon such copy, and that revocation or termination of this power of attorney shall be ineffective as to such third party until actual notice or knowledge of such revocation or termination shall have been received by such third party. I, for myself and for my heirs, executors, legal representatives and assigns, agree to indemnify and hold harmless any such third party from any and all claims that may arise against such third party by reason of such third party having relied on the provisions of this power of attorney. This power of attorney shall not be effective in the event of my future disability or incapacity. This power of attorney may be revoked by me at any time and is automatically revoked upon my death. My attorney-in-fact shall no be compensated for his or her services nor shall my attorney-in-fact be liable to me, my estate, heirs, successors, or assigns for acting or refraining from acting under this document, except for willful misconduct or gross negligence.

④ Dated: _____

Signature and Declaration of Principal
⑤
I, _____ (printed name), the principal, sign my name to this power of attorney this _____day of _____ and, being first duly sworn, do declare to the undersigned authority that I sign and execute this instrument as my power of attorney and that I sign it willingly, or willingly direct another to sign for me, that I execute it as my free and voluntary act for the purposes expressed in the power of attorney and that I am eighteen years of age or older, of sound mind and under no constraint or undue influence.

_____
Signature of Principal

Witness Attestation
⑥
I, _____ (printed name), the first witness, and I, _____ (printed name), the second witness, sign my name to the foregoing power of attorney being first duly sworn and do declare to the undersigned authority that the principal signs and executes this instrument as his/her power of attorney and that he\she signs it willingly, or willingly directs another to sign for him/her, and that I, in the presence and hearing of the principal, sign this power of attorney as witness to the principal's signing and that to the best of my knowledge the principal is eighteen years of age or older, of sound mind and under no constraint or undue influence.

_____
Signature of First Witness

_____
Signature of Second Witness

Notary Acknowledgment
⑦
State of _____ County of _____
Subscribed, sworn to and acknowledged before me by _____,
the Principal, and subscribed and sworn to before me by _____,
and _____, the witnesses, this _____ day of

_____ .

_____
Notary Signature
Notary Public,
In and for the County of _____ State of _____
My commission expires: _____ Seal

Acknowledgment and Acceptance of Appointment as Attorney-in-Fact
⑧

I, _____, (printed name) have read the attached power of attorney and am the person identified as the attorney-in-fact for the principal. I hereby acknowledge that I accept my appointment as attorney-in-fact and that when I act as agent I shall exercise the powers for the benefit of the principal; I shall keep the assets of the principal separate from my assets; I shall exercise reasonable caution and prudence; and I shall keep a full and accurate record of all actions, receipts and disbursements on behalf of the principal.

_____   _____
Signature of Attorney-in-Fact   Date

Acknowledgment and Acceptance of Appointment as Successor Attorney-in-Fact
⑨

I, _____, (printed name) have read the attached power of attorney and am the person identified as the successor attorney-in-fact for the principal. I hereby acknowledge that I accept my appointment as successor attorney-in-fact and that, in the absence of a specific provision to the contrary in the power of attorney, when I act as agent I shall exercise the powers for the benefit of the principal; I shall keep the assets of the principal separate from my assets; I shall exercise reasonable caution and prudence; and I shall keep a full and accurate record of all actions, receipts and disbursements on behalf of the principal.

_____   _____
Signature of Successor Attorney-in-Fact   Date

Limited Power of Attorney

Notice: This is an important document. Before signing this document, you should know these important facts. By signing this document, you are not giving up any powers or rights to control your finances and property yourself. In addition to your own powers and rights, you may be giving another person, your attorney-in-fact, broad powers to handle your finances and property. This limited power of attorney may give the person whom you designate (your "attorney-in-fact") broad powers to handle your finances and property, which may include powers to encumber, sell or otherwise dispose of any real or personal property without advance notice to you or approval by you. THE POWERS GRANTED WILL NOT EXIST AFTER YOU BECOME DISABLED, OR INCAPACITATED. This document does not authorize anyone to make medical or other health care decisions for you. If you own complex or special assets such as a business, or if there is anything about this form that you do not understand, you should ask a lawyer to explain this form to you before you sign it. If you wish to change your limited power of attorney, you must complete a new document and revoke this one. You may revoke this document at any time by destroying it, by directing another person to destroy it in your presence or by signing a written and dated statement expressing your intent to revoke this document. If you revoke this document, you should notify your attorney-in-fact and any other person to whom you have given a copy of the form. You also should notify all parties having custody of your assets. These parties have no responsibility to you unless you actually notify them of the revocation. If your attorney-in-fact is your spouse and your marriage is annulled, or you are divorced after signing this document, this document is invalid. Since some 3rd parties or some transactions may not permit use of this document, it is advisable to check in advance, if possible, for any special requirements that may be imposed. You should sign this form only if the attorney-in-fact that you appoint is reliable, trustworthy and competent to manage your affairs. This form must be signed by the Principal (the person appointing the attorney-in-fact), witnessed by two persons other than the notary public, and acknowledged by a notary public.

① I, _____ (printed name),
of (address)_____,
as principal, do grant a limited and specific power of attorney to, and do hereby appoint
② _____ (printed name),
of (address)_____,
to act as my attorney-in-fact and to have the full power and authority to perform only the following acts on my behalf to the same extent that I could do so personally if I were personally present, with respect to the following matter to the extent that I am permitted by law to act through an agent: (list specific acts) ③

If the attorney-in-fact named above is unable or unwilling to serve, I appoint
④ _____ (printed name),
of (address) _____ ,
to be my attorney-in-fact for all purposes hereunder.

To induce any third party to rely upon this power of attorney, I agree that any third party receiving a signed copy or facsimile of this power of attorney may rely upon such copy, and that revocation or termination of this power of attorney shall be ineffective as to such third party until actual notice or knowledge of such revocation or termination shall have been received by such third party. I, for myself and for my heirs, executors, legal representatives and assigns, agree to indemnify and hold harmless any such third party from any and all claims that may arise against such third party by reason of such third party having relied on the provisions of this power of attorney.

This power of attorney shall not be effective in the event of my future disability or incapacity. This limited grant of authority does not authorize my attorney-in-fact to make any decisions regarding my medical or health care. This power of attorney may be revoked by me at any time and is automatically revoked upon my death. My attorney-in-fact shall not be compensated for his or her services nor shall my attorney-in-fact be liable to me, my estate, heirs, successors, or assigns for acting or refraining from acting under this document, except for willful misconduct or gross negligence. My attorney-in-fact accepts this appointment and agrees to act in my best interest as he or she considers advisable. This grant of authority shall include the power and authority to perform any incidental acts which may be reasonably required in order to perform the specific acts stated above.
⑤
Dated: _____

Signature and Declaration of Principal
⑥
I, _____ (printed name), the principal, sign my name to this power of attorney this _____ day of _____ and, being first duly sworn, do declare to the undersigned authority that I sign and execute this instrument as my power of attorney and that I sign it willingly, or willingly direct another to sign for me, that I execute it as my free and voluntary act for the purposes expressed in the power of attorney and that I am eighteen years of age or older, of sound mind and under no constraint or undue influence.

_____
Signature of Principal

Witness Attestation
⑦
I, _____ (printed name), the first witness,
and I, _____ (printed name), the second witness,
sign my name to the foregoing power of attorney being first duly sworn and do declare to the undersigned authority that the principal signs and executes this instrument as his/her power of attorney and that he\she signs it willingly, or willingly directs another to sign for him/her, and that I, in the presence and hearing of the principal, sign this power of attorney as witness to the

principal's signing and that to the best of my knowledge the principal is eighteen years of age or older, of sound mind and under no constraint or undue influence.

_____

Signature of First Witness

_____

Signature of Second Witness

Notary Acknowledgment

⑧

State of _____ County of _____

Subscribed, sworn to and acknowledged before me by _____,

the Principal, and subscribed and sworn to before me by _____,

and _____, the witnesses, this _____ day of

_____ .

_____

Notary Signature

Notary Public,

In and for the County of _____ State of _____

My commission expires: _____ Seal

Acknowledgment and Acceptance of Appointment as Attorney-in-Fact

⑨

I, _____, (printed name) have read the attached power of attorney and am the person identified as the attorney-in-fact for the principal. I hereby acknowledge that I accept my appointment as attorney-in-fact and that when I act as agent I shall exercise the powers for the benefit of the principal; I shall keep the assets of the principal separate from my assets; I shall exercise reasonable caution and prudence; and I shall keep a full and accurate record of all actions, receipts and disbursements on behalf of the principal.

_____   _____

Signature of Attorney-in-Fact   Date

Acknowledgment and Acceptance of Appointment as Successor Attorney-in-Fact

⑩

I, _____, (printed name) have read the attached power of attorney and am the person identified as the successor attorney-in-fact for the principal. I hereby acknowledge that I accept my appointment as successor attorney-in-fact and that, in the absence of a specific provision to the contrary in the power of attorney, when I act as agent I shall exercise the powers for the benefit of the principal; I shall keep the assets of the principal separate from my assets; I shall exercise reasonable caution and prudence; and I shall keep a full and accurate record of all actions, receipts and disbursements on behalf of the principal.

_____   _____

Signature of Successor Attorney-in-Fact   Date

Revocation of Power of Attorney

① I, _____ (printed name) ,
address: _____

② do revoke the power of attorney dated _____ , 20 _____ ,
③ which was granted to _____ (printed name),
address: _____ ,

to act as my attorney-in-fact.

④ This Revocation is dated _____ , 20 _____

⑤ _____
Signature of Person Revoking Power of Attorney

⑥ **Notary Acknowledgement**

State of _____
County of _____

On _____ , 20 _____ , _____ personally
came before me and, being duly sworn, did state that he or she is the person described in the
above document and that he or she signed the above document in my presence.

_____
Signature of Notary Public

Notary Public, In and for the County of _____
State of _____

My commission expires: _____   Notary Seal

Chapter 11

Releases

Releases are a method of acknowledging the satisfaction of an obligation or of releasing parties from liability or claims. Releases are used in various situations in the business world, from releasing a person or company from liability after an accident to a release of liens or claims against property. Releases can be very powerful documents. The various releases contained in this chapter are tailored to meet the most common situations in which a release is used. For a release to be valid, there must be some type of consideration received by the person who is granting the release. Releases should be used carefully as they may prevent any future claims against the party to whom it is granted. In general, a release from claims relating to an accident which causes personal injury should not be signed without a prior examination by a doctor. Also note that a release relating to damage to community property in a "community property" state must be signed by both spouses. Study the various forms provided to determine which one is proper for the use intended.

Instructions for Releases

General Release: This release serves as a full blanket-release from one party to another. It should only be used when all obligations of one party are to be released. The party signing this release is discharging the other party from all of their obligations to the other party stemming from a specific incident or transaction. This form can be used when one party has a claim against another and the other agrees to waive the claim for payment. To complete this form, fill in the following information:

① Name of person granting release
② Address of person granting release
③ Name of person granted release
④ Address of person granted release

⑤ Transaction or incident for which release is being granted
⑥ Date of release
⑦ Signature of person granting release
⑧ Printed name of person granting release

Mutual Release: The mutual release form provides a method for two parties to jointly release each other from their mutual obligations or claims. This form should be used when both parties intend to discharge each other from all of their mutual obligations. It essentially serves the purpose of two reciprocal General Releases.

① Name of first person granting release
② Address of first person granting release
③ Name of second person granting release
④ Address of second person granting release
⑤ Transaction or incident for which release is being granted
⑥ Date of release
⑦ Signature of first person granting release
⑧ Printed name of first person granting release
⑨ Signature of second person granting release
⑩ Printed name of second person granting release

Specific Release: This release form should be used only when a particular claim or obligation is being released, while allowing other liabilities to continue. The obligation being released should be spelled out in careful and precise terms to prevent confusion with any other obligation or claim. In addition, the liabilities or obligations which are not being released, but will survive, should also be carefully noted.

① Name of person granting release
② Address of person granting release
③ Name of person granted release
④ Address of person granted release
⑤ Claim or obligation for which release is being granted (Also note any claims, liabilites, or obligations that are not being released)
⑥ Transaction or incident for which release is being granted
⑦ Date of release
⑧ Signature of person granting release
⑨ Printed name of person granting release

General Release

For consideration, I, ① _____ ,
address: ②

release ③ _____ ,
address: ④

from all claims and obligations, known or unknown, to this date arising from the following transaction or incident: ⑤

The party signing this release has not assigned any claims or obligations covered by this release to any other party.

The party signing this release intends that it both bind and benefit itself and any successors.

Dated ⑥ _____ , 20 _____

⑦ _____
Signature of person granting release

⑧ _____
Printed name of person granting release

Mutual Release

For consideration, ① _____ ,
address: ②

and ③ _____ ,
address: ④

release each other from all claims and obligations, known or unknown, that they may have against each other arising from the following transaction or incident: ⑤

Neither party has assigned any claims or obligations covered by this release to any other party.

Both parties signing this release intend that it both bind and benefit themselves and any successors.

Dated ⑥ _____ , 20 _____

⑦ _____
Signature of 1st person

⑨ _____
Signature of 2nd person

⑧ _____
Printed name of 1st person

⑩ _____
Printed name of 2nd person

Specific Release

For consideration, I, ① _____ ,
address: ②

release ③ _____ ,
address: ④

from the following specific claims and obligations: ⑤

arising from the following transaction or incident: ⑥

Any claims or obligations that are not specifically mentioned are not released by this Specific Release.

The party signing this release has not assigned any claims or obligations covered by this release to any other party.

The party signing this release intends that it both bind and benefit itself and any successors.

Dated ⑦ _____ , 20 _____

⑧ _____
Signature of person granting release

⑨ _____
Printed name of person granting release

Chapter 12

Liens

The documents in this chapter are all related to the use of liens. Liens are a charge or a claim upon a piece of property that makes that property act as the security for the payment of a debt. For example, a mortgage is a lien against a house. If the mortgage is not paid on time, the house can be seized to satisfy the lien. Liens are thus legal claims against a piece of property. When a property which has an outstanding lien is sold, the lien holder is then generally paid the amount that is owed under the lien out of the proceeds of the sale of the property. There are two documents relating to liens included in this chapter. A Claim of Lien is used to impose a lien or obligation on a piece of property based on labor and/or materials provided for work on the property. A Waiver and Discharge of Lien is used to release such a lien.

Instructions

Claim of Lien: This form is used to assert a claim of lien against a particular piece of real estate, for money owed by the owner of the real estate for labor or materials that were provided for improvements to that particular piece of property. A lien is claim against a piece of real estate that must be paid off prior to the property being transferred or sold. This type of lien is often referred to as a mechanic's lien and may, generally, be filed by anyone who has supplied labor and/or materials for the improvement of a piece of real estate. This form must be signed in front of a notary public and then must be filed in the recorder's office of the county in which the property is located. Finally, at the time that you record this Claim of Lien, you will need to make two (2) copies of the Claim of Lien with the recorder's file stamp on them. Keep one copy for your records and mail one copy (on the same day that it was recorded) to the owner of the property, by USPS certified mail, with a return receipt requested. (Note: separate forms for Florida and Georgia are included on the Forms-on-CD).To prepare this Claim of Lien, simply fill in the following information:

① Name of person requesting recording of this claim (you)
② Name of person to whom the recorded claim should be mailed by the recorder's office (generally, you)
③ Street address where claim should be mailed
④ City where claim should be mailed
⑤ State and Zip Code where claim should be mailed
⑥ Name of who prepared document (usually you)
⑦ Address of who prepared document (usually you)
⑧ State and Zip Code of who prepared document (usually you)
⑨ State in which Notary is located
⑩ County in which Notary is located
⑪ Name of person claiming lien (you)
⑫ Description of labor and/or materials provided
⑬ County where labor or materials were provided
⑭ State where labor or materials were provided
⑮ Street address where labor or materials were provided
⑯ Legal description of property (obtain from recorder's office or county tax office)
⑰ Owner of property
⑱ Address of owner of property
⑲ Total value of all labor and/or materials provided
⑳ Value of labor and/or materials that remain unpaid
㉑ Date on which first labor and/or materials were provided
㉒ Date on which last labor and/or materials were provided
㉓ State in which property is located
㉔ Signature of person claiming lien (you)
㉕ Name of person claiming lien
㉖ Address of person claiming lien
㉗ The following section should be completed by a notary public
㉘ Name of person mailing copy of claim of lien (generally, you)
㉙ Date of mailing of claim of lien
㉚ Name of owner of property
㉛ Address of owner of property
㉜ Dated
㉝ Signature of person mailing claim of lien
㉞ Name of person mailing claim of lien
㉟ *Note: California residents must use this California Notary box

Waiver and Release of Lien: This form is used to waive or release a claim of lien against a particular piece of real estate, for money owed by the owner of the real estate for labor or materials that were provided for improvements to that particular piece of property. A lien is claim against a piece of real estate that must be paid off prior to the property being transferred or sold. This type of lien is often referred to as a mechanic's lien and may, generally, be filed by anyone who has supplied labor and/or materials for the improvement of a piece of real estate. This form is used to *waive* a future lien (give up the right to assert a lien), or to *release* a lien (state that the reasons for the lien have now been satisfied). It may be used by a homeowner to make certain that any contractors or subcontractors who have been paid in full will not, in the future, attempt to file a lien against a piece of property. It may also be used by a contractor or subcontractor to release a lien that they, themselves, have filed against a particular piece of real estate. To effectively release a lien, this form must be signed in front of a notary public and then must be filed in the recorder's office of the county in which the property is located. To prepare this Waiver and Release of Lien, simply fill in the following information:

1. Name of person requesting recording of this waiver and release
2. Name of person to whom the recorded waiver and release should be mailed to by the recorder's office
3. Street address where waiver and release should be mailed
4. City where waiver and release should be mailed
5. State and Zip Code where waiver and release should be mailed
6. Name of person preparing document
7. Address of who prepared document (usually you)
8. State and Zip Code of who prepared document (usually you)
9. State in which Notary is located
10. County in which Notary is located
11. Name of person waiving and releasing lien
12. Name of employer
13. Address of employer (your address if self-employed)
14. Description of labor and/or materials provided
15. Street address where labor or materials were provided
16. Legal description of property (obtain from recorder's office or county tax office)
17. Owner of property
18. Address of owner of property
19. Signature of person waiving and releasing lien
20. Name of person waiving and releasing lien
21. Address of person waiving and releasing lien
22. The following section should be completed by a notary public
23. *Note: California residents must use this California Notary box

Recording requested by: (1) _____
When recorded, mail to:

Name: (2) _____

Address: (3) _____

City: (4) _____

State/Zip: (5) _____

Space above reserved for use by Recorder's Office

Document prepared by:

Name (6) _____

Address (7) _____

City/State/Zip (8) _____

Claim of Lien

State of (9) _____

County of (10) _____

I, (11) _____ , being duly sworn, state the following:
In accordance with an agreement to provide labor and/or material, I did furnish the following labor and/or materials: (12)

on the following described real property located in (13) _____ County,
State of (14) _____ , commonly known as: (15) _____

and legally described as: (16)

which property is owned by (17) _____ , whose address is
(18) _____ , of a total value of $ (19) _____ ,
of which there remains unpaid $ (20) _____ , and I further state that I furnished the first of
the items on the date of (21) _____ , and the last of the items on the date of
(22) _____ .

I hereby, under the laws of the State of (23) _____ , claim a lien against the
above-described property in the amount of money, stated above, which remains unpaid to me.

㉔ _____ ㉕ _____
Signature of Person Claiming Lien   Name of Person Claiming Lien

Address of person claiming lien: ㉖ _____

㉗ On _____ , _____ came before
me personally and, under oath, stated that he/she is the person described in the above document and that
he/she signed the above document in my presence.

_____
Notary Signature
Notary Public,
In and for the County of _____ State of _____
My commission expires: _____   Seal

CERTIFICATE OF MAILING

I, ㉘ _____ , certify that on this date, ㉙ _____ , I have mailed a
copy of this Claim of Lien by USPS certified mail, return receipt requested, in accordance with the law, to:
Name: ㉚ _____
Address: ㉛ _____
Date: ㉜ _____

㉝ _____ ㉞ _____
Signature of Person Mailing Claim of Lien   Name of Person Mailing Claim of Lien

㉟ *California residents or persons intending that this document be valid in the*
State of California should use the following California Notary Acknowledgment form:

State of California
County of _____ } S.S.
On _____ , before me, _____
(name and title of notary), personally appeared _____ , who
proved to me on the basis of satisfactory evidence to be the person(s) whose name(s) is/are subscribed to
the above instrument and acknowledged to me that they/he/she executed the instrument in their/his/her
authorized capacity. I certify under penalty of perjury under the laws of the State of California that the
foregoing is true and correct. Witness my hand and official seal.

_____   Seal
Notary Signature

Recording requested by: ①_____
When recorded, mail to:

Name: ②_____

Address: ③_____

City: ④_____

State/Zip: ⑤_____

Space above reserved for use by Recorder's Office

Document prepared by:

Name ⑥_____

Address ⑦_____

City/State/Zip ⑧_____

Waiver & Release of Lien

State of ⑨_____

County of ⑩_____

I, ⑪_____, being duly sworn, state the following:

I am employed by ⑫_____, whose address is ⑬_____

_____, I have furnished labor and/or materials described as:

⑭_____

for work done at the address of ⑮_____,

the legal property description of which is: ⑯

and which is owned by ⑰_____, whose address is ⑱_____

_____, and I do hereby state I have been paid in

full for the above-mentioned labor and/or materials and I do unconditionally waive all liens or claims of

liens relating to this labor and/or materials that I have or had on the foregoing real property.

⑲ _____

Signature of Person Waiving Lien

⑳ _____

Name of Person Waiving Lien

Address of person waiving lien: ㉑

㉒ On _____ , _____ ,

came before me personally and, under oath, stated that he/she is the person described in the above docu-

ment and that he/she signed the above document in my presence.

_____

Notary Signature

Notary Public,

In and for the County of _____ State of _____

My commission expires: _____   Seal

㉓ *California residents or persons intending that this document be valid in the*
State of California should use the following California Notary Acknowledgment form:

State of California

County of _____ } S.S.

On _____ , before me, _____

___ (name and title of notary), personally appeared _____ ,

who

proved to me on the basis of satisfactory evidence to be the person(s) whose name(s) is/are subscribed to

the above instrument and acknowledged to me that they/he/she executed the instrument in their/his/her

authorized capacity. I certify under penalty of perjury under the laws of the State of California that the

foregoing is true and correct. Witness my hand and official seal.

_____   Seal

Notary Signature

Chapter 13

Real Estate Financing Documents

Loans for real estate are a very big business. In 2008, total U.S. mortgage debt reached a record level of $14.6 trillion. Loans for real estate are generally signified by either a *mortgage* or a *deed of trust*. A mortgage is simply a legal instrument in which property serves as security for the repayment of a loan. Arranging a mortgage is seen as the standard method by which individuals or businesses can purchase residential or commercial real estate without the need to pay the full value immediately. In some states, a deed of trust is used rather than a mortgage. This type of document is held by a trustee pending repayment of the loan. The advantage of a deed of trust is that the trustee does not have to go to court to proceed with foreclosure should the borrower default on the loan. There are no documents included in this chapter pertaining to either mortgages or deeds of trust. Loans for real estate, other than a simple promissory note or a Contract for Deed, are generally subject to many more state and federal regulations and, thus, should be handled by a real estate professional or attorney.

Three separate legal theories exist regarding who has the legal title to a piece of mortgaged property. The majority of states specify that the owner (the mortgagor–the one who has mortgaged his or her property) remains the owner of the property and that the mortgage only creates a lien (or claim) against the property. Thus, in these states, the person who has mortgaged his or her property continues to hold title to the property. These states are referred to as *lien theory* states. The remaining states follow rules that specify that the mortgage is actually a type of deed that conveys the property to the lender (mortgagee). Under this theory, the mortgage/deed becomes void once the loan is paid off. Thus, in these states, the financing institution actually holds the title to the mortgaged property. This is known as the *title theory*. Finally, a few states use what is termed the *intermediary theory* states. In these states, the title remains with the borrower, but the lender may take back title to the property if the borrower defaults on the loan.

In the U.S. the process by which a mortgage is secured by a borrower is called origination. This involves the borrower submitting an application and documentation related to his or her financial history to the financing institution. Many banks now offer "no-doc" or "low-doc" loans in which the borrower is required to submit only minimal financial information. These loans carry a slightly higher interest rate (perhaps 0.25% to 0.50% higher) and are available only to borrowers with excellent credit. Sometimes, a third party is involved, such as a mortgage broker. This entity takes the borrower's information and reviews a number of lenders, selecting the ones that will best meet the needs of the consumer. Loans are often sold on the open market to larger investors by the originating mortgage company.

Lenders may charge various fees when giving a mortgage to a mortgagor. These include entry fees, exit fees, administration fees and lender's mortgage insurance. There are also settlement fees (closing costs) that the company handling the closing will charge. In addition, if a third party handles the loan, it may charge other fees as well.

There are many types of mortgages available. The two most common are fixed rate mortgages that applies the same interest rate toward monthly loan payments for the life of the loan, and adjustable rate mortgages that periodically adjust the home buyer's principal and interest payment throughout the life of that loan, based on fluctuations in the interest rate.

Because of the complex nature of real estate financing documents and the numerous state and federal laws that surround such financing, in virtually all instances, such documents will be drafted and completed by the financing institutions themselves. For any questions regarding mortgages or deeds of trust, please consult a real estate professional, a financing institution or an attorney with real estate experience.

Chapter 14

Miscellaneous Real Estate Documents

Included in this chapter are two documents that may be used in circumstances relating to real estate. The forms that are included and the information necessary to prepare them are as follows:

Instructions

Declaration of Homestead: A homestead is the house or mobile home that a person lives in and land on which it sits. The property must be a person's primary residence for it to be eligible for a homestead declaration. The term homestead also includes any improvements to the land, such as a fence. By signing a legal document known as a homestead declaration, home owners can protect at least part of the value of a home against most creditors' claims. A homestead declaration does not, however, prevent all claims against a piece of property. A person who performs repairs or other work on a home or who supplies materials for such work is allowed by law to place a lien against the home if payment is not received for services rendered or supplies provided. A homestead declaration provides no protection in such cases. A financial institution holding a mortgage on the property also has a lien against the property for any unpaid balance on the house. A homestead declaration provides no protection for failure to pay the mortgage. The declaration also will not provide protection in case of bankruptcy unless it was filed before bankruptcy was declared.

After the homestead exemption declaration form is completed, signed and notarized, it should be recorded in the clerk and recorder's office in the county in which the home or mobile home is located. To complete this form, fill in the following:

① Name of person requesting recording of this claim (you)
② Name of person to whom the recorded claim should be mailed by the recorder's office (generally, you)

③ Street address where claim should be mailed
④ City where claim should be mailed
⑤ State and Zip Code where claim should be mailed
⑥ Name of who prepared document (usually you)
⑦ Address of who prepared document (usually you)
⑧ State and Zip Code of who prepared document (usually you)
⑨ Date of signing document
⑩ Name of claimant (the one claiming the homestead exemption)
⑪ State in which homestead property is located
⑫ Legal description of property
⑬ Date of signing declaration of homestead
⑭ Signature of claimant (must sign before a Notary Public)
⑮ Printed name of claimant
⑯ The following section should be completed by a notary public*
Note: California residents must use the California Notary box available on the Forns-on-CD

Easement and Right of Way Agreement: This type of form allows a property owner to grant the right to cross a portion of his or her property to another person. Such an easement is also referred to as a right of way. After the form is completed, signed and notarized, it should be recorded in the clerk and recorder's office in the county in which the property is located. To complete this form, fill in the following:

① Name of person requesting recording of this claim (you)
② Name of person to whom the recorded claim should be mailed by the recorder's office (generally, you)
③ Street address where claim should be mailed
④ City where claim should be mailed
⑤ State and Zip Code where claim should be mailed
⑥ Name of who prepared document (usually you)
⑦ Address of who prepared document (usually you)
⑧ State and Zip Code of who prepared document (usually you)
⑨ Date of signing document
⑩ Name of grantor (the one granting the easement and right of way)
⑪ Address of grantor
⑫ Name of grantee (the one receiving the easement and right of way)
⑬ Address of grantee
⑭ Legal description of grantor's full property over which easement is granted
⑮ Description of actual easement granted (be as specific as possible)
⑯ Date of signing of easement and right of way
⑰ Signature of grantor
⑱ Printed name of grantor
⑲ The following section should be completed by a notary public*
Note: California residents must use the California Notary box available on the Forns-on-CD

Recording requested by: ①_____

When recorded, mail to:

Name: ②_____

Address: ③_____

City: ④_____

State/Zip: ⑤_____

Space above reserved for use by Recorder's Office

Document prepared by:

Name ⑥_____

Address ⑦_____

City/State/Zip: ⑧_____

Declaration of Homestead

This Declaration of Homestead is made on ⑨_____ , 20 _____ ,

by ⑩_____ , claimant, who does reside on and does hereby claim the following described property to be his or her home stead, and to be exempt from attachment or forced sale pursuant to the laws of the State of

⑪_____ .

The homestead property, claimed as exempt, is described as follows: ⑫

together with the dwelling house, or mobile home and improvements and appurtenances thereon.

Dated: ⑬_____ , 20 _____

⑭_____

Signature of Claimant

⑮_____

Printed Name of Claimant

⑯ State of _____
County of _____

On _____ , 20 _____ , _____ personally
came before me and, being duly sworn, did state that he or she is the person described in the
above document and that he or she signed the above document in my presence.

_____
Signature of Notary Public

Notary Public, In and for the County of _____
State of _____

My commission expires: _____   Notary Seal

Recording requested by: ①_____
When recorded, mail to:

Name: ②_____

Address: ③_____

City: ④_____

State/Zip: ⑤_____

Space above reserved for use by Recorder's Office

Document prepared by:

Name ⑥_____

Address ⑦_____

City/State/Zip ⑧_____

Easement and Right of Way Agreement

This Easement and Right of Way Agreement is made on ⑨_____ , 20 _____ ,
between ⑩_____ , grantor,
address: ⑪

and ⑫_____ , grantee, being the
owner of real property adjoining or adjacent to the property described in this Agreement,
and whose address is: ⑬

For valuable consideration, the Grantor hereby grants to the Grantee, their heirs and assigns,
a perpetual easement and right of way to go through, over, and across the following described
real estate: ⑭

Such easement is described as follows: ⑮

Dated: ⑯_____ , 20 _____

⑰_____
Signature of Grantor

⑱_____
Printed Name of Grantor

⑲ State of _____

County of _____

On _____ , 20 _____ , _____ personally
came before me and, being duly sworn, did state that he or she is the person described in the
above document and that he or she signed the above document in my presence.

_____

Signature of Notary Public

Notary Public, In and for the County of _____

State of _____

My commission expires: _____   Notary Seal

Appendix:
State Real Estate Laws

On the following pages are state listings containing relevant information regarding real estate and landlord/tenant law. You are advised to check your state's listing carefully to determine the particular requirements in your jurisdiction. Every state has some differing requirements. Following is an explanation of the listings:

State Landlord-Tenant Statutes: This listing provides a reference to the statute book location that contains each particular state's laws regarding landlord/tenant relations.

State Property Law Statutes: Should you wish to research the law in your state, this lists the name and chapter of the state statute in which the laws regarding real property are found in each state.

State web address: This listing notes the internet web address of each state's online website. For most state sites, you will arrive at the main index for the state and will need to locate the specific site for the state's statute/legislative information by using the references in the listings above, *State Landlord-Tenant Statutes* and *State Property Law Statutes*. These websites were current at the time of this book's publication.

State Real Estate Disclosure Laws: This listing specifies the name of the document that is required to be completed by a seller disclosing their knowledge about the property for sale. At press time, 31 states provided some type of statutory real estate disclosure form. Also noted is the statutory location of real estate disclosure laws.

Landlord's Entry to Real Estate: This listing provides the state requirement surrounding the right of a landlord to enter a rented property.

Security Deposit Amount Limits: Under this listing are noted the various state limits on the amount that a tenant can be charged as a security deposit.

Deadlines for Security Deposit Returns: Details are provided under this listing regarding the time limits imposed by each state for the return of a tenant's security deposit.

Interest Required on Security Deposits: This listing provides each state's requirements regarding whether a landlord must provide interest to the tenant for the holding period of the tenant's security deposit.

Separate Account Required for Security Deposits: This listing specifies whether a landlord is required to keep tenant security deposits in a separate bank account.

Exemption from Security Deposit Laws: This listing specifies which, if any, rental units are exempt from security deposit laws.

Notice Required to Change or Terminate Month-to-Month Tenancy: This listing provides the time limit required of a landlord to provide a tenant with notice that a month-to-month tenancy is being changed or terminated.

Rent Late Fees: This listing provides state requirements surrounding the ability of a landlord to impose fees for the late payment of rent and any restrictions as to the amount of those fees.

Required Landlord Disclosures: This section provides information regarding any state requirements for landlord disclosures.

When and Where Rent is Due: This listing identifies the statutes containing any requirements regarding when and where rent is due and if there are any grace periods for late rental payments.

Notary Acknowledgment: This listing provides additional state requirements to the standard Notary Block.

Lien: This listing provides additional state requirements to the standard Claim of Lien.

Other Recording Requirements: Unless otherwise noted, all of the following items are the standard state requirements for the recording of deeds and/or other recordable documents. Although not all of these items are mandatory for all states, however, they are highly recommended as the document will then be valid and recordable in any state. Any additional state-specific requirements which may be necessary are noted under the individual state listings in the following Appendix.

• Document must be in writing and signed and dated by the grantor.
• Document must identify grantor and grantee and provide their addresses.
• If document is deed, it must contain words of conveyance and adequately describe land conveyed (generally both by a street address and also a valid legal description that is exactly the same as the description on the current deed).
• Document must be on 8 1/2" x 11" paper of at least 20# weight.
• Document must have 1" margins at sides and bottom, and a 3" margin at the top.
• Grantor's signature must be notarized and witnessed by two persons.
• Name of person requesting recording of document must be noted.
• Name of address of person who prepared document must be noted.
• Name and address of the person or entity to which the recorded document should be mailed to upon recording must be noted.

Alabama

State Landlord-Tenant Statutes: The Code of Alabama, Title 35, Chapter 9. **State Property Laws Statutes:** The Code of Alabama, Title 35.

State Law Website: http://www.alabama.gov/

State Real Estate Disclosure Laws: No statutory form. Use basic Real Estate Disclosure Form in Chapter 4 and on the Forms-on-CD.

Landlord's Entry to Real Estate: No statute.

Security Deposit Amount Limits: None.

Deadlines for Security Deposit Returns: No statute.

Interest Required on Security Deposit: No statute.

Separate Account required for Security Deposit: No statute.

Exemption from Security Deposit Laws: No statute.

Notice Required to Change or Terminate Month-to-Month Tenancy: 10 days to terminate. No statute to change rent. (The Code of Alabama, Section 35-9-3).

Rent Late Fees: No statute.

Required Landlord Disclosures: Landlord must disclose the name and address the manager of the property and the name and address for the purpose of receiving notices. (Code of Alabama, Section 35,-9A-202).

When and Where Rent is Due: Details of when and where rent is due. (Code of Alabama, Section 35,-9A-161(c)).

Notary Acknowledgment: Standard Notary Block acceptable. (The Code of Alabama, Section 35-4-29).

Lien: Standard Claim of Lien form acceptable. (The Code of Alabama, Section 35-11-1+).

Other Recording Requirements: Disclosure of marital status of all grantors on all conveyances of land. (The Code of Alabama, Section 35-4-73). Where a married person coneys the homestead, his or her spouse must sign the conveyance. (The Code of Alabama, Section 6-10-03).

Alaska

State Landlord-Tenant Statutes: Alaska Statutes, Sections 34.03.010 to 34.03.380.

State Property Laws Statutes: Alaska Statutes, Title 34.

State Law Website: http://www.state.ak.us/

State Real Estate Disclosure Laws: Residential Real Property Transfer Disclosure Statement. (Alaska Statutes, Title 34, Chapter 70). Disclosures in Residential Real Property Transfers. (This form is provided on the Forms-on-CD).

Landlord's Entry to Real Estate: Immediate access for emergency. 24 hour notice for inspection, repairs, viewing of property and if tenant is absent for long periods. (Alaska Statutes, Section 34.03.140).

Security Deposit Amount Limits: 2 months rent. (Alaska Statutes, Section 34.03.070).

Deadlines for Security Deposit Returns: 14 days if the tenant gives proper notice to terminate rent. 30 days if tenant does not give proper notice. (Alaska Statutes, Section 34.03.070).

Interest Required on Security Deposit: No. (Alaska Statutes, Section 34.03.070).

Separate Account required for Security Deposit: Yes. (Alaska Statutes, Section 34.03.070).

Exemption from Security Deposit Laws: Rental units that cost more than $2,000 per month are exempt. (Alaska Statutes, Section 34.03.070).

Notice Required to Change or Terminate Month-to-Month Tenancy: 30 days to terminate or change rent. (Alaska Statutes, Section 34.03.290(b)).

Rent Late Fees: No statute.

Required Landlord Disclosures: Landlord must disclose the name and address the manager of the property and the name and address for the purpose of receiving notices. (Alaska Statutes, Section 34.03.080)

When and Where Rent is Due: Details of when and where rent is due. (Alaska Statutes, Section 34.03.020(c))

Notary Acknowledgment: Standard Notary Block acceptable. (Alaska Statutes Section, 09-63-100).

Lien: Standard Claim of Lien form acceptable. (Alaska Statutes Section, 34-35-005+).

Other Recording Requirements: Document must be accompanied by or contain the name of the recording district in which it is to be recorded. Also, an exact or fully conformed copy of an original document must be accompanied by an affidavit of the person offering the document. (Alaska Statutes Section, 40-17-030).

Arizona

State Landlord-Tenant Statutes: Arizona Revised Statutes, Sections 33-1301 to 33-1381 and 12-1171 to 12-1183.

State Property Laws Statutes: Arizona Revised Statutes, Title 33.

State Law Website: http://www.azleg.state.az.us/

State Real Estate Disclosure Laws: Affidavit of Disclosure. (This form is provided on the Forms-on-CD). May also additionally use basic Real Estate Disclosure Form in Chapter 4 and on the Forms-on-CD. (Arizona Revised Statutes, Section 33-422).

Landlord's Entry to Real Estate: Immediate access for emergency. 2 days notice for inspection, repairs, viewing of property and if tenant is absent for long periods. (Arizona Revised Statutes, Section 33-1343).

Security Deposit Amount Limits: 1 ½ month's rent. Landlord can charge more only if renter agrees. (Arizona Revised Statutes, Section 33-1321).

Deadlines for Security Deposit Returns: 14 days. (Arizona Revised Statutes, Section 33-1321).

Interest Required on Security Deposit: No. (Arizona Revised Statutes, Section 33-1321).

Separate Account required for Security Deposit: No. (Arizona Revised Statutes, Section 33-1321).

Exemption from Security Deposit Laws: None. (Arizona Revised Statutes, Section 33-1321).

Notice Required to Change or Terminate Month-to-Month Tenancy: 30 days to terminate or change rent. (Arizona Revised Statutes, Section 33-1375).

Rent Late Fees: Reasonable amount of late fee after nonpayment of rent for 5 days. (Arizona Revised Statutes, Section 33-1368(B)).

Required Landlord Disclosures: Landlord must disclose the name and address the manager of the property and the name and address for the purpose of receiving notices. Any non-refundable fees must be stated in the lease. Separate utility charges by the landlord must be stated in the lease. A move-in/move-out checklist is required and the tenant has the right to be present at the move-out inspection. (Arizona Revised Statutes, Section 33-1321).

When and Where Rent is Due: Details of when and where rent is due. (Arizona Revised Statutes, Section 33-1314(C) and 33-1368(B)).

Notary Acknowledgment: Standard Notary Block acceptable. (Arizona Revised Statutes, Section 33-506).

Lien: Standard Claim of Lien form acceptable. (Arizona Revised Statutes, Section 33-981+).

Other Recording Requirements: An affidavit of legal value must be attached to the conveyance. (Arizona Revised Statutes, 11-1133).

Arkansas

State Landlord-Tenant Statutes: Arkansas Code, Sections 18-16-101 to 18-16-306.

State Property Laws Statutes: Arkansas Code, Title 18.

State Law Website: http://www.arkleg.state.ar.us/

State Real Estate Disclosure Laws: No statutory form. Use basic Real Estate Disclosure Form in Chapter 4 and on the Forms-on-CD.

Landlord's Entry to Real Estate: No Statute.

Security Deposit Amount Limits: 2 month's rent. (Arkansas Code, Section 18-16-303 to 18-16-306).

Deadlines for Security Deposit Returns: 30 days. (Arkansas Code, Section 18-16-303 to 18-16-306).

Interest Required on Security Deposit: No. (Arkansas Code, Section 18-16-303 to 18-16-306).

Separate Account required for Security Deposit: No. (Arkansas Code, Section 18-16-303 to 18-16-306).

Exemption from Security Deposit Laws: Does not apply to a landlord who owns 5 or less units. It does apply if the units are managed by another party for a fee. (Arkansas Code, Section 18-16-303 to 18-16-306).

Notice Required to Change or Terminate Month-to-Month Tenancy: 10 days to terminate or change rent. (Arkansas Code, Section 18-16-101).

Rent Late Fees: No statute.

Required Landlord Disclosures: None.

When and Where Rent is Due: Details of when and where rent is due. (Arkansas Code, Section 18-17-401); state law also provides for rental grace periods (Arkansas Code, Section 18-17-401, 18-17-701, and 18-17-901).

Notary Acknowledgment: Standard Notary Block acceptable. (Arkansas Code, Section 16-47-207).

Lien: Standard Claim of Lien form acceptable. (Arkansas Code, Section 18-44-101+).

Other Recording Requirements: Where a married person conveys the homestead, his or her spouse must sign the conveyance. (18-12-403). Document must have a two and one-half inch margin at the bottom of the last page. (14-15-402). Document must be acknowledged pursuant to 16-47-207. (14-15-402). Must provide proof of payment of tax. (26-60-110).

California

State Landlord-Tenant Statutes: California Civil Code, Sections 1940 to 1954.1 and 1954.50 to 1954.535 and 1961 to 1962.7.

State Property Laws Statutes: California Civil Code, Division 2, Part 2. Real or Immovable Property.

State Law Website: http://www.state.ca.us/**State Real Estate Disclosure Laws:** Smoke Detector Statement of Compliance, (CA Health and Safety Code 13113.8(b)). Military Ordnance Disclosure (Civil Code 1102.15). Industrial Use Disclosure, (Civil Code 1102.17). Earthquake Hazards Disclosure and Homeowner's Guide to Earthquake Safety, (CA Business and Professions Code 10149). Real Estate Transfer Disclosure Statement, (Civil Code Section 1102-1102.18). Natural Hazard Disclosure Statement, (Civil Code Section 1103-1103.14). (The last two forms are provided on the Forms-on-CD).

Landlord's Entry to Real Estate: Immediate access for emergency. 24 hour notice repairs and viewing of property. 48 hours for move out inspection. (California Civil Code, Section 1950 and 1954).

Security Deposit Amount Limits: 2 months rent if unfurnished. 2 ½ month's rent if unfurnished and renter has a waterbed. 3 months rent if furnished. 3 ½ months rent if furnished with a waterbed. (California Civil Code, Sections 1950.5 and 1940.5(g)).

Deadlines for Security Deposit Returns: 3 weeks. (California Civil Code, Sections 1950.5 and 1940.5(g)).

Interest Required on Security Deposit: No. (California Civil Code, Sections 1950.5 and 1940.5(g)).

Separate Account required for Security Deposit: No. (California Civil Code, Sections 1950.5 and 1940.5(g)).

Exemption from Security Deposit Laws: No. (California Civil Code, Sections 1950.5 and 1940.5(g)).

Notice Required to Change or Terminate Month-to-Month Tenancy: 30 days for tenant to terminate or change rent. 30 days for landlord to terminate or change rent. 60 days for landlord when raising rent or if tenancy is for over 1 year. (California Civil Code, Sections 1946, 827a, and 827b).

Rent Late Fees: No statute. Late fees are unenforceable under California case law.

Required Landlord Disclosures: The following notice must be included in all leases: "Notice-Pursuant to Section 290.46 of the California Penal Code, information about specified registered sex offenders is made available to the public via an Internet Web site maintained by the Department of Justice at www.meganslaw.co.gov. Depending on an offender's criminal history, this information will include either the address at which the offender resides or the community of residence and Zip Code in which he or she resides." In addition, landlord must disclose the name and address the manager of the property and the name and address for the purpose of receiving notices. Landlord also must disclose whether utilities to the property also serve other properties and how the costs are allocated. Landlord must also give written notice to prospective tenants of any pending demolition permits, known locations of former federal or state ordnance, any known toxic mold, and any pest control disclosures. (California Civil Code, Section 1950.5(m), 1940.6, 1940.7, 1940.8, and 2079.10a; California Health & Safety Code, Sections 26147 and 26148; California Business and Professional Code, Section 8538).

When and Where Rent is Due: Details of when and where rent is due. (California Civil Code, Sections 1947 and 1962).

Notary Acknowledgment: In addition to standard Notary Block, the following language is necessary: Under penalty of perjury. (California Civil Code, Section 1189).

Lien: Standard Claim of Lien form acceptable. (California Civil Code, Section 3082+).

Other Recording Requirements: Document must be legible, photographically, reproducible, in English or translated, capable of being indexed, contain title of document, have the left 3 1/2" for the name of the person requesting recording and return address and the right 5" left blank for the recorders stamp. (Government Code §§ 27200 et seq.).

Colorado

State Landlord-Tenant Statutes: (Colorado Revised Statutes, Sections 38-12-101 to 38-12-104, 38-12-301 to 38-12-302).

State Property Laws Statutes: Colorado Revised Statutes, Title 38.

State Law Website: http://www.leg.state.co.us/

State Real Estate Disclosure Laws: Seller's Property Disclosure (Colorado Real Estate Commission SPD 19-10-05). (This form is provided on the Forms-on-CD).

Landlord's Entry to Real Estate: No Statute.

Security Deposit Amount Limits: No limit in statute. (Colorado Revised Statutes, Section 38-12-102 to 38-12-104).

Deadlines for Security Deposit Returns: 1 month unless rental agreement states otherwise, no more than 60 days. 72 hours if a hazardous situation concerning gas equipment requires renter to vacate property. (Colorado Revised Statutes, Section 38-12-102 to 38-12-104).

Interest Required on Security Deposit: No. (Colorado Revised Statutes, Section 38-12-102 to 38-12-104).

Separate Account required for Security Deposit: No. (Colorado Revised Statutes, Section 38-12-102 to 38-12-104).

Exemption from Security Deposit Laws: None. (Colorado Revised Statutes, Section 38-12-102 to 38-12-104).

Notice Required to Change or Terminate Month-to-Month Tenancy: No statute.

Rent Late Fees: No statute.

Required Landlord Disclosures: None.

When and Where Rent is Due: None.

Notary Acknowledgment: Standard Notary Block acceptable. (Colorado Revised Statutes, Section 12-55-208).

Lien: Standard Claim of Lien form acceptable. (Colorado Revised Statutes, Section 38-22-101+).

Other Recording Requirements: Disclosure Statement. (1) Every contract for the purchase and sale of residential real property shall contain a disclosure statement in bold-faced type which is clearly legible and in substantially the following form: "Special taxing district may be subject to general obligation indebtedness that is paid by revenues produced from annual tax levies and excessive tax burdens to support the servicing of such debt where circumstances arise resulting in the inability of such a district to discharge such indebtedness without such an increase in mill levies. Purchasers should investigate the debt financing requirements of the authorized general obligation indebtedness of such districts, existing mill levies of such district servicing such indebtedness, and the potential for an increase in such mill levies." (Colorado revised statutes, section 38-35.7-101). One or after january 1, 2007, every contract for the purchase and sale of residential real property in a common interest community shall contain a disclosure statement in bold-faced type that is clearly legible and in substantially the following form: "the property is located within a common interest community and is subject to the declaration for such community. The owner of the property will be required to be a member of the owner's association for the community and will be subject to the bylaws and rules and regulations of the association. The declaration, bylaws, and rules and regulations will impose financial obligations upon the owner of the property, including an obligation to pay assessments of the association. If the owner does not pay these assessments, the association could place a lien on the property and possibly sell it to pay the debt. The declaration, bylaws, and rules and regulations of the community may prohibit the owner from making changes to the property without an architectural review by the association (or a committee of the association) and the approval of the association. Purchasers of property within the common interest community should investigate the financial obligations of members of the association. Purchasers should carefully read the declaration for the community and the bylaws and rules and regulations of the association." (Colorado Revised Statutes, Section 38-35.7-102).

Connecticut

State Landlord-Tenant Statutes: Connecticut General Statutes, Sections 47a-1 to 47a-51.

State Property Laws Statutes: Connecticut General Statutes (see Volume 12, Section 47 and 47a).

State Law Website: http://www.ct.gov

State Real Estate Disclosure Laws: Residential Property Condition Disclosure Report. (Connecticut General Statutes, Sections 20-327b). (This form is provided on the Forms-on-CD).

Landlord's Entry to Real Estate: Immediate access for emergency. Reasonable notice for inspection, repairs, viewing of property and if tenant is absent for long periods. (Connecticut General Statutes, Section 47a-16 to 47a-16a).

Security Deposit Amount Limits: 2 month's rent. 1 month's rent if renter is over the age of 62. (Connecticut General Statutes, Section 47a-21).

Deadlines for Security Deposit Returns: 30 days or within 15 days of receiving the renter's forwarding address. (Connecticut General Statutes, Section 47a-21).

Interest Required on Security Deposit: Yes. (Connecticut General Statutes, Section 47a-21).

Separate Account required for Security Deposit: Yes.. (Connecticut General Statutes, Section 47a-21).

Exemption from Security Deposit Laws: None. (Connecticut General Statutes, Section 47a-21).

Notice Required to Change or Terminate Month-to-Month Tenancy: No statute.

Rent Late Fees: 9 days after rent is due. (Connecticut General Statutes, Section 47a-15a).

Required Landlord Disclosures: Landlord must provide written notice if property is a 'common-interest community'. Landlord must disclose the name and address the manager of the property and the name and address for the purpose of receiving notices. (Connecticut General Statutes, Sections 47a-3e and 47a-6).

When and Where Rent is Due: Details of when and where rent is due. (Connecticut General Statutes, Section 47a-3a); state law also provides for rental grace periods (Connecticut General Statutes, Section 47a-15a).

Notary Acknowledgment: Standard Notary Block acceptable. (Connecticut General Statutes, Section 1-62).

Lien: Standard Claim of Lien form acceptable. (Connecticut General Statutes, Section 49-33+).

Other Recording Requirements: Two witnesses required for conveyances of land. Acknowledgement required. (Connecticut General Statutes, Section 47-5).

Delaware

State Landlord-Tenant Statutes: Delaware Code, Title 25, Sections 5101-7013.

State Property Laws Statutes: Delaware Code, Title 25.

State Law Website: http://www.delaware.gov/

State Real Estate Disclosure Laws: Seller's Disclosure of Real Property Condition Report. (Delaware Code, Title 6, Chapter 25, Subtitle VII, Buyer Property Protection Act. Sections, 2571-2578).(This form is provided on the Forms-on-CD).

Landlord's Entry to Real Estate: Immediate access for emergency. 2 days notice for inspection, repairs and viewing of property and if tenant is absent for long periods. (Delaware Code, Title 25, Sections, 5509 & 5510).

Security Deposit Amount Limits: 1 month's rent for rental agreements for one year or more. No limit on month-to-month rental agreements. Pet deposit can be up to an additional month's rent. (Delaware Code, Title 25, Section 5514).

Deadlines for Security Deposit Returns: 20 days. (Delaware Code, Title 25, Section 5514).

Interest Required on Security Deposit: No. (Delaware Code, Title 25, Section 5514).

Separate Account required for Security Deposit: Yes. (Delaware Code, Title 25, Section 5514).

Exemption from Security Deposit Laws: None. (Delaware Code, Title 25, Section 5514).

Notice Required to Change or Terminate Month-to-Month Tenancy: 60 days to terminate or change rent. Renter had 45 days to terminate tenancy after changes. (Delaware Code, Title 25, Sections 5106 & 5107).

Rent Late Fees: Cannot exceed 5% of rent after rent is more than 5 days late. (Delaware Code, Title 25, Section 5501(d)).

Required Landlord Disclosures: Landlord must disclose the name and address the manager of the property and the name and address for the purpose of receiving notices. Landlord must provide tenant with a copy of the Summary of Residential Landlord-Tenant Code (found at: **attorneygeneral .delaware.gov/consumers/protection/brochure/ landlordcode.pdf**)

When and Where Rent is Due: Details of when and where rent is due. (Delaware Code, Title 25, Section 5501(b)); state law also provides for rental grace periods (Delaware Code, Title 25, section 5501(d)).

Notary Acknowledgment: Standard Notary Block acceptable. (Delaware Code, Title 29, Section 4328).

Lien: Standard Claim of Lien form acceptable. (Delaware Code, Title 25, Section 2701+).

Other Recording Requirements: Acknowledgement required. (Delaware Code, Title 25, Section 154). The recorders are authorized to set format and size of document. (Delaware Code, Title 9, Section 9605). Affidavit of residence and gain (Delaware Code, Title 9, Section 9605). Recorder shall not accept for recording any deed until the recorder has received payment of all state and municipal realty transfer tax due on the transfer. (Delaware Code, Title 9, Section 9605).

District of Columbia (Washington D.C.)

State Landlord-Tenant Statutes: District of Columbia Code Annotated, Section 42-3201 to 42-4097.

State Property Laws Statutes: District of Columbia Code Annotated, Personal Property, Title 41 and Real Property, Title 42.

State Law Website: http://dccouncil.washington.dc.us/

State Real Estate Disclosure Laws: No statutory form. Use basic Real Estate Disclosure Form in Chapter 4 and on the Forms-on-CD. (District of Columbia Code Annotated, Section 42-1301).

Landlord's Entry to Real Estate: No statute.

Security Deposit Amount Limits: 1 month's rent. (District of Columbia Code Annotated, Section 42-3502-17 and District of Columbia Municipal Regulations, Title 14, Sections, 308 to 311).

Deadlines for Security Deposit Returns: 45 days. (District of Columbia Code Annotated, Section 42-3502-17 and District of Columbia Municipal Regulations, Title 14, Sections, 308 to 311).

Interest Required on Security Deposit: Yes. (District of Columbia Code Annotated, Section 42-3502-17 and District of Columbia Municipal Regulations, Title 14, Sections, 308 to 311).

Separate Account required for Security Deposit: Yes (District of Columbia Code Annotated, Section 42.3502.17 and District of Columbia Municipal Regulations, Title 14, Sections, 308 to 311).

Exemption from Security Deposit Laws: None. (District of Columbia Code Annotated, Section 42-3502-17 and District of Columbia Municipal Regulations, Title 14, Sections, 308 to 311).

Notice Required to Change or Terminate Month-to-Month Tenancy: 30 days to terminate or change rent. (District of Columbia Code Annotated, Section 42-3202).

Rent Late Fees: No statute.

Required Landlord Disclosures: Landlord must provide the tenant with a copy of the DC Landlord and Tenant Law, Landlord and Tenant Civil Enforcement Policy; and Landlord and Tenant Notification of Tenant's Concerning Violations (14 D.C. Municipal Regulations, Section 300).

When and Where Rent is Due: None.

Notary Acknowledgment: Standard Notary Block acceptable. (District of Columbia Code Annotated, Section 42-148).

Lien: Standard Claim of Lien form acceptable. (District of Columbia Code Annotated, Section 40-301-01).

Other Recording Requirements: Must be acknowledged, under seal. (District of Columbia Code Annotated, Section 42-401). Nothing will be recorded if taxes are owing under Chapter 11 of Title 42. (District of Columbia Code Annotated, Section 42-407). The Recorder of Deeds shall not accept for recordation any instrument unless the instrument is executed and acknowledged by the person granting his/her right, title, or interest in the land or any instrument for property against which a lien for delinquent water, sanitary, sewer, or meter service charges has been assessed. (District of Columbia Code Annotated, Section 42-407 and Section 34-2407.02). All documents by which legal title to real property, or an estate for life or a lease for a term of at least 30 years is transferred must be recorded with the Recorder of Deeds within 30 days of execution. (District of Columbia Code Annotated, Section 47-1431(a). Failure to record within the 30 day period will result in a $250 penalty. (District of Columbia Code Annotated, Section 47-1433(c)).

Florida

State Landlord-Tenant Statutes: Florida Statutes, Sections 83.40-83.682.

State Property Laws Statutes: Florida Statutes, Title XL., Chapters 689-723.

State Law Website: http://www.leg.state.fl.us/

State Real Estate Disclosure Laws: No statutory form. Use basic Real Estate Disclosure Form in Chapter 4 and on the Forms-on-CD.

Landlord's Entry to Real Estate: Immediate access for emergency. 12 hour notice for inspection, repairs and viewing of property and if tenant is absent for long periods. (Florida Statutes, Section 83.53).

Security Deposit Amount Limits: No limit in statute. (Florida Statutes, Section 83.53).

Deadlines for Security Deposit Returns: 15 to 60 days. This depends on if renter argues deductions.

(Florida Statutes, Section 83.49).

Interest Required on Security Deposit: Are not required. (Florida Statutes, Section 83.49).

Separate Account required for Security Deposit: Yes. (Florida Statutes, Section 83.49).

Exemption from Security Deposit Laws: None. (Florida Statutes, Section 83.49).

Notice Required to Change or Terminate Month-to-Month Tenancy: 15 days to terminate or change rent. (Florida Statutes, Section 83.57).

Rent Late Fees: No statute.

Required Landlord Disclosures: Landlord must disclose the name and address the manager of the property and the name and address for the purpose of receiving notices. If property is over 3 stories, landlord must provide information about fire protection. (Florida Statutes, Section 83.50).

When and Where Rent is Due: Details of when rent is due. (Florida Statutes, Section 83.46(1)).

Notary Acknowledgment: Standard Notary Block acceptable. (Florida Statutes, Section 117.05).

Lien: In addition to standard Claim of Lien form, the following language is necessary: "Warning! This legal document reflects that a construction lien has been placed on the real property listed herein. Unless the owner of such property takes action to shorten the time period, this lien may remain valid for one year from the date of recording, and shall expire and become null and void thereafter unless legal proceedings have been commenced to foreclose or to discharge this lien." (Florida Statutes, Section 713.08).

Other Recording Requirements: Clerks of the Circuit Court will not accept for recordation instruments unless there is a 3" x 3" blank space at the top right-hand corner of the first page and a 1" x 3" blank space at the top right-hand corner of each subsequent page. (Florida Statutes, Section 695.26(1)(e)).

Georgia

State Landlord-Tenant Statutes: Georgia Code, Sections 44-7-1 to 44-7-81.

State Property Laws Statutes: Georgia Code, Title 44.

State Law Website: http://www.legis.state.ga.us/

State Real Estate Disclosure Laws: No statutory form. Use basic Real Estate Disclosure Form in Chapter 4 and on the Forms-on-CD.

Landlord's Entry to Real Estate: No statute.

Security Deposit Amount Limits: No limit in statute. (Georgia Code, Sections 44-7-30 to 44-7-37).

Deadlines for Security Deposit Returns: 1 month. (Georgia Code, Sections 44-7-30 to 44-7-37).

Interest Required on Security Deposit: No. (Georgia Code, Sections 44-7-30 to 44-7-37).

Separate Account required for Security Deposit: Yes. (Georgia Code, Sections 44-7-30 to 44-7-37).

Exemption from Security Deposit Laws: Exemption for landlord who owns 10 or less rental units. Exemption does not apply if rental units are managed by an outside agency. (Georgia Code, Sections 44-7-30 to 44-7-37).

Notice Required to Change or Terminate Month-to-Month Tenancy: 30 days for tenant to terminate or change rent. 60 days for landlord to terminate or change rent. (Georgia Code, Sections 44-7-7).

Rent Late Fees: No statute.

Required Landlord Disclosures: Prior to collecting any security deposit, landlord must provide tenant a list of pre-existing conditions. Landlord must also disclose if property has flooded more than 3 times in the last 5 years. (Georgia Code, Section 44-7-20).

When and Where Rent is Due: None.

Notary Acknowledgment: Standard Notary Block acceptable. (Georgia Code, Sections 45-17-1).

Lien: In addition to standard Claim of Lien form, the following language is necessary: This claim of lien expires and is void 395 days from the date of filing of the claim of lien if no notice of commencement of lien action is filed in that time period. (Georgia Code, Sections 44-14-367). When explaining when the claim became due, the phrase which is the last date the labor, services or materials were supplied to the premises must be used. (Georgia Code, Sections 44-14-361.1). Further, there must be notice in the claim to the owner that he has the right to contest the lien. Georgia Code, Sections 44-14-368).

Other Recording Requirements: Document must contain two witnesses, one of who must be a notary with his seal affixed, or if one of the two witnesses is not a notary, then there must be an acknowledgment by a notary attached to the deed. (Georgia Code, Section 44-2-21 and Section 4402014). In order to record a warranty deed or quitclaim deed a real estate transfer tax form must be presented to the clerk at the time of filing with the deed. (Georgia Code, Section 48-6-4).

Hawaii

State Landlord-Tenant Statutes: Hawaii Revised Statutes, Sections 521-1 to 521-78.

State Property Laws Statutes: Hawaii Revised Statutes, Volume 12, Chapter 0501 to 0588.

State Law Website:
http://www.capitol.hawaii.gov

State Real Estate Disclosure Laws: No statutory form. Use basic Real Estate Disclosure Form in Chapter 4 and on the Forms-on-CD. (Hawaii Revised Statutes 508D-4(2)).

Landlord's Entry to Real Estate: Immediate access for emergency. 2 day notice for inspection, repairs and viewing of property and if tenant is absent for long periods. (Hawaii Revised Statutes, Sections 521-53 to 521-70(b)).

Security Deposit Amount Limits: 1 month's rent. Landlord may not require any other fees from tenant, other than first month's rent.. (Hawaii Revised Statutes, Section 521-43 and 521-44).

Deadlines for Security Deposit Returns: 14 days. (Hawaii Revised Statutes, Section 521-44).

Interest Required on Security Deposit: No. (Hawaii Revised Statutes, Section 521-44).

Separate Account required for Security Deposit: No. (Hawaii Revised Statutes, Section 521-44).

Exemption from Security Deposit Laws: None. (Hawaii Revised Statutes, Section 521-44).

Notice Required to Change or Terminate Month-to-Month Tenancy: 28 days for tenant to terminate or change rent. 45 days for landlord to terminate or change rent. (Hawaii Revised Statutes, Section 521-71, 521-21(d)).

Rent Late Fees: No statute.

Required Landlord Disclosures: Landlord must disclose the name and address the manager of the property; if manager is off-island, must provide name and address of on-island agent. Move-in/move-out checklist is required. Landlord must provide tenant with tax excise number so tenant can claim low-income tax credit. (Hawaii Revised Statutes, Sections 521-42 and 521-43).

When and Where Rent is Due: Details of when and where rent is due. (Hawaii Revised Statutes, Section 521-21(b).

Notary Acknowledgment: Standard Notary Block acceptable. (Hawaii Revised Statutes, Section 502-41).

Lien: Standard Claim of Lien form acceptable. (Hawaii Revised Statutes, Section 507-42+).

Other Recording Requirements: Acknowledgment required, interlineations, erasures and changes must be initialed by the notary. The marital status of all parties must be stated, the full name of the spouse must be stated if a party is married and the instrument must contain a reference to the current Transfer Certificate of Title affected by the instrument. (Hawaii Revised Statutes, Section 502-31 and Section 501-108).

Idaho

State Landlord-Tenant Statutes: Idaho Code, Sections 55-201 to 55-313 and 6-301 to 6-324.
State Property Laws Statutes: Idaho Code, Title 55.
State Law Website: http://www.state.id.us/**State Real Estate Disclosure Laws:** Seller Property Disclosure Form. (Idaho Code, Section 55-2501). (This form is provided on the Forms-on-CD).
Landlord's Entry to Real Estate: No statute.
Security Deposit Amount Limits: No limit in statute. (Idaho Code, Section 6-321).
Deadlines for Security Deposit Returns: 21 days. Up to 30 days if both parties agree. (Idaho Code, Section 6-321).
Interest Required on Security Deposit: No. (Idaho Code, Section 6-321).
Separate Account required for Security Deposit: No. (Idaho Code, Section 6-321).
Exemption from Security Deposit Laws: None. (Idaho Code, Section 6-321).
Notice Required to Change or Terminate Month-to-Month Tenancy: 1 month notice for tenant to terminate or change rent. 1 month notice for landlord to terminate rent. Landlord must provide 15 day's notice to increase rent or change tenancy. (Idaho Code, Sections 55-208 and 55-307).
Rent Late Fees: No statute.
Required Landlord Disclosures: None.
When and Where Rent is Due: None.
Notary Acknowledgment: Standard Notary Block acceptable. (Idaho Code, Section 51-109).
Lien: Standard Claim of Lien form acceptable. (Idaho Code, Section 45-501+).
Other Recording Requirements: None.

Illinois

State Landlord-Tenant Statutes: Illinois Compiled Statutes, Chapter. 765, Sections 705/0.01 to 740/5.
State Property Laws Statutes: Illinois Compiled Statutes, Chapter 765.
State Law Website: http://www.illinois.gov/government/
State Real Estate Disclosure Laws: Residential Real Property Disclosure Report. (Illinois Compiled Statutes, Chapter. 765 ILCS 77). (This form provided on the Forms-on-CD).
Landlord's Entry to Real Estate: No statute.
Security Deposit Amount Limits: No limit in statute. (Illinois Compiled Statutes, Chapter. 765, Sections 710/0.01 to 715/3).
Deadlines for Security Deposit Returns: 30 days. Up to 45 days if renter argues deductions. (Illinois Compiled Statutes, Chapter. 765, Sections 710/0.01 to 715/3).
Interest Required on Security Deposit: Required for landlords with more than 25 rental units. (Illinois Compiled Statutes, Chapter. 765, Sections 710/0.01 to 715/3).
Separate Account required for Security Deposit: No. (Illinois Compiled Statutes, Chapter. 765, Sections 710/0.01 to 715/3).
Exemption from Security Deposit Laws: Landlords with 4 or less rental units are exempt. (Illinois Compiled Statutes, Chapter. 765, Sections 710/0.01 to 715/3).
Notice Required to Change or Terminate Month-to-Month Tenancy: 30 days to terminate or change rent. (Illinois Compiled Statutes, Chapter. 735, Section 5/9-207).
Rent Late Fees: No statute.
Required Landlord Disclosures: If landlord pays a master metered utility, tenant must be provided with written information regarding the formula used to allocate tenant amounts. Any rent concessions must be noted in lease, with letters not less than 1/2" high stating "Concession Granted. (Illinois

Compiled Statutes, Chapter. 765, Section 730/0 to 730-6, and 740/5).

When and Where Rent is Due: Details of when rent is due. (Illinois Compiled Statutes, Chapter 765, Section 705/3).

Notary Acknowledgment: Standard Notary Block acceptable. (Illinois Compiled Statutes, Chapter. 5, Section 312/6-105).

Lien: Standard Claim of Lien form acceptable. (Illinois Compiled Statutes, Chapter. 770, Section 60/0.01+).

Other Recording Requirements: Proper notary/acknowledgement and property index number (PIN) required. (Illinois Compiled Statutes, Chapter 765, Section 5).

Indiana

State Landlord-Tenant Statutes: Indiana Code, Sections 32-31-1-1 to 32-31-8-6.

State Property Laws Statutes: Indiana Code, Title 32.

State Law Website: http://www.state.in.us/**State Real Estate Disclosure Laws:** Seller's Residential Real Estate Sales Disclosure. (Indiana Code, Section 32-21-5). (This form is provided on the Forms-on-CD).

Landlord's Entry to Real Estate: No statute.

Security Deposit Amount Limits: No limits in statute. (Indiana Code, Sections 32-31-3-9 to 32-31-3-19).

Deadlines for Security Deposit Returns: 45 days. (Indiana Code, Sections 32-31-3-9 to 32-31-3-19).

Interest Required on Security Deposit: No. (Indiana Code, Sections 32-31-3-9 to 32-31-3-19).

Separate Account required for Security Deposit: No. (Indiana Code, Sections 32-31-3-9 to 32-31-3-19).

Exemption from Security Deposit Laws: None. (Indiana Code, Sections 32-31-3-9 to 32-31-3-19).

Notice Required to Change or Terminate Month-to-Month Tenancy: 1 month to terminate

or change rent. (Indiana Code, Sections 32-31-1-1).

Rent Late Fees: No statute.

Required Landlord Disclosures: Landlord must disclose the name and address of an Indiana resident manager of the property and the name and address for the purpose of receiving notices. (Indiana Code, Section 32-31-3-18).

When and Where Rent is Due: Details of when rent is due. (No statute. Found in Indiana case law.)

Notary Acknowledgment: Standard Notary Block acceptable. (Indiana Code, Sections 33-42-1+).

Lien: Standard Claim of Lien form acceptable. (Indiana Code, Sections 32-28-3-1+).

Other Recording Requirements: Permanently bound documents and continuous form paper is forbidden. (Indiana Code, Section 36-2-11-16.5). A standard Sales Disclosure form must be filed with the Auditor's office at a filing fee of $10.00 when a conveyance document is filed with the Auditor's office. (Indiana Code, Section 6-1.1-5.5).

Iowa

State Landlord-Tenant Statutes: Iowa Code Annotated, Sections 562A.1-.36.

State Property Laws Statutes: Iowa Code, Title XIV.

State Law Website: www.legis.state.ia.us/ **State Real Estate Disclosure Laws:** Residential Property Seller Disclosure Statement. (Iowa Code Annotated, Section 558A.1). (This form is provided on the Forms-on-CD).

Landlord's Entry to Real Estate: Immediate access for emergency. 24 hour notice for inspection, repairs, viewing of property and if tenant is absent for long periods. (Iowa Code Annotated, Sections 562A.19, 562A.28 and 562A.29).

Security Deposit Amount Limits:
2 month's rent. (Iowa Code Annotated, Section 562A.12).

Deadlines for Security Deposit Returns: 30 days. (Iowa Code Annotated, Section 562A.12).

Interest Required on Security Deposit: Interest payments are not required. (Iowa Code Annotated, Section 562A.12).

Separate Account required for Security Deposit: Yes. (Iowa Code Annotated, Section 562A.12).

Exemption from Security Deposit Laws: None. (Iowa Code Annotated, Section 562A.12).

Notice Required to Change or Terminate Month-to-Month Tenancy: 30 days to terminate or change rent. (Iowa Code Annotated, Sections 562A.34 and 562A.13(5)).

Rent Late Fees: Late fees cannot exceed $10.00 per day or $40.00 a month. (Iowa Code Annotated, Section 535.2(7)).

Required Landlord Disclosures: Landlord must disclose the name and address of the manager of the property and the name and address for the purpose of receiving notices. If utilities are shared, landlord must disclose how utilities are allocated. Landlord must disclose if property is listed in any federal environmental contamination register system. (Iowa Code, Section 562A.13).

When and Where Rent is Due: Details of when and where rent is due. (Iowa Code Annotated, Section 562A.9(3).

Notary Acknowledgment: Standard Notary Block acceptable. (Iowa Code Annotated, Section 1-4-9E.15).

Lien: Standard Claim of Lien form acceptable. (Iowa Code Annotated, Section 572.1+).

Other Recording Requirements: None.

Kansas

State Landlord-Tenant Statutes: Kansas Statutes, Sections 58-2501 to 58-2573.

State Property Laws Statutes: Kansas Statutes, Chapters 58 and 67.

State Law Website:
http://www.accesskansas.org/

State Real Estate Disclosure Laws: No statutory form. Use basic Real Estate Disclosure Form in Chapter 4 and on the Forms-on-CD.

Landlord's Entry to Real Estate: Immediate access for emergency. "Reasonable" notice for inspection, repairs, viewing of property and if tenant is absent for long periods. (Kansas Statutes, Sections 58-2557 and 58-2565).

Security Deposit Amount Limits: 1 month's rent unfurnished. 1 ½ month's rent furnished. Additional ½ month's rent for pet deposit. (Kansas Statutes, Section 58-2550).

Deadlines for Security Deposit Returns: 30 days. (Kansas Statutes, Section 58-2550).

Interest Required on Security Deposit: No. (Kansas Statutes, Section 58-2550).

Separate Account required for Security Deposit: No. (Kansas Statutes, Section 58-2550).

Exemption from Security Deposit Laws: None. (Kansas Statutes, Section 58-2550).

Notice Required to Change or Terminate Month-to-Month Tenancy: 30 days to terminate rent. No amount of notice in statute for changing rent. (Kansas Statutes, Section 58-2550).

Rent Late Fees: No statute.

Required Landlord Disclosures: Landlord must disclose the name and address of the manager of the property and the name and address for the purpose of receiving notices. Within 5 days of move-in, landlord and tenant must complete an inventory of the property. (Kansas Statutes, Section 58-2548).

When and Where Rent is Due: Details of when and where rent is due. (Kansas Statutes, Section 58-2545(c).

Notary Acknowledgment: Standard Notary Block acceptable. (Kansas Statutes, Section 53-509).

Lien: Standard Claim of Lien form acceptable. However, must include a detailed itemized statement. (Kansas Statutes, Section 60-1101+).

Other Recording Requirements: None.

Kentucky

State Landlord-Tenant Statutes: Kentucky Revised Statutes, Sections 383.010 to 383.715.

State Property Laws Statutes: Kentucky Revised Statutes, Title XXXII.

State Law Website: http://www.lrc.state.ky.us/

State Real Estate Disclosure Laws: Seller's Disclosure of Property Conditions. (Kentucky Revised Statutes, Section 324.360). (This form is provided on the Forms-on-CD).

Landlord's Entry to Real Estate: Immediate access for emergency. 2 day notice for inspection, repairs and viewing of property and if tenant is absent for long periods. (Kentucky Revised Statutes, Section 383.615).

Security Deposit Amount Limits: No limit in statute, but see also .

Deadlines for Security Deposit Returns: 30 days. Up to 60 days if renter argues deductions. (Kentucky Revised Statutes, Section 383.580).

Interest Required on Security Deposit: No. (Kentucky Revised Statutes, Section 383.580).

Separate Account required for Security Deposit: Yes. (Kentucky Revised Statutes, Section 383.580).

Exemption from Security Deposit Laws: None. (Kentucky Revised Statutes, Section 383.580).

Notice Required to Change or Terminate Month-to-Month Tenancy: 30 days to terminate or change rent. (Kentucky Revised Statutes, Section 383.695).

Rent Late Fees: No statute.

Required Landlord Disclosures: Landlord must disclose the name and address of the manager of the property and the name and address for the purpose of receiving notices. Landlord and tenant must complete an inventory of the property before landlord can collect any security deposit. (Kentucky Revised Statutes, Sections 383.580 and 383.585).

When and Where Rent is Due: Details of when and where rent is due. (Kentucky Revised Statutes, Section 383.565(2)).

Notary Acknowledgment: Standard Notary Block acceptable. (Kentucky Revised Statutes, Section 423.160).

Lien: Standard Claim of Lien form acceptable. (Kentucky Revised Statutes, Section 376.010+).

Other Recording Requirements: Grantor's signature must be notarized, consideration must be given, grantor's source of title must be described, consideration certificate must be completed, deed must be subscribed, and must contain preparer's certification. (Kentucky Revised States, Sections 382.110)

Louisiana

State Landlord-Tenant Statutes: Louisiana Revised Statutes Annotated, Sections 9:3201 to 9:3259 and Louisiana Civil Code Annotated Article 2669 to 2729.

State Property Laws Statutes: Louisiana Revised Statutes Annotated, Title 9, Civil Code Ancillaries, Louisiana Civil Code, Louisiana Code of Civil procedure.

State Law Website: www.legis.state.la.us/

State Real Estate Disclosure Laws: Property Disclosure Document for Residential Real Estate. (Louisiana Revised Statutes Annotated, Title 9, Civil Code Ancillaries, Section 9:3198). (This form is provided on the Forms-on-CD).

Landlord's Entry to Real Estate: No statute.

Security Deposit Amount Limits: No limit in statute. (Louisiana Revised Statutes Annotated, Sections 9:3251 to 9:3254).

Deadlines for Security Deposit Returns: 1 month. (Louisiana Revised Statutes Annotated, Sections 9:3251 to 9:3254).

Interest Required on Security Deposit: No. (Louisiana Revised Statutes Annotated, Sections 9:3251 to 9:3254).

Separate Account required for Security Deposit: No. (Louisiana Revised Statutes Annotated, Sections 9:3251 to 9:3254).

Exemption from Security Deposit Laws: None. (Louisiana Revised Statutes Annotated, Sections 9:3251 to 9:3254).

Notice Required to Change or Terminate Month-to-Month Tenancy: 10 days to terminate or change rent. (Louisiana Civil Code Annotated, Article 2686).

Rent Late Fees: No statute.

Required Landlord Disclosures: None.

When and Where Rent is Due: Details of when and where rent is due. (Louisiana Civil Code, Article 2703(1)).

Notary Acknowledgment: Standard Notary Block acceptable. (Louisiana Revised Statutes Annotated, Sections 35-8-511).

Lien: Standard Claim of Lien form acceptable. (Louisiana Revised Statutes Annotated, Sections 9:4801+).

Other Recording Requirements: Any waiver of warranty must be specifically and expressly included in the document. (Louisiana Civil Code Annotated, Article 3340). The marital status including name of present spouse must be included. (Louisiana Civil Code Annotated, Article 3352).

Maine

State Landlord-Tenant Statutes: Maine Revised Statutes, Title 14, Sections 6021 to 6046.

State Property Laws Statutes: Maine Revised Statutes Title 33.

State Law Website: janus.state.me.us/legis/

State Real Estate Disclosure Laws: Property Disclosure Statement. (Maine Revised Statutes, Section 33-7-1A-171) (This form is provided on the Forms-on-CD)..

Landlord's Entry to Real Estate: Immediate access for emergency. 24 hour notice for inspection, repairs and viewing of property and if tenant is absent for long periods. (Maine Revised Statutes, Title 14, Section 6025).

Security Deposit Amount Limits: 2 month's rent. (Maine Revised Statutes, Title 14, Sections 6031 to 6038).

Deadlines for Security Deposit Returns: 30 days if rental agreement is in writing. 21 days if agreement is verbal. (Maine Revised Statutes, Title 14, Sections 6031 to 6038).

Interest Required on Security Deposit: No. (Maine Revised Statutes, Title 14, Sections 6031 to 6038).

Separate Account required for Security Deposit: Yes. (Maine Revised Statutes, Title 14, Sections 6031 to 6038).

Exemption from Security Deposit Laws: Exemption if rental structure has 5 or less rental units and the landlord is also living in one of the rental units. (Maine Revised Statutes, Title 14, Sections 6031 to 6038).

Notice Required to Change or Terminate Month-to-Month Tenancy: 30 days to terminate rent. Landlord must provide 45 day's notice to increase rent. (Maine Revised Statutes, Title 14, Sections 6002 and 6015).

Rent Late Fees: Late fees cannot exceed 4% of the amount due for 30 days. Landlord must notify in writing any late fee at the start of tenancy and cannot impose it until rent is 15 days late. (Maine Revised Statutes, Title 14, Section 6028).

Required Landlord Disclosures: If property is a multi-unit with common area utilities, must be written agreement regarding tenant share of common utilities. Landlord must provide tenant with a residential energy efficiency disclosure statement and landlord and tenant must sign this disclosure. Maine Revised Statutes, Title 14, Section 6030(c)).

When and Where Rent is Due: None. However, there are grace periods for rent payments. (Maine Revised Statutes, Title 14, Section 6028).

Notary Acknowledgment: Standard Notary Block acceptable. (Maine Revised Statutes, Title 4, Section 1016).

Lien: Standard Claim of Lien form acceptable. (Maine Revised Statutes, Title 10, Section 3251+).

Other Recording Requirements: None.

Maryland

State Landlord-Tenant Statutes: Maryland Code, Real Property, Sections 8-101 to 8-604.

State Property Laws Statutes: Maryland Code, Real Property.

State Law Website: http://www.maryland.gov/

State Real Estate Disclosure Laws: Residential Property Disclosure and Disclaimer Statement. (Maryland Code, Real Property, Section 10-702). (This form is provided on the Forms-on-CD).

Landlord's Entry to Real Estate: No statute.

Security Deposit Amount Limits: 2 month's rent. (Maryland Code, Real Property, Sections 8-203 to 8-203.1).

Deadlines for Security Deposit Returns: 30 days. Up to 45 days if renter was evicted or abandoned the rental unit. (Maryland Code, Real Property, Sections 8-203 to 8-203.1).

Interest Required on Security Deposit: Yes. (Maryland Code, Real Property, Sections 8-203 to 8-203.1).

Separate Account required for Security Deposit: Yes. (Maryland Code, Real Property, Sections 8-203 to 8-203.1).

Exemption from Security Deposit Laws: None. (Maryland Code, Real Property, Sections 8-203 to 8-203.1).

Notice Required to Change or Terminate Month-to-Month Tenancy: 1 month to terminate or change rent. 2 month's notice in Montgomery County. Does not apply to Baltimore. (Maryland Code, Real Property, Sections 8-402(b)(3) and 8-402(b)(4)).

Rent Late Fees: Late fees cannot exceed 5% of the rent due. (Maryland Code, Real Property, Sections 8-208(d)(3)).

Required Landlord Disclosures: Landlord must disclose the name and address of the manager of the property and the name and address for the purpose of receiving notices. Landlord and tenant must complete an inventory of the property before landlord can collect any security deposit. Lease must contain statement that the premises are habitable, if that is the reason for rental, and a statement regarding tenant's responsibilities for utilities and repairs. (Maryland Code, Real Property, Sections 8-203.1, 8-20, and 8-210).

When and Where Rent is Due: None.

Notary Acknowledgment: Standard Notary Block acceptable. (Maryland Code, State Government, Section 19-107).

Lien: Standard Claim of Lien form acceptable. (Maryland Code, Real Property, Sections 9-101+).

Other Recording Requirements: All real estate taxes and assessments must be paid prior to recordation. (Maryland Code, Real Property, Section 3-104(b)). All deeds must recite the amount of consideration payable. (Maryland Code, Real Property, Section 3-104(g)). Must include a Certification of Preparation indicating that the instrument has been prepared by an attorney or under an attorney's supervision, or a certificate that the instrument was prepared by one of the parties named in the instrument. (Maryland Code, Real Property, Section 3-104(f)). There are also local requirements as to certain counties in Maryland.

Massachusetts

State Landlord-Tenant Statutes: Massachusetts General Laws, Chapter 186, Section 1-21.

State Property Laws Statutes: Massachusetts General Laws, Part I, Real And Personal Property And Domestic Relations, Chapters 183-189.

State Law Website: www.mass.gov/legis

State Real Estate Disclosure Laws: No statutory form. Use basic Real Estate Disclosure Form in Chapter 4 and on the Forms-on-CD.

Landlord's Entry to Real Estate: Immediate access for emergencies; may enter for inspections for damages during last 30 days of lease; may enter if property appears abandoned. Lease may provide landlord access for repairs, reasonable inspections, and to show the premises to a prospective tenant or buyer. (Massachusetts General Laws, Chapter 186, Section 15B(1)(a)).

Security Deposit Amount Limits: 1 month's rent. (Massachusetts General Laws, Chapter 186, Section 15B).

Deadlines for Security Deposit Returns: 30 days. (Massachusetts General Laws, Chapter 186, Section 15B).

Interest Required on Security Deposit: Yes. (Massachusetts General Laws, Chapter 186, Section 15B).

Separate Account required for Security Deposit: Yes. (Massachusetts General Laws, Chapter 186, Section 15B).

Exemption from Security Deposit Laws: None. (Massachusetts General Laws, Chapter 186, Section 15B).

Notice Required to Change or Terminate Month-to-Month Tenancy: Length of tenancy period or 30 days (whichever is longer). (Massachusetts General Laws, Chapter 186, Section 12).

Rent Late Fees: Late fees, including interest on late rent, cannot be imposed until the rent is 30 days late. (Massachusetts General Laws, Chapter 186, Section 15B(1)(c)).

Required Landlord Disclosures: Upon tenant's request, landlord must provide name and coverages for any insurance policies in force for loss or damage by fire. . (Massachusetts General Laws, Chapter 186, Section 15-B(2)(c) and 21).

When and Where Rent is Due: None. However, there are provisions for rental payment grace periods. (Massachusetts General Laws, Chapter 186, Section 15-B(1)(c)).

Notary Acknowledgment: Standard Notary Block acceptable. (Revised Executive Order No. 455 (04-04).

Lien: Standard Claim of Lien form acceptable. (Massachusetts General Laws, Chapter 254, Section 1+).

Other Recording Requirements: All deeds must be acknowledged. Notaries taken outside the Commonwealth of Massachusetts must be seal and notaries taken outside of the country must be accompanied by a Certificate of Authority. (Massachusetts General Laws, Chapter 183, Section 29). Full consideration must be paid with state excise of documentary stamps affixed. (Massachusetts General Laws, Chapter 183, Section 6). Other instruments such as Affidavits, Powers of Attorney and Trustee's Certificates must all be executed and acknowledged. (Massachusetts General Laws, Chapter 183, Section 29-40).

Michigan

State Landlord-Tenant Statutes: Michigan Compiled Laws, Section 554.601-.640.

State Property Laws Statutes: Michigan Compiled Laws, Chapters 554 to 570.

State Law Website: www.michiganlegislature.org

State Real Estate Disclosure Laws: Seller's Disclosure Statement. (Michigan Compiled Laws, Section 565.957). (This form is provided on the Forms-on-CD).

Landlord's Entry to Real Estate: No statute.

Security Deposit Amount Limits: 1 ½ month's rent. (Michigan Compiled Laws, Sections 554.602 to 554.613).

Deadlines for Security Deposit Returns: 30 days. (Michigan Compiled Laws, Sections 554.602 to 554.613).

Interest Required on Security Deposit: No. (Michigan Compiled Laws, Sections 554.602 to 554.613).

Separate Account required for Security Deposit: Yes. (Michigan Compiled Laws, Sections 554.602 to 554.613).

Exemption from Security Deposit Laws: None. (Michigan Compiled Laws, Sections 554.602 to 554.613).

Notice Required to Change or Terminate Month-to-Month Tenancy: Length of tenancy period. (Michigan Compiled Laws, Sections 554.134).

Rent Late Fees: No statute.

Required Landlord Disclosures: Landlord must disclose the name and address of the manager of the property and the name and address for the purpose of receiving notices. Move-in/move-out checklists are required. Lease must state in at least 12 point type the following: "NOTICE: Michigan law establishes rights and obligations for parties to rental agreements. This rental agreement is required to comply with the Truth in Rental Act. If you have a question about the interpretation or legality of a provision of this agreement, you may want to seek the assistance of a lawyer or other qualified person." (Michigan Compiled Laws, Sections 554.608 and 554.634).

When and Where Rent is Due: Details of when rent is due. (No statute, but details in Michigan case law).

Notary Acknowledgment: Standard Notary Block acceptable. (Michigan Compiled Laws, Sections 565.267).

Lien: Standard Claim of Lien form acceptable. (Michigan Compiled Laws, Sections 570.1101+).

Other Recording Requirements: Requirements include notarial certificate, two witnesses, name and business addresses of individual drafter/preparer, reference number, and marital status of all male grantors. (Michigan Compiled Laws, Section 565.8). Every deed must contain a recital of consideration given. (Michigan Compiled Laws, Section 565.151).

Minnesota

State Landlord-Tenant Statutes: Minnesota Statutes Sections 504B.001 to 504B.471.

State Property Laws Statutes: Minnesota Statutes, Chapters 500-566.

State Law Website: http://www.leg.state.mn.us/

State Real Estate Disclosure Laws: No statutory form. Use basic Real Estate Disclosure Form in Chapter 4 and on the Forms-on-CD.

Landlord's Entry to Real Estate: Immediate access for emergency. "Reasonable" notice for inspection, repairs and viewing of property. (Minnesota Statutes, Section 504B.211).

Security Deposit Amount Limits: No limit in statute. (Minnesota Statutes, Sections 504B.175 to 504B.178).

Deadlines for Security Deposit Returns: 3 weeks. 5 days if rental unit is condemned. (Minnesota Statutes, Sections 504B.175 to 504B.178).

Interest Required on Security Deposit: Yes. (Minnesota Statutes, Sections 504B.175 to 504B.178).

Separate Account required for Security Deposit: No. (Minnesota Statutes, Sections 504B.175 to 504B.178).

Exemption from Security Deposit Laws: None. (Minnesota Statutes, Sections 504B.175 to 504B.178).

Notice Required to Change or Terminate Month-to-Month Tenancy: Length between time rent is due. (Minnesota Statutes, Section 504B.135).

Rent Late Fees: No statute.

Required Landlord Disclosures: Landlord must disclose the name and address of the manager of the property and the name and address for the purpose of receiving notices. (Minnesota Statutes, Section 504B.151, 504B.181 and 504B.195).

When and Where Rent is Due: None.

Notary Acknowledgment: Standard Notary Block acceptable. (Minnesota Statutes, Section 358.48).

Lien: Standard Claim of Lien form acceptable. (Minnesota Statutes, Section 514.01+).

Other Recording Requirements: Title of the document must be prominently displayed at the top of the first page and no additional sheet shall be attached or affixed to a page that covers up any information or printed part of the form. (Minnesota Statutes, Section 507.151). Must pay a transfer tax. (Minnesota Statutes, Sections 287.21-287.33).

Mississippi

State Landlord-Tenant Statutes: Mississippi Code, Sections 89-8-1 to 89-8-27.

State Property Laws Statutes: Mississippi Code, Title 89.

State Law Website: http://www.mscode.com/

State Real Estate Disclosure Laws: Seller's Disclosure Statement. (Mississippi Code, Section 89-1-501). (This form is provided on the Forms-on-CD).

Landlord's Entry to Real Estate: No statute.

Security Deposit Amount Limits: No limit in statute. (Mississippi Code, Section 89-8-21).

Deadlines for Security Deposit Returns: 45 days. (Mississippi Code, Section 89-8-21).

Interest Required on Security Deposit: No. (Mississippi Code, Section 89-8-21).

Separate Account required for Security Deposit: No. (Mississippi Code, Section 89-8-21).

Exemption from Security Deposit Laws: None. (Mississippi Code, Section 89-8-21).

Notice Required to Change or Terminate Month-to-Month Tenancy: 30 days to terminate or change rent. (Mississippi Code, Section 89-8-19).

Rent Late Fees: No statute.

Required Landlord Disclosures: None.

When and Where Rent is Due: None.

Notary Acknowledgment: Standard Notary Block acceptable. (Mississippi Code, Section 89-3-7).

Lien: Standard Claim of Lien form acceptable. (Mississippi Code, Section 85-7-131+).

Other Recording Requirements: Must be properly acknowledged, must contain instructions as to how the instrument is to be indexed, and the name, address and telephone number of the person, firm, or entity preparing the document must be included. (Mississippi Code, Section 89-5-1).

Missouri

State Landlord-Tenant Statutes: Missouri Revised Statutes, Sections 441.005 to 441.880 and 535.150 to 535.300.

State Property Laws Statutes: Missouri Revised Statutes, Title 29.

State Law Website: www.mo.gov/

State Real Estate Disclosure Laws: No statutory form. Use basic Real Estate Disclosure Form in Chapter 4 and on the Forms-on-CD.

Landlord's Entry to Real Estate: No statute.

Security Deposit Amount Limits: 2 month's rent. (Missouri Revised Statutes, Section 535.300).

Deadlines for Security Deposit Returns: 30 days. (Missouri Revised Statutes, Section 535.300).

Interest Required on Security Deposit: No. (Missouri Revised Statutes, Section 535.300).

Separate Account required for Security Deposit: No. (Missouri Revised Statutes, Section 535.300).

Exemption from Security Deposit Laws: None. (Missouri Revised Statutes, Section 535.300).

Notice Required to Change or Terminate Month-to-Month Tenancy: 1 month to terminate or change rent. (Missouri Revised Statutes, Section 441.060).

Rent Late Fees: No statute.

Required Landlord Disclosures: None.

When and Where Rent is Due: Details of when rent is due. (Missouri Revised Statutes. Section 535.060).

Notary Acknowledgment: Standard Notary Block acceptable. (Missouri Revised Statutes, Section 486.330).

Lien: Standard Claim of Lien form acceptable. (Missouri Revised Statutes, Section 429.010+).

Other Recording Requirements: None.

Montana

State Landlord-Tenant Statutes: Montana Code, Sections 70-24-101 to 70-25-206.

State Property Laws Statutes: Montana Code, Title 70.

State Law Website: http://leg.state.mt.gov

State Real Estate Disclosure Laws: No statutory form. Use basic Real Estate Disclosure Form in Chapter 4 and on the Forms-on-CD.

Landlord's Entry to Real Estate: Immediate access for emergency. 24 hour notice for inspection, repairs and viewing of property and if tenant is absent for long periods. (Montana Code, Section 70-24-312).

Security Deposit Amount Limits: No limit in statute. (Montana Code, Sections 70-25-101 to 70-25-206).

Deadlines for Security Deposit Returns: 30

days. 10 days if no deductions are made. (Montana Code Sections 70-25-101 to 70-25-206).

Interest Required on Security Deposit: No. (Montana Code Sections 70-25-101 to 70-25-206).

Separate Account required for Security Deposit: No. (Montana Code Sections 70-25-101 to 70-25-206).

Exemption from Security Deposit Laws: None. (Montana Code Sections 70-25-101 to 70-25-206).

Notice Required to Change or Terminate Month-to-Month Tenancy: 30 days to terminate or change rent. (Montana Code, Section 70-24-441).

Rent Late Fees: No statute.

Required Landlord Disclosures: Landlord must disclose the name and address the manager of the property and the name and address for the purpose of receiving notices. Landlord and tenant must complete an inventory of the property before landlord can collect any security deposit. No non-refundable fees, such as a cleaning fee, are permitted. (Montana Code, Section 70-24-301, 70-25-101(40) and 70-25-206)).

When and Where Rent is Due: Details of when and where rent is due. (Montana Code, Section 70-24-201(2)(b) and 70-24-201(2)(c)).

Notary Acknowledgment: Standard Notary Block acceptable. (Montana Code, Section 1-5-610).

Lien: Standard Claim of Lien form acceptable. (Montana Code, Section 71-3-521).

Other Recording Requirements: Check the Montana Subdivision and Platting Act when attempting to transfer title to any parcel of land less than 160 acres in size which has not previously been transferred of record such that the current description cannot be referenced to a tract of record. (Montana Code, Section 76-3-101+).

Nebraska

State Landlord-Tenant Statutes: Nebraska Statutes, Sections 76-1401 to 76-1449.

State Property Laws Statutes: Nebraska Statutes, Chapters 69 and 76.

State Law Website:
http://www.unicam.state.ne.us/

State Real Estate Disclosure Laws: Seller Property Condition Disclosure Statement. (Nebraska Statutes, Section 76-2,120). (This form is provided on the Forms-on-CD).

Landlord's Entry to Real Estate: Immediate access for emergency. 1 day notice for inspection, repairs and viewing of property and if tenant is absent for long periods. (Nebraska Statutes, Section 76-1423).

Security Deposit Amount Limits: No limit in statute. (Nebraska Statutes, Section 76-1416).

Deadlines for Security Deposit Returns: 14 days. (Nebraska Statutes, Section 76-1416).

Interest Required on Security Deposit: No. (Nebraska Statutes, Section 76-1416).

Separate Account required for Security Deposit: No. (Nebraska Statutes, Section 76-1416).

Exemption from Security Deposit Laws: None. (Nebraska Statutes, Section 76-1416).

Notice Required to Change or Terminate Month-to-Month Tenancy: 30 days to terminate or change rent. (Nebraska Statutes, Section 76-1437).

Rent Late Fees: No statute.

Required Landlord Disclosures: Landlord must disclose the name and address the manager of the property and the name and address for the purpose of receiving notices. (Nebraska Statutes, Section 76-1416).

When and Where Rent is Due: Details of when and where rent is due. (Nebraska Statutes, Section 76-1414(3)).

Notary Acknowledgment: Standard Notary Block acceptable. (Nebraska Statutes, Section 64-206).

Lien: Standard Claim of Lien form acceptable. (Nebraska Statutes, Section 52-125+).

Other Recording Requirements: Tax statement required. (Nebraska Statutes, Section 76-214). Acknowledgment required. (Nebraska Statutes, Section 76-216).

Nevada

State Landlord-Tenant Statutes: Nevada Revised Statute Annotated, Sections 118A.010 - 118A.520.

State Property Laws Statutes: Nevada Revised Statute Annotated, Title 10.

State Law Website: http://www.leg.state.nv.us/

State Real Estate Disclosure Laws: Seller's Real Property Disclosure Form. (Nevada Revised Statute Annotated, Section 113.060-113.080). (This form is provided on the Forms-on-CD).

Landlord's Entry to Real Estate: Immediate access for emergency. 24 hour notice for inspection, repairs and viewing of property and if tenant is absent for long periods. (Nevada Revised Statute Annotated, Section 118A.330).

Security Deposit Amount Limits: 3 month's rent. (Nevada Revised Statute Annotated, Sections 118A.240 to 118A.250).

Deadlines for Security Deposit Returns: 30 days. (Nevada Revised Statute Annotated, Sections 118A.240 to 118A.250).

Interest Required on Security Deposit: No. (Nevada Revised Statute Annotated, Sections 118A.240 to 118A.250).

Separate Account required for Security Deposit: No. (Nevada Revised Statute Annotated, Sections 118A.240 to 118A.250).

Exemption from Security Deposit Laws: None. (Nevada Revised Statute Annotated, Sections 118A.240 to 118A.250).

Notice Required to Change or Terminate Month-to-Month Tenancy: 30 days to terminate. Landlord must give 45 day notice to raise rent. (Nevada Revised Statute Annotated, Sections 40.251 and 118A.300).

Rent Late Fees: Must be in writing. (Nevada Revised Statute Annotated, Sections 118A.200(3)(g) and 118A.200(4)(c)).

Required Landlord Disclosures: Lease must contain the following: 1) information regarding the right of tenant to display U.S. flag, 2) information regarding tenant's reporting of building, safety, or health code violations; and 3) summary of penalties for maintaining a nuisance. Non-refundable fees are permitted if explained in lease. Lease must also contain a signed inventory and record of the condition of the property. (Nevada Revised Statutes Annotated, Sections 118A.200, 118A.325, and 202.470).

When and Where Rent is Due: Details of when and where rent is due. (Nevada Revised Statute Annotated, Sections 118A.210).

Notary Acknowledgment: Standard Notary Block acceptable. (Nevada Revised Statute Annotated, Sections 240.167+).

Lien: Standard Claim of Lien form acceptable. (Nevada Revised Statute Annotated, Sections 108.221+).

Other Recording Requirements: Acknowledgment required and the mailing address of the grantee and the assessor's parcel number required. (Nevada Revised Statutes, Section 111.312).

New Hampshire

State Landlord-Tenant Statutes: New Hampshire Revised Statutes, Sections 540:1 to 540:29 and 540-A:1 to 540-A:8.

State Property Laws Statutes: New Hampshire Revised Statutes, Titles 46 to 48.

State Law Website: http://www.nh.gov/

State Real Estate Disclosure Laws: No statutory form. Use basic Real Estate Disclosure Form in Chapter 4 and on the Forms-on-CD.

Landlord's Entry to Real Estate: Immediate access for emergency. "Reasonable" notice and prior consent are required for inspection, repairs, viewing of property and entry if tenant is absent for long periods. (New Hampshire Revised Statutes, Section 540-A:3).

Security Deposit Amount Limits: 1 month's rent or $100.00 (which ever is greater). No limit but in writing, if owner resides on the premises. (New Hampshire Revised Statutes, Sections 540-A:5 to 540-A:8 and 540-B:10).

Deadlines for Security Deposit Returns: 30

days. If it is a shared facility and if it is more than 1 month's rent, an agreement must be written stating how much the deposit is and when it will be returned. If no written agreement, deposit must be returned within 20 days. (New Hampshire Revised Statutes, Sections 540-A:5 to 540-A:8 and 540-B:10).

Interest Required on Security Deposit: Yes. (New Hampshire Revised Statutes, Sections 540-A:5 to 540-A:8 and 540-B:10).

Separate Account required for Security Deposit: Yes. (New Hampshire Revised Statutes, Sections 540-A:5 to 540-A:8 and 540-B:10).

Exemption from Security Deposit Laws: Exemption for a person who rents or leases a single family residence and owns no other rental property or who rents or leases rental units in an owner-occupied building of 5 units or less shall not be considered a "landlord" for the purposes of this subdivision, except for any individual unit in such building which is occupied by a person or persons 60 years of age or older. Exemption also applies for vacation property. (New Hampshire Revised Statutes, Section 540-A:5).

Notice Required to Change or Terminate Month-to-Month Tenancy: 30 days to terminate or change rent. Landlord must have "just cause" for termination. (New Hampshire Revised Statutes, Section 540:2 and 540:3).

Rent Late Fees: No statute.

Required Landlord Disclosures: Tenant may note any conditions that need repair on the security deposit receipt or on lease. (New Hampshire Revised Statutes, Section 540-A:6).

When and Where Rent is Due: None.

Notary Acknowledgment: Standard Notary Block acceptable. (New Hampshire Revised Statutes, Section 456-B:8).

Lien: Standard Claim of Lien form acceptable. (New Hampshire Revised Statutes, Section 447:1+).

Other Recording Requirements: None.

New Jersey

State Landlord-Tenant Statutes: New Jersey Statutes Annotated, Sections 2A:18-61.40 to 2A:18-61.52.

State Property Laws Statutes: New Jersey Statutes Annotated, Title 46.

State Law Website: www.njleg.state.nj.us

State Real Estate Disclosure Laws: No statutory form. Use basic Real Estate Disclosure Form in Chapter 4 and on the Forms-on-CD.

Landlord's Entry to Real Estate: No statute.

Security Deposit Amount Limits: 1 ½ month's rent. (New Jersey Statutes Annotated, Sections 46:8-19 to 46:8-26).

Deadlines for Security Deposit Returns: 30 days. Return deposit in 5 days in case of fire, flood, condemnation or evacuation. (New Jersey Statutes Annotated, Sections 46:8-19 to 46:8-26).

Interest Required on Security Deposit: Yes. (New Jersey Statutes Annotated, Sections 46:8-19 to 46:8-26).

Separate Account required for Security Deposit: Yes. (New Jersey Statutes Annotated, Sections 46:8-19 to 46:8-26).

Exemption from Security Deposit Laws: Rental units in owner-occupied buildings that have no more than two units other than the owner-landlord's unit.unless tenants in have sent a 30-day written notice to the landlord stating that he or she wants the landlord to comply with the law's provisions. (New Jersey Statutes Annotated, Section 46:8-19 to 46:8-26).

Notice Required to Change or Terminate Month-to-Month Tenancy: No statute.

Rent Late Fees: Landlord must wait until 5 days to charge late fee. (New Jersey Statutes Annotated, Section 2A:42-6.1).

Required Landlord Disclosures: Land lord must provide tenant with copy of landlord and tenants rights from the Department of Consumer Affairs website -see below. Landlord must also inform tenant if property is in flood zone. (New Jersey Statutes Annotated, Section 46:8-50 and http://www.state.nj.us/dca/codes/lt/pdf/landlord_regs.pdf)

When and Where Rent is Due: Details of when rent is due. There is a grace period allowed for rental payments. (New Jersey Statutes Annotated, Section 2A:42-6.1)

Notary Acknowledgment: Standard Notary Block acceptable. (New Jersey Statutes Annotated, Section 52:1-7+).

Lien: Standard Claim of Lien form acceptable. (New Jersey Statutes Annotated, Section 2A: 44A-1+).

Other Recording Requirements: The instrument must be in English or accompanied by an English translation, be acknowledged, contain a statement as to consideration for realty transfer tax purposes, and contain the municipal tax lot and block designation of property. (New Jersey Statutes Annotated, Section 46:15-1.1). For deeds conveying real property on which there has been new construction must have the words "New Construction" printed at the top of the first page of the deed in upper case lettering along with an affidavit by the grantor stating that there is new construction. (New Jersey Statutes Annotated, Section 46:15-1.1).

New Mexico

State Landlord-Tenant Statutes: New Mexico Statutes Annotated, Sections 47-8-1 to 47-8-51 (rev. 01/06).

State Property Laws Statutes: New Mexico Statutes Annotated, Chapter 42.

State Law Website: http://legis.state.nm.us

State Real Estate Disclosure Laws: No statutory form. Use basic Real Estate Disclosure Form in Chapter 4 and on the Forms-on-CD.

Landlord's Entry to Real Estate: Immediate access for emergency. 24 hour notice for inspection, repairs, viewing and entry if tenant is absent for long periods. (New Mexico Statutes Annotated, Section 47-8-24).

Security Deposit Amount Limits: 1 month's rent for rental agreements less than a year. No limit for leases over one year. (New Mexico Statutes An-

notated, Section 47-8-18).

Deadlines for Security Deposit Returns: 30 days. (New Mexico Statutes Annotated, Section 47-8-18).

Interest Required on Security Deposit: Yes. (New Mexico Statutes Annotated, Section 47-8-18).

Separate Account required for Security Deposit: No. (New Mexico Statutes Annotated, Section 47-8-18).

Exemption from Security Deposit Laws: None. (New Mexico Statutes Annotated, Section 47-8-18).

Notice Required to Change or Terminate Month-to-Month Tenancy: 30 days to terminate or change rent. (New Mexico Statutes Annotated, Section 47-8-37 and 47-8-15(F)).

Rent Late Fees: Late fee cannot exceed 10% of the rent. (New Mexico Statutes Annotated, Section 47-8-15(D)).

Required Landlord Disclosures: Landlord must disclose the name and address the manager of the property and the name and address for the purpose of receiving notices. (New Mexico Statutes Annotated, Section 47-8-19).

When and Where Rent is Due: Details of when and where rent is due. (New Mexico Statutes Annotated, Section 47-8-15(B)).

Notary Acknowledgment: Standard Notary Block acceptable. (New Mexico Statutes Annotated, Section 14-14-8).

Lien: Standard Claim of Lien form acceptable. (New Mexico Statutes Annotated, Section 48-2-1+).

Other Recording Requirements: Acknowledgment required. (New Mexico Statutes Annotated, Section 14-9-1+).

New York

State Landlord-Tenant Statutes: New York Consolidated Laws Real Property Law (RPP) Sections 220-238; Real Property Actions and Proceedings Law (RPA) Sections 701-881; Multiple Dwelling

Law (MDW) all; Multiple Residence Law (MRE) all; General Obligation Law (GOL) Sections 7-101- 7-109.

State Property Laws Statutes: New York Consolidated Laws, Real Property (RPP).

State Law Website: http://assembly.state.ny.us/

State Real Estate Disclosure Laws: Property Condition Disclosure Statement. (New York Consolidated Laws, Real Property (RPP) 14-460). (This form is provided on the Forms-on-CD).

Landlord's Entry to Real Estate: No statute. A landlord, however, may enter a tenant's apartment with reasonable prior notice, and at a reasonable time: (a) to provide necessary or agreed upon repairs or services; or (b) in accordance with the lease; or (c) to show the apartment to prospective purchasers or tenants. In emergencies, such as fires, the landlord may enter the apartment without the tenant's consent. (Tenant's Rights Guide, New York State Attorney General Office).

Security Deposit Amount Limits: No limit in statutes for non-regulated units. (New York Consolidated General Obligation Law (GOL), Sections 7-101 to 7-109).

Deadlines for Security Deposit Returns: Within a reasonable amount of time. (New York Consolidated General Obligation Law (GOL), Sections 7-101 to 7-109).

Interest Required on Security Deposit: Yes. (New York Consolidated General Obligation Law (GOL), Sections 7-101 to 7-109).

Separate Account required for Security Deposit: Yes. (New York Consolidated General Obligation Law (GOL), Sections 7-101 to 7-109).

Exemption from Security Deposit Laws: Landlords are exempt who rent out non-regulated units in buildings with 5 or fewer units. (New York Consolidated General Obligation Law (GOL), Sections 7-101 to 7-109).

Notice Required to Change or Terminate Month-to-Month Tenancy: 1 month to terminate or change rent. (New York Consolidated Laws, Real Property Law, Section 232-a and 232-b).

Rent Late Fees: No statute.

Required Landlord Disclosures: None.

When and Where Rent is Due: None.

Notary Acknowledgment: Standard Notary Block acceptable. (New York Consolidated Laws, Real Property Law, Section 309+).

Lien: Standard Claim of Lien form acceptable. (New York Consolidated Laws, Lien Law, Section 1+).

Other Recording Requirements: Acknowledgment required. (New York Consolidated Laws, Real Property (RPP), Section 291). Must be in English and contain the tax map section including block and lot. (New York Consolidated Laws, Real Property (RPP), Section 333). Real Property Transfer Tax Forms are required and can be obtained from www.tax.state.ny.us. There are special requirements for Chautauqua county. (New York Consolidated Laws, Real Property (RPP), Section 291-A). There are special requirements for Cattaraugus county. (New York Consolidated Laws, Real Property (RPP), Section 291-B).

North Carolina

State Landlord-Tenant Statutes: North Carolina General Statutes, Sections 42-1 to 42-76.

State Property Laws Statutes: North Carolina General Statutes, Chapters 47B to 47F and 116A to 116B.

State Law Website: www.ncga.state.nc.us/

State Real Estate Disclosure Laws: Residential Property Disclosure Statement. (North Carolina General Statutes, Section 47E). (This form is provided on the Forms-on-CD).

Landlord's Entry to Real Estate: No statute.

Security Deposit Amount Limits: 1 ½ month's rent for month-to-month rental agreements. 2 month's rent if agreement is longer than 2 months. (North Carolina General Statutes, Sections 42-50 to 42-56).

Deadlines for Security Deposit Returns: 30 days. (North Carolina General Statutes, Sections 42-50 to 42-56).

Interest Required on Security Deposit: No. (North Carolina General Statutes, Sections 42-50 to 42-56).

Separate Account required for Security Deposit: Yes. (North Carolina General Statutes, Sections 42-50 to 42-56).

Exemption from Security Deposit Laws: None. (North Carolina General Statutes, Sections 42-50 to 42-56).

Notice Required to Change or Terminate Month-to-Month Tenancy: 7 days to terminate or change rent. (North Carolina General Statutes, Section 42-14).

Rent Late Fees: Late fee cannot exceed $15.00 or 5% of rent (whichever is greater). Landlord cannot impose this fee until rent is 5 days late. (North Carolina General Statutes, Section 42-46).

Required Landlord Disclosures: None.

When and Where Rent is Due: None. However, grace periods are allowed for rental payments. (North Carolina General Statutes, Section 42-46).

Notary Acknowledgment: Standard Notary Block acceptable. (North Carolina General Statutes, Section 47 and 10B).

Lien: Standard Claim of Lien form acceptable. (North Carolina General Statutes, Section 44A-7+).

Other Recording Requirements: Documents must be executed and acknowledged in strict compliance with the North Carolina statutory requirements for acknowledgments. (North Carolina General Statutes, Section 45-21.16). Some counties require affidavits of consideration. (North Carolina General Statutes, Section 45-37).

North Dakota

State Landlord-Tenant Statutes: North Dakota Century Code, Sections 47-16-01 to 47-16-41.

State Property Laws Statutes: North Dakota Century Code, Title 47.

State Law Website: http://www.nd.gov/

State Real Estate Disclosure Laws: No statutory form. Use basic Real Estate Disclosure Form in Chapter 4 and on the Forms-on-CD.

Landlord's Entry to Real Estate: Immediate access for emergency. "Reasonable" notice required for inspection, repairs, viewing of property and entry if tenant is absent for long periods. (North Dakota Century Code, Section 47-16-07.3).

Security Deposit Amount Limits: 1 month's rent. $2,500.00 if renter has a pet. (North Dakota Century Code Section 47-16-07.1).

Deadlines for Security Deposit Returns: 30 days. (North Dakota Century Code, Section 47-16-07.1).

Interest Required on Security Deposit: Yes. (North Dakota Century Code, Section 47-16-07.1).

Separate Account required for Security Deposit: Yes. (North Dakota Century Code, Section 47-16-07.1).

Exemption from Security Deposit Laws: None. (North Dakota Century Code, Section 47-16-07.1).

Notice Required to Change or Terminate Month-to-Month Tenancy: 30 days to terminate or change rent. (North Dakota Century Code, Section 47-16-15).

Rent Late Fees: No statute.

Required Landlord Disclosures: Landlord and tenant must complete an inventory of the property and both parties must sign at time lease is signed. (North Dakota Century Code, Section 47-16-07.2).

When and Where Rent is Due: Details of when rent is due. (North Dakota Century Code, Section 47-16-07).

Notary Acknowledgment: Standard Notary Block acceptable. (North Dakota Century Code, Section 47-19-14.6).

Lien: Standard Claim of Lien form acceptable. (North Dakota Century Code, Section 35-27-01+).

Other Recording Requirements: Before an instrument can be recorded, its execution must be established by an acknowledgment, subscribing witness, or another way prescribed by law. (North Dakota Century Code, Section 47-19-03).

Ohio

State Landlord-Tenant Statutes: Ohio Revised Code, Sections 5321.01 to 5321.19.

State Property Laws Statutes: Ohio Revised Code, Title 53.

State Law Website: http://www.ohio.gov/

State Real Estate Disclosure Laws: Residential Property Disclosure Form. (Ohio Revised Code, Section 5302.30). (This form is provided on the Forms-on-CD).

Landlord's Entry to Real Estate: Immediate access for emergency. 24 hour notice required for inspection, repairs, viewing of property and entry if tenant is absent for long periods. (Ohio Revised Code, Sections 5321.04(A)(8) and 5321.05(B)).

Security Deposit Amount Limits: No limit in statute. (Ohio Revised Code, Sections 5321.16).

Deadlines for Security Deposit Returns: 30 days. (Ohio Revised Code, Sections 5321.16).

Interest Required on Security Deposit: Yes. (Ohio Revised Code, Sections 5321.16).

Separate Account required for Security Deposit: No. (Ohio Revised Code, Sections 5321.16).

Exemption from Security Deposit Laws: None. (Ohio Revised Code, Sections 5321.16).

Notice Required to Change or Terminate Month-to-Month Tenancy: 30 days to terminate or change rent. (Ohio Revised Code, Sections 5321.17).

Rent Late Fees: No statute.

Required Landlord Disclosures: Landlord must disclose the name and address the manager of the property and the name and address for the purpose of receiving notices. (Ohio Revised Code, Sections 5321.18).

When and Where Rent is Due: None.

Notary Acknowledgment: Standard Notary Block acceptable. (Ohio Revised Code, Sections 147.55).

Lien: Standard Claim of Lien form acceptable. (Ohio Revised Code, Sections 1311.01+).

Other Recording Requirements: Acknowledgment required. (Ohio Revised Code, Sections 5301.01).

Oklahoma

State Landlord-Tenant Statutes: Oklahoma Statutes, Title 41, Sections 1-136.

State Property Laws Statutes: Oklahoma Statutes, Title 60.

State Law Website: http://www.oklahoma.gov/

State Real Estate Disclosure Laws: Residential Property Condition Disclosure Statement. (Oklahoma Statutes, Section 60-831). (This form is provided on the Forms-on-CD).

Landlord's Entry to Real Estate: Immediate access for emergency. 1 day notice required for inspection, repairs, viewing of property. (Oklahoma Statutes, Section 41-128).

Security Deposit Amount Limits: No limit in statute. (Oklahoma Statutes, Section 41-115).

Deadlines for Security Deposit Returns: 30 days. (Oklahoma Statutes, Section 41-115).

Interest Required on Security Deposit: No. (Oklahoma Statutes, Section 41-115).

Separate Account required for Security Deposit: Yes. (Oklahoma Statutes, Section 41-115).

Exemption from Security Deposit Laws: None. (Oklahoma Statutes, Section 41-115).

Notice Required to Change or Terminate Month-to-Month Tenancy: 30 days to terminate or change rent .(Oklahoma Statutes, Section 41-111).

Rent Late Fees: Preset late fees are not valid. (Oklahoma Case Law).

Required Landlord Disclosures: Landlord must disclose the name and address the manager of the property and the name and address for the purpose of receiving notices. If the property has flooded within the last 5 years, this must be stated in the lease. Oklahoma Statutes, Section 113A-116).

When and Where Rent is Due: Details of when and where rent is due. Grace periods are allowed for rental payments. ((Oklahoma Statutes, Section 41-109 and 41-132(B)).

Notary Acknowledgment: Standard Notary Block acceptable. (Oklahoma Statutes, Section 49-119).

Lien: Standard Claim of Lien form acceptable. (Oklahoma Statutes, Section 42-141+).

Other Recording Requirements: Acknowledgment required. (Oklahoma Statutes, Title 19, Section 284+).

Oregon

State Landlord-Tenant Statutes: Oregon Revised Statutes, Sections 90.100 to 90.440.

State Property Laws Statutes: Oregon Revised Statutes, Chapters 90-93.

State Law Website: http://www.leg.state.or.us/

State Real Estate Disclosure Laws: Seller's Property Disclosure Statement. (Oregon Revised Statutes, Section 105.462). (This form is provided on the Forms-on-CD).

Landlord's Entry to Real Estate: Immediate access for emergency. 24 hour notice required for inspection, repairs, viewing of property. (Oregon Revised Statutes, Section 90.322).

Security Deposit Amount Limits: No limit in statute. (Oregon Revised Statutes, Section 90.300).

Deadlines for Security Deposit Returns: 31 days. (Oregon Revised Statutes, Section 90.300).

Interest Required on Security Deposit: No. (Oregon Revised Statutes, Section 90.300).

Separate Account required for Security Deposit: No. (Oregon Revised Statutes, Section 90.300).

Exemption from Security Deposit Laws: None. (Oregon Revised Statutes, Section 90.300).

Notice Required to Change or Terminate Month-to-Month Tenancy: 30 days to terminate or change rent. (Oregon Revised Statutes, Section 90.070).

Rent Late Fees: A reasonable late fee may be charged after 5 days if specified in the lease. (Oregon Revised Statutes, Section 90.260).

Required Landlord Disclosures: Landlord must disclose the name and address the manager of the property and the name and address for the purpose of receiving notices. Non-refundable fees may be allowed for reasonably anticipated landlord expense. For rentals of more than 4 units, landlord must disclose any outstanding actions for foreclosure or notices of defaults under mortgages or contracts for sale. Landlord must also disclose to tenant how utilities for property are paid and assessed, including for any common areas. In addition, Landlord must inform tenant of opportunity for recycling. (Oregon Revised Statutes, Section 90.302 and 90.305).

When and Where Rent is Due: Details of when and where rent is due. Grace periods are provided for rent payments. (Oregon Revised Statutes, Section 90.220 and 90.260).

Notary Acknowledgment: Standard Notary Block acceptable. (Oregon Revised Statutes, Section 194.575).

Lien: Standard Claim of Lien form acceptable. (Oregon Revised Statutes, Section 7.001+).

Other Recording Requirements: The first page should show to whom and where the recorder should return the document after recording. A conveyance or contract to convey must have a statement of the actual consideration paid, a statutory land use warning, and an addressee and address for tax statements. Every instrument must be sufficiently legible to reproduce a readable photographic record meaning that the recorder can reject an instrument because of highlighting on text, encroachment of a notary seal into the test of an acknowledgment, smudged notary seal, or faxed or photocopied exhibits of poor legibility. (Oregon Revised Statutes, Section 93.010+).

Pennsylvania

State Landlord-Tenant Statutes: Pennsylvania Consolidated Statutes, Title 68, Section 250.101 to 250.510-B.

State Property Laws Statutes: Pennsylvania Consolidated Statutes, Title 68.

State Law Website: http://www.state.pa.us/

State Real Estate Disclosure Laws: Seller's Property Disclosure Statement. (Pennsylvania

Consolidated Statutes, Section 68-7301). (This form is provided on the Forms-on-CD).

Landlord's Entry to Real Estate: No statute.

Security Deposit Amount Limits: 2 month's rent for first year, 1 month's rent for every year after. (Pennsylvania Consolidated Statutes, Sections 68-250.511a to 68-250.512).

Deadlines for Security Deposit Returns: 30 days. (Pennsylvania Consolidated Statutes, Sections 68-250.511a to 68-250.512).

Interest Required on Security Deposit: Yes. (Pennsylvania Consolidated Statutes, Sections 68-250.511a to 68-250.512).

Separate Account required for Security Deposit: Yes. (Pennsylvania Consolidated Statutes, Sections 68-250.511a to 68-250.512).

Exemption from Security Deposit Laws: None. (Pennsylvania Consolidated Statutes, Sections 68-250.511a to 68-250.512).

Notice Required to Change or Terminate Month-to-Month Tenancy: No statute.

Rent Late Fees: No statute.

Required Landlord Disclosures: None.

When and Where Rent is Due: None.

Notary Acknowledgment: Standard Notary Block acceptable. (Pennsylvania Consolidated Statutes, Section 21-291.7).

Lien: Standard Claim of Lien form acceptable. However, must include a detailed itemized statement. (Pennsylvania Consolidated Statutes, Section 49-1503).

Other Recording Requirements: The deed must include the Uniform Parcel Identifier. (Pennsylvania Consolidated Statutes, 16 PS Section 9781.1.). Consideration must be stated on deed or an original and conformed copy of an Affidavit of Value must accompany the deed. (Pennsylvania Consolidated Statutes, 42 PS Section 21053). Must report transfers to tax assessment authorities. (Pennsylvania Consolidated Statutes, 16 PS Section 9781).

Rhode Island

State Landlord-Tenant Statutes: Rhode Island General Laws, Sections 34-18-1 to 34-18-57.

State Property Laws Statutes: Rhode Island General Laws, Title 34.

State Law Website: http://www.state.ri.us/

State Real Estate Disclosure Laws: No statutory form. Use basic Real Estate Disclosure Form in Chapter 4 and on the Forms-on-CD. (Rhode Island General Laws, Section 5-20.8-1).

Landlord's Entry to Real Estate: Immediate access for emergency. 2 days notice required for inspection, repairs, viewing of property and entry if tenant is absent for long periods. (Rhode Island General Laws Section 34-18-26).

Security Deposit Amount Limits: 1 month's rent. (Rhode Island General Laws, Section 34-18-19).

Deadlines for Security Deposit Returns: 20 days .(Rhode Island General Laws, Section 34-18-19).

Interest Required on Security Deposit: No. (Rhode Island General Laws, Section 34-18-19).

Separate Account required for Security Deposit: No .(Rhode Island General Laws, Section 34-18-19).

Exemption from Security Deposit Laws: None. (Rhode Island General Laws, Section 34-18-19).

Notice Required to Change or Terminate Month-to-Month Tenancy: 30 days to terminate or change rent. (Rhode Island General Laws, Sections 34-18-16.1 and 34-18-37).

Rent Late Fees: No statute.

Required Landlord Disclosures: Landlord must disclose the name and address the manager of the property and the name and address for the purpose of receiving notices. Landlord must inform tenant of any housing code violations. (Rhode Island General Laws, Section 34-18-20 and 34-18-22.1).

When and Where Rent is Due: Details of when and where rent is due. Grace periods are provided for rent payments. (Rhode Island General Laws, Section 34-18-15(c) and 34-18-35).

Notary Acknowledgment: Standard Notary Block acceptable. (Rhode Island General Laws, Sections

34-12-1+).

Lien: Standard Claim of Lien form acceptable. (Rhode Island General Laws, Sections 34-28-1+).

Other Recording Requirements: Rhode Island does NOT record by county. Recordings are sent to the appropriate recording office of the property address. Check city websites for special requirements. For example, the City of Newport's website is http://www.ci.newport.ri.us/departments/city-clerk/pdf/2008_probate_fees.amended2.pdf.

South Carolina

State Landlord-Tenant Statutes: South Carolina Code of Laws, Sections 27-40-10 to 27-40-910.

State Property Laws Statutes: South Carolina Code of Laws, Title 27 and 30.

State Law Website: http://www.sc.gov

State Real Estate Disclosure Laws: Residential Property Condition Disclosure Statement. (South Carolina Code of Laws, Section 27-50-10). (This form is provided on the Forms-on-CD).

Landlord's Entry to Real Estate: Immediate access for emergency. 24 hour notice required for inspection, repairs, viewing of property and entry if tenant is absent for long periods. (South Carolina Code of Laws, Section 27-40-530).

Security Deposit Amount Limits: No limit in statute. (South Carolina Code of Laws, Section 27-40-410).

Deadlines for Security Deposit Returns: 30 days. (South Carolina Code of Laws, Section 27-40-410).

Interest Required on Security Deposit: No. (South Carolina Code of Laws, Section 27-40-410).

Separate Account required for Security Deposit: No .(South Carolina Code of Laws, Section 27-40-410).

Exemption from Security Deposit Laws: None .(South Carolina Code of Laws, Section 27-40-410).

Notice Required to Change or Terminate

Month-to-Month Tenancy: 30 days to terminate or change rent. (South Carolina Code of Laws, Section 27-40-770).

Rent Late Fees: No statute.

Required Landlord Disclosures: Landlord must disclose the name and address the manager of the property and the name and address for the purpose of receiving notices. ((South Carolina Code of Laws, Section 27-40-420).

When and Where Rent is Due: Details of when and where rent is due. ((South Carolina Code of Laws, Section 27-40-310(c)).

Notary Acknowledgment: Standard Notary Block acceptable. (South Carolina Code of Laws, Section 26-3-70).

Lien: Standard Claim of Lien form acceptable. (South Carolina Code of Laws, Section 29-5-10+).

Other Recording Requirements: Signature and seal of the party whose interest is being conveyed or dealt with is required. (South Carolina Code of Laws, Section 30-5-30). Deeds and mortgages must contain a statutory derivation clause stating the name of the grantor and recording date of the prior deed. (South Carolina Code of Laws, Section 30-5-35).

South Dakota

State Landlord-Tenant Statutes: South Dakota Codified Laws, Sections 43-32-1 to 43-32-29.

State Property Laws Statutes: South Dakota Codified Laws, Title 43.

State Law Website: http://www.state.sd.us/

State Real Estate Disclosure Laws: Seller's Property Condition Disclosure Statement. (South Dakota Codified Laws, Section 43-4-37). (This form is provided on the Forms-on-CD).

Landlord's Entry to Real Estate: No statute.

Security Deposit Amount Limits: 1 month's rent unless special conditions warrant more. (South Dakota Codified Laws, Sections 43-32-6.1 and 43-32-24).

Deadlines for Security Deposit Returns: 2

weeks to return entire deposit or portion with written reasons for deductions. (South Dakota Codified Laws, Sections 43-32-6.1 and 43-32-24).

Interest Required on Security Deposit: No. (South Dakota Codified Laws, Sections 43-32-6.1 and 43-32-24).

Separate Account required for Security Deposit: No. (South Dakota Codified Laws, Sections 43-32-6.1 and 43-32-24).

Exemption from Security Deposit Laws: None. (South Dakota Codified Laws, Sections 43-32-6.1 and 43-32-24).

Notice Required to Change or Terminate Month-to-Month Tenancy: 1 month to terminate or change rent. Renter has 15 days to terminate after receiving landlord's modification of agreement. (South Dakota Codified Laws, Sections 43-32-13 and 43-8-8).

Rent Late Fees: No statute.

Required Landlord Disclosures: Landlord must disclose knowledge of the existence of any prior manufacturing of methamphetamines on the property. (South Dakota Codified Laws, Sections 43-32-30).

When and Where Rent is Due: Details of when rent is due. (South Dakota Codified Laws, Sections 43-32-12).

Notary Acknowledgment: Standard Notary Block acceptable. (South Dakota Codified Laws, Section 18-5-8+).

Lien: Standard Claim of Lien form acceptable. (South Dakota Codified Laws, Section 44-1-1+).

Other Recording Requirements: Certificate of value required. (South Dakota Codified Laws, Section 7-9-7(4)).

Tennessee

State Landlord-Tenant Statutes: Tennessee Code, Sections 66-28-101 to 66-28-520.

State Property Laws Statutes: Tennessee Code, Title 66.

State Law Website: http://www.tennessee.gov/

State Real Estate Disclosure Laws: Residential Property Condition Disclosure. (Tennessee Code, Title 66, Chapter 5, Part 2). (This form is provided on the Forms-on-CD).

Landlord's Entry to Real Estate: Immediate access for emergency or abandonment. "Reasonable notice required for inspection, repairs and viewing of property. (Tennessee Code, Section 66-28-403).

Security Deposit Amount Limits: No limit in statute. (Tennessee Code, Section 66-28-301).

Deadlines for Security Deposit Returns: No deadline in statute. (Tennessee Code, Section 66-28-403).

Interest Required on Security Deposit: No. (Tennessee Code, Section 66-28-403).

Separate Account required for Security Deposit: Yes. (Tennessee Code, Section 66-28-403).

Exemption from Security Deposit Laws: None. (Tennessee Code, Section 66-28-403).

Notice Required to Change or Terminate Month-to-Month Tenancy: 30 days to terminate or change rent. (Tennessee Code, Section 66-28-512).

Rent Late Fees: Landlord must wait until rent is 5 days late to impose late fee. Late fee cannot exceed 10% of the amount due. (Tennessee Code, Sections 66-28-201(d)).

Required Landlord Disclosures: Landlord must disclose the name and address the manager of the property and the name and address for the purpose of receiving notices. (Tennessee Code, Sections 66-22-302).

When and Where Rent is Due: Details of when and where rent is due. Grace periods are provided for rental payments. ((Tennessee Code, Section 66-28-201(c) and 66-28-201(d)).

Notary Acknowledgment: Standard Notary Block acceptable. (Tennessee Code, Sections 66-22-107+).

Lien: Standard Claim of Lien form acceptable. (Tennessee Code, Sections 66-11-101+).

Other Recording Requirements: Designation of grantor's source of title and the tax assessor's parcel number required. (Tennessee Code, Sections 66-24-110 and 66-24-122).

Texas

State Landlord-Tenant Statutes: Texas Statutes, Property Code, Sections 91.001 - 91.006 and 92.001-92.354.

State Property Laws Statutes: Texas Statutes, Property Code.

State Law Website: http://www.state.tx.us/

State Real Estate Disclosure Laws: Seller's Disclosure of Property Condition. (Texas Statutes, Property Code, Sections 5.008). (This form is provided on the Forms-on-CD).

Landlord's Entry to Real Estate: No statute.

Security Deposit Amount Limits: No limit in statute. (Texas Statutes, Property Code, Sections 92.101 to 92.109).

Deadlines for Security Deposit Returns: 30 days. If landlord wishes to require tenant to give advance notice of surrender of property prior to return of security deposit, this must be stated in writing in the lease in bold or underlined. (Texas Statutes, Property Code, Sections 92.101 to 92.109 and 92.201).

Interest Required on Security Deposit: No. (Texas Statutes, Property Code, Sections 92.101 to 92.109).

Separate Account required for Security Deposit: No. (Texas Statutes, Property Code, Sections 92.101 to 92.109).

Exemption from Security Deposit Laws: None. Texas Statutes: (Texas Statutes, Property Code, Sections 92.101 to 92.109).

Notice Required to Change or Terminate Month-to-Month Tenancy: 1 month to terminate or change rent. (Texas Statutes, Property Code, Section 91.001).

Rent Late Fees: No statute.

Required Landlord Disclosures: Landlord must disclose the name and address the manager of the property and the name and address for the purpose of receiving notices. If landlord wants tenant requests for security devices in writing, this must be stated in lease in bold or underlined. (Texas Statutes, Property Code, Section 92.103 and 92.159).

When and Where Rent is Due: None.

Notary Acknowledgment: Standard Notary Block acceptable. (Texas Statutes, Property Code, Section 121.007+).

Lien: Standard Claim of Lien form acceptable. (Texas Statutes, Property Code, Section 53.001+).

Other Recording Requirements: Must be in English. (Texas Statutes, Property Code, Section 11.002). Must be acknowledged or sworn to by the grantor in the presence of two or more credible subscribing witnesses or acknowledged or sworn to with a proper jurat before and certified by an officer authorized to take acknowledgment or oaths. (Texas Statutes, Property Code, Section 12.001). A plat or replat of a subdivision of real property may not be filed for record unless it is approved as provided by law by the appropriate governmental authority and unless the plat or replat has attached to it the documents required by the Local Government Code. (Texas Statutes, Property Code, Section 12.002).

Utah

State Landlord-Tenant Statutes: Utah Code, Sections 57-17-1 to 57-17-5 and 57-22-1 to 57-22-6.

State Property Laws Statutes: Utah Code, Title 57.

State Law Website: http://www.utah.gov/**State Real Estate Disclosure Laws:** No statutory form. Use basic Real Estate Disclosure Form in Chapter 4 and on the Forms-on-CD.

Landlord's Entry to Real Estate: Immediate access for emergency. No renter can deny access for repairs. (Utah Code, Section 57-22-5(2)(c)).

Security Deposit Amount Limits: No limit in statute. (Utah Code, Sections 57-17-1 to 57-17-5).

Deadlines for Security Deposit Returns: 30 days or 15 days after receiving tenant's forwarding address (whichever is longer). (Utah Code, Sections 57-17-1 to 57-17-5).

Interest Required on Security Deposit: No.

(Utah Code, Sections 57-17-1 to 57-17-5).

Separate Account required for Security Deposit: No. (Utah Code, Sections 57-17-1 to 57-17-5).

Exemption from Security Deposit Laws: None. (Utah Code, Sections 57-17-1 to 57-17-5).

Notice Required to Change or Terminate Month-to-Month Tenancy: No statute.

Rent Late Fees: No statute.

Required Landlord Disclosures: None.

When and Where Rent is Due: None.

Notary Acknowledgment: Standard Notary Block acceptable. (Utah Code, Sections 57-2a-7).

Lien: Standard Claim of Lien form acceptable. (Utah Code, Sections 38-1-1+).

Other Recording Requirements: Certificate of acknowledgment or other proof of execution is required. (Utah Code, Section 57-3-101).

Vermont

State Landlord-Tenant Statutes: Vermont Statutes, Title 9, Sections 4451 to 4468.

State Property Laws Statutes: Vermont Statutes, Title 27.

State Law Website: www.leg.state.vt.us/

State Real Estate Disclosure Laws: No statutory form. Use basic Real Estate Disclosure Form in Chapter 4 and on the Forms-on-CD.

Landlord's Entry to Real Estate: Immediate access for emergency. 48 hour notice for inspection, repairs and viewing of property. (Vermont Statutes, Title 9, Section 4460).

Security Deposit Amount Limits: No limit in statute. (Vermont Statutes, Title 9, Section 4461).

Deadlines for Security Deposit Returns: 14 days. (Vermont Statutes, Title 9, Section 4461).

Interest Required on Security Deposit: No. (Vermont Statutes, Title 9, Section 4461).

Separate Account required for Security Deposit: No. (Vermont Statutes, Title 9, Section 4461).

Exemption from Security Deposit Laws: None. (Vermont Statutes, Title 9, Section 4461).

Notice Required to Change or Terminate Month-to-Month Tenancy: Renter has 1 rental period to terminate or change rent. Landlord has 30 days to terminate or change rent. If there is no written agreement, the landlord has 60 days if tenant has rented for 2 years or less, 90 days if tenant has rented for more than 2 years. (Vermont Statutes, Title 9, Sections 4467 and 4456(d)).

Rent Late Fees: No statute.

Required Landlord Disclosures: None.

When and Where Rent is Due: Details of when rent is due. (Vermont Statutes, Title 9, Sections 4455).

Notary Acknowledgment: Standard Notary Block acceptable. (Vermont Statutes, Title 24, Section 441+).

Lien: Standard Claim of Lien form acceptable. (Vermont Statutes, Title 9, Section 1921+).

Other Recording Requirements: Must be witness and acknowledged by the grantor. (Vermont Statutes, Title 27, Section 341).

Virginia

State Landlord-Tenant Statutes: Code of Virginia, Sections 55-218.1 to 55-248.40.

State Property Laws Statutes: Code of Virginia, Title 55.

State Law Website: http://www.virginia.gov/

State Real Estate Disclosure Laws: Residential Property Disclosure Statement.(Code of Virginia, Section 55-517). (This form is provided on the Forms-on-CD).

Landlord's Entry to Real Estate: Immediate access for emergency. 24 hours required for inspection, repairs, viewing of property and entry if tenant is absent for long periods. (Code of Virginia, Section 55-248.18).

Security Deposit Amount Limits: 2 month's rent. (Code of Virginia, Section 55-248.15:1).

Deadlines for Security Deposit Returns: 45 days. (Code of Virginia, Section 55-248.15:1).

Interest Required on Security Deposit: Yes. (Code of Virginia, Section 55-248.15:1).

Separate Account required for Security Deposit: No. (Code of Virginia, Section 55-248.15:1).

Exemption from Security Deposit Laws: None. (Code of Virginia, Section 55-248.15:1).

Notice Required to Change or Terminate Month-to-Month Tenancy: 30 days to terminate or change rent. Renter must approve in writing of any change. (Code of Virginia, Sections 55-248.37 and 55-248.7).

Rent Late Fees: No statute.

Required Landlord Disclosures: A written move-in report must be provided to tenant within 5 days of move-in. Landlord must disclose presence of mold if known. Landlord must disclose the name and address the manager of the property and the name and address for the purpose of receiving notices. Landlord must disclose to tenant notice if property is near military air installation noise or accident zone. (Code of Virginia, Sections 55-248.11: 1, 55-248.11:2, and 55-248.12:1).

When and Where Rent is Due: Details of when and where rent is due. (Code of Virginia, Sections 55-248.7(C)).

Notary Acknowledgment: Standard Notary Block acceptable. (Code of Virginia, Section 55-118.6+).

Lien: Standard Claim of Lien form acceptable. (Code of Virginia, Section 43-1+).

Other Recording Requirements: Circuit Court Clerks may require that any deed or other instrument must be filed with a cover sheet. (Code of Virginia, Sections 17.1-227.1). Circuit Court Clerks in localities with a unique parcel identification system shall require that any deed or instrument must have tax map reference number or parcel identification number (PIN). (Code of Virginia, Sections 17.1-252). Acknowledgment required. (Code of Virginia, Section 17.1-223).

Washington

State Landlord-Tenant Statutes: Revised Code of Washington, Sections 59.04.010 to 59.04.900 and 59.18.010 to 59.18.911.

State Property Laws Statutes: Revised Code of Washington, Titles 63-65.

State Law Website: http://www1.leg.wa.gov/legislature/

State Real Estate Disclosure Laws: Seller's Residential Property Disclosures Statement. (Revised Code of Washington, Section 64.06.005). (This form is provided on the Forms-on-CD).

Landlord's Entry to Real Estate: Immediate access for emergency. 2 days required for inspection, repairs and viewing of property. (Revised Code of Washington, Section 59.18.150).

Security Deposit Amount Limits: No limit in statutes. (Revised Code of Washington, Sections 59.18.260 to 59.18.285).

Deadlines for Security Deposit Returns: 14 days .(Revised Code of Washington, Sections 59.18.260 to 59.18.285).

Interest Required on Security Deposit: No. (Revised Code of Washington, Sections 59.18.260 to 59.18.285).

Separate Account required for Security Deposit: Yes .(Revised Code of Washington, Sections 59.18.260 to 59.18.285).

Exemption from Security Deposit Laws: None. (Revised Code of Washington, Sections 59.18.260 to 59.18.285).

Notice Required to Change or Terminate Month-to-Month Tenancy: 30 days for renter to terminate or change rent. 20 days for landlord to terminate rent and 30 days to change rent. (Revised Code of Washington, Sections 59.18.200 and 59.18.140).

Rent Late Fees: No statute.

Required Landlord Disclosures: A move-in checklist is required. Non-refundable fees are permitted if clearly disclosed in lease. Landlord must disclose the name and address the manager of the property and the name and address for the purpose of receiving notices. Landlord must disclose tenant information about the health hazards of mold; about fire protection and safety information; whether building has smoking policy, an emergency notification plan, or evacuation plan. Landlord must disclose whether he or she has a policy of renting to known criminal offenders. (Revised Code of Washington, Sections 59.18.060, 59.18.260, 59.18.285, and 59.18.600).

When and Where Rent is Due: None.

Notary Acknowledgment: Standard Notary Block acceptable. (Revised Code of Washington, Sections 42.44.100).

Lien: Standard Claim of Lien form acceptable. (Revised Code of Washington, Sections 60.04.010+).

Other Recording Requirements: Acknowledgment required. (Revised Code of Washington, Section 65.08.070). Assessor's property tax parcel or account number, a return address within the top left margin, the title(s) of the instrument indicating the kind(s) of documents or transaction are required. (Revised Code of Washington, Section 65.04.045).

West Virginia

State Landlord-Tenant Statutes: West Virginia Code, Sections 37-6-1 to 37-6-30.

State Property Laws Statutes: West Virginia Code, Chapters 32A, 34, 35, 36, and 39.

State Law Website: http://www.legis.state.wv.us/

State Real Estate Disclosure Laws: No statutory form. Use basic Real Estate Disclosure Form in Chapter 4 and on the Forms-on-CD.

Landlord's Entry to Real Estate: No statute.

Security Deposit Amount Limits: No statute.

Deadlines for Security Deposit Returns: No statute.

Interest Required on Security Deposit: No statute.

Separate Account required for Security Deposit: No statute.

Exemption from Security Deposit Laws: No statute.

Notice Required to Change or Terminate Month-to-Month Tenancy: 1 month to terminate or change rent. (West Virginia Code, Sections 37-6-5).

Rent Late Fees: No statute.

Required Landlord Disclosures: None.

When and Where Rent is Due: None.

Notary Acknowledgment: Standard Notary Block acceptable. (West Virginia Code, Sections 39-1A-6).

Lien: Standard Claim of Lien form acceptable. (West Virginia Code, Sections 38-2-1+).

Other Recording Requirements: Acknowledgment required. (West Virginia Code, Section 39-1-2). Must set forth legibly the name of the person who prepared the deed. (West Virginia Code, Section 39-1-2a). Must contain a declaration of consideration or value and a Sales Listing form must be presented to the clerk. (West Virginia Code, Section 11-22-6).

Wisconsin

State Landlord-Tenant Statutes: Wisconsin Statutes & Annotations, Sections 704.01 to 704.45.

State Property Laws Statutes: Wisconsin Statutes & Annotations, Chapters 700-710.

State Law Website: www.legis.state.wi.us/

State Real Estate Disclosure Laws: Real Estate Condition Report. (Wisconsin Statutes & Annotations, Section 709.01). (This form is provided on the Forms-on-CD).

Landlord's Entry to Real Estate: Immediate access for emergency. "Reasonable" notice required for inspection, repairs and viewing of property. If landlord wishes to enter property for other purposes, such authority must be disclosed to tenant, before lease is signed, in a separate written document entitled "NONSTANDARD RENTAL PROVISIONS". (Wisconsin Statutes & Annotations, Sections 134.06 and 704.05(2)).

Security Deposit Amount Limits: No limit in statute. (Wisconsin Administrative Code ATCP, Section 134.06).

Deadlines for Security Deposit Returns: 21 days. (Wisconsin Administrative Code ATCP, Section 134.06).

Interest Required on Security Deposit: No. (Wisconsin Administrative Code ATCP, Section 134.06).

Separate Account required for Security Deposit: No. (Wisconsin Administrative Code ATCP, Section 134.06).

Exemption from Security Deposit Laws: None. (Wisconsin Administrative Code ATCP, Section 134.06).

Notice Required to Change or Terminate Month-to-Month Tenancy: 28 days to terminate or change rent. (Wisconsin Statutes & Annotations, Sections 704.19).

Rent Late Fees: No statute.

Required Landlord Disclosures: Landlord must disclose the name and address the manager of the property and the name and address for the purpose of receiving notices. Tenant has right to inspect property and provide landlord with list of defects and also receive a list of prior tenants' damages. Landlord must disclose any uncorrected building and housing code violations or any other serious problems affecting the habitability of the property before accepting a deposit or signing a lease. If utility charges are not included in the rent, landlord must disclose this before accepting a deposit or signing a lease, including any utilities for common areas and how the amounts due are calculated. (Wisconsin Administrative Code ATCP, Section 134.04, 134.06, and 134.09).

When and Where Rent is Due: None.

Notary Acknowledgment: Standard Notary Block acceptable. (Wisconsin Statutes & Annotations, Sections 706.07).

Lien: Standard Claim of Lien form acceptable. (Wisconsin Statutes & Annotations, Sections 779.01+).

Other Recording Requirements: Acknowledgment required. (Wisconsin Statutes &Annotations, Section 706.02). Must be signed or joined in by a separate conveyance by or on behalf of both spouses if the conveyance alienates any interest of a married person in a homestead unless it is a conveyance between spouses. (Wisconsin Statutes & Annotations, Section 706.02). All documents must have a name, certain areas must be blank for register's use, must have parcel identification number (PIN), the ink must be black or red, except for signatures. (Wisconsin Statutes & Annotations, Section 59.43).

Wyoming

State Landlord-Tenant Statutes: Wyoming Statutes, Sections 1-21-1201 to 1-21-1211 and 34-2-128 to 34-2-129.

State Property Laws Statutes: Wyoming Statutes, Title 34.

State Law Website:
http://legisweb.state.wy.us/

State Real Estate Disclosure Laws: No statutory form. Use basic Real Estate Disclosure Form in Chapter 4 and on the Forms-on-CD.

Landlord's Entry to Real Estate: No statute.

Security Deposit Amount Limits: No limit in statute. (Wyoming Statutes, Sections 1-21-1207 to 1-21-1208).

Deadlines for Security Deposit Returns: 30 days or 15 days after receiving renter's forwarding address (whichever is later). 60 days if there are deductions for damages.(Wyoming Statutes, Sections 1-21-1207 to 1-21-1208).

Interest Required on Security Deposit: No. (Wyoming Statutes, Sections 1-21-1207 & 1208).

Separate Account required for Security Deposit: No. (Wyoming Statutes, Sections 1-21-1207 to 1-21-1208).

Exemption from Security Deposit Laws: None. (Wyoming Statutes, Sections 1-21-1207 to 1-21-1208).

Notice Required to Change or Terminate Month-to-Month Tenancy: No statute.

Rent Late Fees: No statute.

Required Landlord Disclosures: Non-refundable fees are permitted if disclosed in the lease. (Wyoming Statutes, Section 1-21-1207).

When and Where Rent is Due: None.

Notary Acknowledgment: Standard Notary Block acceptable. (Wyoming Statutes, Section 34-26-108).

Lien: Standard Claim of Lien form acceptable. (Wyoming Statutes, Section 29-1-201+).

Other Recording Requirements: Acknowledgment required. (Wyoming Statutes, Section 34-1-113). Statement of Consideration required. (Wyoming Statutes, Section 34-1-142).

Glossary

Abstract of title: A historical summary provided by a title insurance company of all records affecting the title to a property.

Acceleration clause: Allows a lender to declare the entire outstanding balance of a loan immediately due and payable should a borrower violate specific loan provisions or default on the loan.

Adjustable rate mortgage (ARM): A variable or flexible rate mortgage with an interest rate that varies according to the financial index it is based upon. To limit the borrower's risk, the ARM may have a payment or rate cap. See also *cap*.

Amenities: Features of your home that fit your preferences and can increase the value of your property. Some examples include the number of bedrooms, bathrooms, or vicinity to public transportation.

Amortization: The liquidation of a debt by regular, usually monthly, installments of principal and interest. An amortization schedule is a table showing the payment amount, interest, principal and unpaid balance for the entire term of the loan.

Annual cap: See *cap*.

Annual percentage rate (APR): The actual interest rate, taking into account points and other finance charges, for the projected life of a mortgage. Disclosure of APR is required by the *Truth-in-Lending Law* and allows borrowers to compare the actual costs of different mortgage loans.

Appraisal: An estimate of a property's value as of a given date, determined by a qualified professional appraiser. The value may be based on replacement cost, the sales of comparable properties or the property's ability to produce income.

Appreciation: A property's increase in value due to inflation or economic factors.

APR: See *annual percentage rate*.

ARM: See *adjustable rate mortgage*.

Assessment: Charges levied against a property for tax purposes or to pay for municipality or association improvements such as curbs, sewers, or grounds maintenance.

Assignment: The transfer of a contract or a right to buy property at given rates and terms from a mortgagee to another person.

Assumption: An agreement between a buyer and a seller, requiring lender approval, where the buyer takes over the payments for a mortgage and accepts the liability. Assuming a loan can be advantageous for a buyer because there are no closing costs and the loan's interest rate may be lower than current market rates.

Balloon mortgage: Mortgage with a final lump sum payment that is greater than preceding payments and pays the loan in full.

Biweekly mortgage: A loan requiring payments of principal and interest at two-week intervals. This type of loan amortizes much faster than monthly payment loans. The payment for a biweekly mortgage is half what a monthly payment would be.

Bond: A certificate serving as security for payment of a debt. Bonds backed by mortgage loans are pooled together and sold in the secondary market.

Bridge loan: A loan to "bridge" the gap between the termination of one mortgage and the beginning of another, such as when a borrower purchases a new home before receiving cash proceeds from the sale of a prior home. Also known as a "swing loan."

Broker: An intermediary between the borrower and the lender. The broker may represent several lending sources and charges a fee or commission for services.

Buy-down: Where the buyer pays additional discount points or makes a substantial down payment in return for a below market interest rate; or the seller offers 3-2-1 interest payment plans or pays closing costs such as the origination fee.

Cap: A limit in how much an adjustable rate mortgage's monthly payment or interest rate can increase. A cap is meant to protect the borrower from large increases and may be a payment cap, an interest cap, a life-of-loan cap or an annual cap. A payment cap is a limit on the monthly payment. An interest cap is a limit on the amount of the interest rate. A life-of-loan cap restricts the amount the interest rate can increase over the entire term of the loan. An annual cap limits the amount the interest rate can increase over a twelve-month period.

Certificate of reasonable value (CRV): A Veteran's Administration appraisal that establishes the maximum VA mortgage loan amount for a specified property.

Certificate of title: Document rendering an opinion on the status of a property's title based on public records.

Closed-end mortgage: A mortgage principal amount that is fixed and cannot be increased during the life of the loan. See also *open-end mortgage*.

Closing costs: Costs payable by both seller and buyer at the time of settlement, when the purchase of a property is finalized.

Cloud: A claim to the title of a property that, if valid, would prevent a purchaser from obtaining a clear title.

Collateral: Something of value pledged as security for a loan. In mortgage lending, the property itself serves as collateral for a mortgage loan.

Commitment fee: A fee charged when an agreement is reached between a lender and a borrower for a loan at a specific rate and points and the lender guarantees to lock in that rate.

Co-mortgagor: One who is individually and jointly obligated to repay a mortgage loan and shares ownership of the property with one or more borrowers. See also *co-signer*.

Condominium: An individually owned unit within a multi-unit building where others or a condominium owners association share ownership of common areas such as the grounds, the parking facilities, hallways, etc.

Conforming loan: A loan that conforms to *Federal National Mortgage Association (FNMA)* or *Federal Home Loan Mortgage Corporation (FHLMC)* guidelines. See also *non-conforming loan*.

Construction loan: A short-term loan financing improvements to real estate, such as the building of a new home. The lender advances funds to the borrower as needed while construction progresses. Upon completion of the construction, the borrower must obtain permanent financing or pay the construction loan in full.

Consumer handbook on adjustable rate mortgages *(CHARM)*: A disclosure required by the federal government to be given to any borrower applying for an adjustable rate mortgage (ARM).

Conventional loan: A mortgage loan that is not insured, guaranteed or funded by the *Veterans Administration* (VA), the *Federal Housing Administration* (FHA) or *Rural Economic Community Development* (RECD) (formerly *Farmers Home Administration*).

Convertible mortgage: An adjustable rate mortgage (ARM) that allows a borrower to switch to a fixed-rate mortgage at a specified point in the loan term.

Co-signer: One who is obligated to repay a mortgage loan should the borrower default but who does not share ownership in the property. See also *co-mortgagor*.

Covenants: Rules and restrictions governing the use of property.

CRV: See *certificate of reasonable value*.

Curtailments: The borrower's privilege to make payments on a loan's principal before they are due. Paying off a mortgage before it is due may incur a penalty if so specified in the mortgage's prepayment clause.

Debt: Money owed to repay someone.

Debt-to-income ratio: The ratio between a borrower's monthly payment obligations divided by his or her net effective income (FHA or VA loans) or gross monthly income (conventional loans).

Deed of trust: A document, used in many states in place of a mortgage, held by a trustee pending repayment of the loan. The advantage of a deed of trust is that the trustee does not have to go to court to proceed with foreclosure should the borrower default on the loan.

Department of Housing and Urban Development (HUD): The U. S. government agency that administers FHA, GNMA and other housing programs.

Discount points: Amounts paid to the lender based on the loan amount to buy the interest rate down. Each point is one percent of the loan amount; for example, two points on a $100,000 mortgage is $2,000.

Down payment: The difference between the purchase price and mortgage amount. The down payment becomes the property equity. Typically it should be cash savings, but it can also be a gift that is not to be repaid or a borrowed amount secured by assets.

Due-on-sale: A clause in a mortgage or deed of trust allowing a lender to require immediate payment of the balance of the loan if the property is sold (subject to the terms of the security instrument).

Duplex: Dwelling divided into two units.

Earnest money: Deposit in the form of cash or a note, given to a seller by a buyer as good faith assurance that the buyer intends to go through with the purchase of a property.

Easement: The right one party has in regard to the property of another, such as the right of a public utility company to lay lines.

Equal Credit Opportunity Act: A federal law prohibiting lenders and other creditors from discrimination based on race, color, sex, religion, national origin, age, marital status, receipt of public assistance or because an applicant has exercised his or her rights under the *Consumer Credit Protection Act*.

Equity: The value of a property beyond any liens against it. Also referred to as "owner's interest."

Escape clause: A provision allowing one party or more to cancel all or part of the contract if certain events fail to happen, such as the ability of the buyer to obtain financing within a specified period.

Escrow: Money placed with a third party for safekeeping either for final closing on a property or for payment of taxes and insurance throughout the year.

Fair market value: The price a property can realistically sell for, based upon comparable selling prices of other properties in the same area.

Fannie Mae: Nickname for *Federal National Mortgage Association (FNMA)*.

Federal Home Loan Mortgage Corporation *(FHLMC or Freddie Mac)*: A quasi-governmental, federally-sponsored organization that acts as a secondary market investor to buy and sell mortgage loans. FHLMC sets many of the guidelines for conventional mortgage loans, as does FNMA.

Federal Housing Administration (FHA): An agency within the *Department of Housing and Urban Development* that sets standards for underwriting and insures residential mortgage loans made by private lenders. One of FHA's objectives is to ensure affordable mortgages to those with low or moderate income. FHA loans may be high loan-to-value, and they are limited by loan amount.

Federal National Mortgage Association (*FNMA or Fannie Mae*): A private corporation that acts as a secondary market investor to buy and sell mortgage loans. FNMA sets many of the guidelines for conventional mortgage loans, as does FHLMC. The major purpose of this organization is to make mortgage money more affordable and more available.

Fee simple: The maximum form of ownership, with the right to occupy a property and sell it to a buyer at any time. Upon the death of the owner, the property goes to the owner's designated heirs. Also known as "fee absolute."

FHA: See *Federal Housing Administration*.

Fifteen-year mortgage: A loan with a term of 15 years. Although the monthly payment on a 15-year mortgage is higher than that of a 30-year mortgage, the amount of interest paid over the life of the loan is substantially less.

Fixed-rate mortgage: A mortgage whose rate remains constant throughout the life of the mortgage.

Flood insurance: The *Federal Flood Disaster Protection Act of 1973* requires that federally-regulated lenders determine if real estate to be used to secure a loan is located in a *Specially Flood Hazard Area (SFHA)*. If the property is located in a SFHA area, the borrower must obtain and maintain flood insurance on the property. Most insurance agents can assist in obtaining flood insurance.

FNMA: See *Federal National Mortgage Association*.

Freddie Mac: Nickname for *Federal Home Loan Mortgage Corporation (FHLMC)*.

Gift: This includes amounts from a relative or a grant from the borrower's employer, a municipality, non-profit religious organization, or non-profit community organization that does not have to be repaid.

Ginnie Mae: Nickname for *Government National Mortgage Association (GNMA)*.

Good faith: Estimate on closing costs and monthly mortgage payments provided by the lender to the homebuyer within 3 days of applying for a loan.

Government National Mortgage Association (*GNMA or Ginnie Mae)*: A government organization that participates in the secondary market, securitizing pools of FHA, VA, and RHS loans.

Graduated payment mortgage (GPM): A fixed-interest loan with lower payments in the early years than the later years. The amount of the payment gradually increases over a period of time and then levels off at a payment sufficient to pay off the loan over the remaining amortization period.

Hazard insurance: A form of insurance that protects the insured property against physical damage such as fire and tornadoes. Mortgage lenders often require a borrower to maintain an amount of hazard insurance on the property that is equal at least to the amount of the mortgage loan.

Home equity loan: A mortgage on the borrower's principal residence, usually for the purpose of making home improvements or debt consolidation.

Home inspection: A thorough review of the physical aspects and condition of a home by a professional home inspector. This inspection should be completed prior to closing so that any repairs or changes can be completed before the home is sold.

Homeowners insurance: A form of insurance that protects the insured property against loss from theft, liability and most common disasters.

Housing and Urban Development (HUD): The U. S. government agency that administers FHA, GNMA and other housing programs.

Housing affordability index: Indicates what proportion of homebuyers can afford to buy an average-priced home in specified areas. The most well known housing affordability index is published by the National Association of Realtors.

Housing expenses-to-income ratio: See *debt-to-income ratio*.

HUD: See *Housing and Urban Development*.

Income approach to value: A method used by real estate appraisers to predict a property's anticipated future income. Income property includes shopping centers, hotels, motels, restaurants, apartment buildings, office space and so forth.

Income-to-debt ratio: See *debt-to-income ratio*.

Index: A published interest rate compiled from other indicators such as U.S. Treasury bills or the monthly average interest rate on loans closed by savings and loan organizations. Mortgage lenders use the index figure to establish rates on adjustable rate mortgages (ARMs).

Insurance: As a part of PITI, the amount of the monthly mortgage payment that does not include the principal, interest, and taxes. See also *homeowners insurance*.

Interest: The amount of the entire mortgage loan which does not include the principal. Also, as a part of PITI, the amount of the monthly mortgage payment which does not include the principal, taxes, and insurance.

Interest cap: See *cap*.

Interest rate: The simple interest rate, stated as a percentage, charged by a lender on the principal amount of borrowed money. See also *Annual Percentage Rate*.

Joint tenancy: See *tenancy*.

Jumbo loan: A nonconforming loan that is larger than the limits set by the *Federal National Mortgage Association* (FNMA) or *Federal Home Loan Mortgage Corporation* (FHLMC) guidelines.

Key lot: Real estate deemed highly valuable because of its location.

Lien: A claim against a property for the payment of a debt. A mortgage is a lien; other types of liens a property might have include a tax lien for overdue taxes or a mechanics lien for unpaid debt to a subcontractor.

Life-of-loan cap: See *cap*.

Liquidity: The capability of an asset to be readily converted into cash.

Loan discount: See *points*.

Loan origination fee: See *origination fee*.

Loan-to-value ratio (LTV): The relationship, expressed as a percentage, between the amount of the proposed loan and a property's appraised value. For example, a $75,000 loan on a property appraised at $100,000 is a 75 percent loan-to-value.

Lock-in: The guarantee of a specific interest rate and/or points for a specific period of time. Some lenders will charge a fee for locking in an interest rate.

Maintenance costs: The cost of the upkeep of the house. These costs may be minor in cost and nature (replacing washers in the faucets) or major in cost and nature (new heating system or a new roof) and can apply to either the interior or exterior of the house.

Margin: The amount a lender adds to the index of an adjustable rate mortgage to establish an adjusted interest rate. For example, a margin of 1. 50 added to a 7 percent index establishes an adjusted interest rate of 8. 50 percent.

Market value: The price a property can realistically sell for, based upon comparable selling prices of other properties in the same area.

Modification: A change in the terms of the mortgage note, such as a reduction in the interest rate or change in maturity date.

Mortgage: A legal instrument in which property serves as security for the repayment of a loan. In some states, a deed of trust is used rather than a mortgage.

Mortgage banker: A lender that originates, closes, services and sells mortgage loans to the secondary market.

Mortgage broker: An intermediary between a borrower and a lender. A broker's expertise is to help borrowers find financing that they might not otherwise find themselves.

Mortgage insurance: Money paid to insure the lender against loss due to foreclosure or loan default. Mortgage insurance is required on conventional loans with less than a 20 percent down payment.

Mortgage interest: Interest rate charge for borrowing the money for the mortgage. It is a used to calculate the interest payment on the mortgage each month.

Mortgage term: The length of time that a mortgage is scheduled to exist. Example: a 30-year mortgage term is for 30 years.

Mortgagee: The lender.

Mortgagor: The borrower.

Negative amortization: A situation in which a borrower is paying less interest than what is actually being charged for a mortgage loan. The unpaid interest is added to the loan's principal. The borrower may end up owing more than the original amount of the mortgage.

Non-assumption clause: In a mortgage contract, a statement that prohibits a new buyer from assuming a mortgage loan without the approval of the lender.

Non-conforming loan: A loan that does not conform to *Federal National Mortgage Association* (FNMA) or *Federal Home Loan Mortgage Corporation* (FHLMC) guidelines. Jumbo loans are nonconforming. See also *conforming loan*.

Note: A signed document that acknowledges a debt and shows the borrower is obligated to pay it.

Open-end mortgage: A mortgage allowing the borrower to receive advances of principal from the lender during the life of the loan. See also *closed-end mortgage*.

Origination fee: The amount charged by a lender to originate and close a mortgage loan. Origination fees are usually expressed in points.

Payment cap: See *cap*.

P&I: Abbreviation for principal and interest.

PITI: Abbreviation for principal, interest, taxes and insurance.

Points: Charges levied by the lender based on the loan amount. Each point equals one percent of the loan amount; for example, two points on a $100,000 mortgage is $2,000. Discount points are used to buy down the interest rate. Points can also include a loan origination fee, which is usually one point.

Pre-qualification: Tentative establishment of a borrower's qualification for a mortgage loan amount of a specific range, based on the borrower's assets, debts, and income.

Prime rate: The interest rate commercial banks charge their most creditworthy customers.

Principal: The amount of the entire mortgage loan, not counting interest. Also, as a part of PITI, the amount of the monthly mortgage payment which does not include the interest, insurance, and taxes.

Private mortgage insurance (PMI): See *mortgage insurance*.

Property appraisal: See *appraisal*.

Property tax: The amount which the state and/or locality assesses as a tax on a piece of property.

Prorate: To proportionally divide amounts owed by the buyer and the seller at closing.

Qualification: As determined by a lender, the ability of the borrower to repay a mortgage loan based on the borrower's credit history, employment history, assets, debts and income.

Rate cap: See *cap*.

RESPA: Abbreviation for the *Real Estate Settlement Procedures Act*, which allows consumers to review settlement costs at application and once again prior to closing.

Reverse annuity mortgage: A type of mortgage loan in which the lender makes periodic payments to the borrower. The borrower's equity in the home is used as security for the loan.

RHCDS: *Rural Housing and Community Service*.

Right of first refusal: Purchasing a property under conditions and terms made by another buyer and accepted by the seller.

Right of rescission: When a borrower's principal dwelling is going to secure a loan, the borrower has three business days following signing of the loan documents to rescind or cancel the transaction. Any and all money paid by the borrower must be refunded upon rescission. The right to rescind does not apply to loans to purchase real estate or to refinance a loan under the same terms and conditions where no additional funds will be added to the existing loan.

Rural Housing and Community Development Service: A federal agency that administers mortgage loans for buyers in rural areas.

Second mortgage: A loan that is junior to a primary or first mortgage and often has a higher interest rate and a shorter term.

Secondary market: A market comprising investors like GNMA, FHLMC and FNMA, which buy large numbers of mortgages from the primary lenders and sell them to other investors.

Servicing: The responsibility of collecting monthly mortgage payments and properly crediting them to the principal, taxes and insurance, as well as keeping the borrower informed of any changes in the status of the loan.

Settlement costs: See *closing costs*.

Survey: A physical measurement of property done by a registered professional showing the dimensions and location of any buildings as well as easements, rights of way, roads, etc.

Tax deed: A written document conveying title to property repossessed by the government due to default on tax payments.

Tax savings: The amount of money that the homeowner is not required to pay the government in taxes because he or she owns a home.

Taxes: As a part of PITI, the amount of the monthly mortgage payment which does not include the principal, interest, and insurance.

Tenancy: *Joint tenancy:* equal ownership of property by two or more parties, each with the right of survivorship. *Tenancy by the entireties:* ownership of property only between husband and wife in which neither can sell without the consent of the other and the property is owned by the survivor in the event of death of either party. *Tenancy in common:* equal ownership of property by two or more parties without the right of survivorship. *Tenancy in severalty:* ownership of property by one legal entity or a sole party. *Tenancy at will:* a license to use or occupy a property at the will of the owner.

Title: A formal document establishing ownership of property.

Title insurance: A policy issued by a title insurance company insuring the purchaser against any errors in the title search. The cost of title insurance may be paid for by the buyer, the seller or both.

Trust deed: See *deed of trust*.

Truth In Lending Act: The *Truth In Lending Act* requires lenders to disclose the Annual Percentage Rate and other associated costs to homebuyers within three working days of the loan application.

Underwriter: A professional who approves or denies a loan to a potential homebuyer based on the homebuyer's credit history, employment history, assets, debts and other factors such as loan guidelines.

Uniform Settlement Statement: A standard document prescribed by the *Real Estate Settlement Procedures Act* containing information for closing which must be supplied to both buyer and seller.

Utility costs: Periodic housing costs for water, electricity, natural gas, heating oil, etc.

VA loan: See *Veterans Administration*.

Vacation home: See *secondary residence*.

Variable rate mortgage (VRM): See *adjustable rate mortgage*.

Veterans Administration (VA): The federal agency responsible for the VA loan guarantee program as well as other services for eligible veterans. In general, qualified veterans can apply for home loans with no down payment and a funding fee of 1 percent of the loan amount.

Walk-through: An inspection of a property by the prospective buyer prior to closing on a mortgage.

Warranty deed: A document protecting a homebuyer against any and all claims to the property.

Yield: The rate of earnings from an investment.

Zoning: The ability of local governments to specify the use of private property in order to control development within designated areas of land. For example, some areas of a neighborhood may be designated only for residential use and others for commercial use such as stores, gas stations, etc.

Index

Nova Publishing Company
Small Business and Consumer Legal Books and Software

Legal Toolkit Series

Estate Planning Toolkit	ISBN 13: 978-1-892949-44-8	Book w/CD	$39.95
Business Start-Up Toolkit	ISBN 13: 978-1-892949-43-1	Book w/CD	$39.95
Legal Forms Toolkit	ISBN 13: 978-1-892949-48-6	Book w/CD	$39.95
No-Fault Divorce Toolkit	ISBN 13: 978-1-892949-35-6	Book w/CD	$39.95
Personal Bankruptcy Toolkit	ISBN 13: 978-1-892949-42-4	Book w/CD	$29.95
Will and Living Will Toolkit	ISBN 13: 978-1-892949-47-9	Book w/CD	$29.95

Law Made Simple Series

Advance Health Care Directives	ISBN 13: 978-1-892949-23-3	Book w/CD	$24.95
Living Trusts Simplified	ISBN 0-935755-51-9	Book w/CD	$28.95
Personal Legal Forms Simplified (3rd Edition)	ISBN 0-935755-97-7	Book w/CD	$28.95
Powers of Attorney Simplified	ISBN 13: 978-1-892949-40-0	Book w/CD	$24.95

Small Business Made Simple Series

Corporation: Small Business Start-up Kit (2nd Edition)	ISBN 1-892949-06-7	Book w/CD	$29.95
Employer Legal Forms	ISBN 13: 978-1-892949-26-4	Book w/CD	$24.95
Landlord Legal Forms	ISBN 13: 978-1-892949-24-0	Book w/CD	$24.95
Limited Liability Company: Start-up Kit (3rd Edition)	ISBN 13: 978-1-892949-37-0	Book w/CD	$29.95
Partnership: Start-up Kit (2nd Edition)	ISBN 1-892949-07-5	Book w/CD	$29.95
Real Estate Forms Simplified (2nd Edition)	ISBN 13: 978-1-892949-49-3	Book w/CD	$29.95
S-Corporation: Small Business Start-up Kit (3rd Edition)	ISBN 13: 978-1-892949-36-3	Book w/CD	$29.95
Small Business Accounting Simplified (5th Edition)	ISBN 13: 978-1-892949-50-9	Book only	$29.95
Small Business Bookkeeping System Simplified	ISBN 0-935755-74-8	Book only	$14.95
Small Business Legal Forms Simplified (4th Edition)	ISBN 0-935755-98-5	Book w/CD	$29.95
Small Business Payroll System Simplified	ISBN 0-935755-55-1	Book only	$14.95
Sole Proprietorship: Start-up Kit (2nd Edition)	ISBN 1-892949-08-3	Book w/CD	$29.95

Legal Self-Help Series

Divorce Yourself: The National Divorce Kit (6th Edition)	ISBN 1-892949-12-1	Book w/CD	$39.95
Prepare Your Own Will: The National Will Kit (6th Edition)	ISBN 1-892949-15-6	Book w/CD	$29.95

National Legal Kits

Simplified Divorce Kit (3rd Edition)	ISBN 13: 978-1-892949-39-4	Book w/CD	$19.95
Simplified Family Legal Forms Kit (2nd Edition)	ISBN 13: 978-1-892949-41-7	Bookw/CD	$19.95
Simplified Incorporation Kit	ISBN 1-892949-33-4	Book w/CD	$19.95
Simplified Limited Liability Company Kit	ISBN 1-892949-32-6	Book w/CD	$19.95
Simplified Living Will Kit (2nd Edition)	ISBN 13: 978-1-892949-45-5	Book w/CD	$19.95
Simplified S-Corporation Kit	ISBN 1-892949-31-8	Book w/CD	$19.95
Simplified Will Kit (3rd Edition)	ISBN 1-892949-38-5	Book w/CD	$19.95

Ordering Information

Distributed by:
National Book Network
4501 Forbes Blvd. Suite 200
Lanham MD 20706

Shipping: $4.50 for first & $.75 for additionall
Phone orders with Visa/MC: (800) 462-6420
Fax orders with Visa/MC: (800) 338-4550
Internet: www.novapublishing.com
Free shipping on all internet orders (within in the U.S.)